BOOK 2

PAPER MONEY
AND
THE BANKING SYSTEM
IN ACTION
Illustrated And Explained

By
Sharif Rahman & Amy Norwood

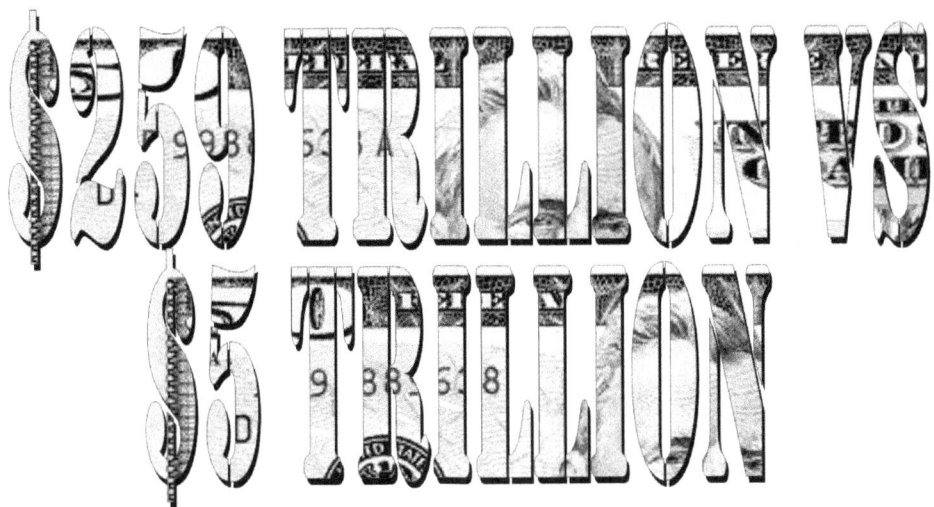

$259 TRILLION VS $5 TRILLION

Why America Is Far From Bankrupt,
Money Out Of Thin Air Explained,
The Workings Of Our Banks &
The Money System
Illustrated & Explained

BOOK 2

By

Sharif Rahman & Amy Norwood

"The United States Government is the sole issuer of money and the government is the first in line to spend this newly issued money.

The issuance of this money via the debt instrument is free and at no cost to the government because all of the interest payable to the Fed on the so called 'debt' is returned to the government and relabeled as 'profits'.

In 2010, the Federal Reserve returned USD 89,000,000,000.00 (89 billion dollars) of profits to its only shareholder, the United States Government. This totally negate the interest payable on the so called 'mountains of debt' that is due to the money supply issuance."

This second book is full of colored illustrations covering the simulation of the banking system in action plus many more. Plenty of detail explanations such as why interest need to be paid and why a central bank is required in our modern banking system is provided, among others.

DEDICATION

We would like to dedicate this book to our readers.
Don't give up hope.

ACKNOWLEDGMENTS

We would like to credit the followings for the use of their materials which were made public by them. We have taken pains on checking the licenses for the images/ artwork/clipart/vectors use in this book and used only commercial free arts. We thank them for their efforts and generosity.

Credit to Florian Hirzinger for the US Treasury Building used in the cover. Image was obtained from Wikimedia Commons. Thank you. Eagle image used on the cover is from Microsoft Clipart.

Thanks a million to All-Silhouettes.com for making a lot of the silhouettes used in our illustrations and also other artists and sites that gave their arts freely (fuzzimo.com, vectorlady.com). Clipart and images from Microsoft ClipArt (trademark of Microsoft Corp) are used with permission and images from Wikimedia Commons are appropriately credited when used..

The use of their work does not mean they endorse our book in any way.

All illustrations composition are of our own works

A lot of data used in our analysis, charts and graphs came from the United States government (Federal Reserve, FDIC, Treasury, Labor Department, etc.). We're very impressed with the data collection and archiving efforts made by the US Gov. including the Fed. There are no stinginess on their part to which, only benefits to all is the outcome. We thank them and all those who made their contribution. Historical inflation data and wealth/investment calculator is from MeasuringWorth.com and are used with permission.

Other quotes from various internet articles and books were used to illustrate a point or disagreement on certain issues and were not intended as an endorsement from those authors nor to infringe on their copyright.

ALSO IN THE SERIES:

BOOK 1

THE CONUNDRUM OF ASSETS & MONEY

(Released in Oct 2011 – Kindle Edition)
(Released in Nov 2011 – Printed Edition (Color/Normal))

BOOK 3

WEALTH OF THE UNITED STATES
Plus Major Questions Since The Financial Crisis
(Slated for release in February 2012)

By

Sharif Rahman & Amy Norwood

Table Of Contents

FOREWORD

$\mathcal{D}$ear Readers,

We hope that you had learned greatly from Book 1 of the **259 Trillion Vs. 5 Trillion series**. As promised, Book 2 will explain more about our current usage of paper money, and our banks. We also tried our best in keeping the promise of making the book as simple as we can. Therefore, you will not find complicated stuff in this book other than easy to follow tables of simulations. Please take your time to go through them. There will also be three more additional lessons to go through for better understanding- and don't forget to get your interactive lessons plus bonus materials at our website that will increase your learning level even further.

This book will jump right into Section 3 without delay, as promised earlier in Book 1.

Last but not least, request your free digital copy whenever you purchase a full price printed edition (Normal or Color). Details are at our website. Drop us a note at our official site if you have any question.

Thank you.

Don't Give Up!

Sharif Rahman & Amy Norwood Maine

SECTION 3: PAPER – THE NEW MONEY

TOPICS INSIDE :

~ EVOLUTION AND TRANSFORMATION OF MONEY

~ "MONEY IS BACKED BY DEBT" AND "MONEY OUT OF THIN
AIR" EXPLAINED

~ EXPONENTIAL GROWTH EXPLAINED

~ SHRINKING OF PURCHASING POWER OF PAPER MONEY IS
EXPLAINED

~ REMOVAL OF THE GOLD STANDARD ALLOWS FOR STABLE
AND THRIVING ECONOMY

EVOLUTION AND TRANSFORMATION OF MONEY

$\mathcal{T}$hroughout the ages, the role of money in our world hardly changes, despite numerous transformation of the money's physical form. Money is still used primarily as a medium of exchange, while its secondary role is as a temporary store of value. From the use of rare materials such as seashells, elephant husks, gold and silver, papers, rocks, to the use of common and widely available materials such as cocoa beans, sea salt, wheat, rice and many others, the one and common consistency between them all is that the form of money is changing all the time. Whatever the form money has taken; it has been tried. History has shown that there were hundreds of different forms of money being experimented with, some with good success, and some with total failure. Each form of money was later superseded by another, better form of money. It normally happens when the existing form of money is failing due to mismanagement, or simply due to the limitation of that aging form of money imposes, that a more improved version emerges. Advancement in manufacturing and technology make it more practical and natural for the new form of money to win easy acceptance.

The natural evolution of money in history was progressing

steadily towards three ideal common characteristics; First is the impossibility of being copied, second is that it can be made or removed from circulation as needed, and the third is of course, cheap to produce. Notice that 'rare' or 'expensive' is not even in the list of the ideal characteristics of money because it is actually a drawback, not a plus.

With each successive evolution of the physical form of money, the world moved closer to the three ideal characteristics of a perfect money. Back when seashells were chosen by a community as money due to its rare status, several problems occurred which cannot be solved, that is when more is needed, little can be found. They were cheap to obtain, yet they can be found by anyone or no one at all. Seashells failed to fulfill all of the three ideal characteristics of money, despite its scarcity. Sea salt on the other hand was easily and abundantly available, cheap to make, yet due to its uncontrollable production nature (read as —really easily copied), its value eventually drops to almost zero. Since then, it cannot be used as money. Again, sea salt could only fulfill two of the three ideal requirements of money. Gold and silver, were also used as money, with varying degrees of success and failures, until it outlived its function, and was superseded by a more superior form of money for use in the modern economy. Gold and silver, despite their glitter, cannot fulfill any of the three ideal characteristics of money. Hundreds of years ago, gold can only be found, not mined like today and just like seashells, it cannot be made or removed when needed. In today's world, gold is mined, at great costs, can be copied, made, and still, just like old times, cannot be removed when needed, unless gold is made illegal for everyone else except the government.

With great improvements in technology, paper money made a comeback. This form of money was used repeatedly before in history, yet it has largely failed, despite having at least one essential characteristic of good money (cheap to make) and sometimes, two (can be added and removed from circulation as needed). The second characteristic is at the hands of governments, who knew very well how to add money into the economy when required, yet no government knows how to remove money when it is needed, leading to massive mismatch between monetary demand and supply, eventually leading to total collapse.

 The failure to remove money from circulation whenever required, is one of the reasons why paper money received a bad image. Because of the mismatch, hyperinflation tends to occur since governments then only know how to inject, but not remove money from circulation. This bad press prevented the world from adopting and embracing paper money in full until the 70's.

The ascent of fractional reserve banking, overseen by a master bank (the central bank) eventually made it possible for ease of issuance and removal of money from the economy. This ability guarantees the stability of the value of the money, despite great changes in demand, during wars, large calamities and other events. This enabled paper money to obtain two of the required characteristics of ideal money. The final characteristic was soon obtained, when new anti-counterfeit technology was invented, preventing paper money from being copied and produced by anyone. With a very low production cost and the ability to be issued or removed at will, paper money has finally fulfilled the ideal form of money sought after for thousands of years. No form of money in history has ever attained all three characteristics of ideal money at the same time. A new dawn of the world's economic system was then finally upon us. **Paper money automatically became the natural choice as the ideal form of money.**

Despite its clear advantages, paper money was used only as a loose replacement for gold-based money for many decades. Paper money was linked to gold and its production was limited by how much gold can be produced. The improvements of every facet of our economic life, from central banks to tax systems, to world trade, require more money to function as economic activities expanded. Eventually economic growth was threatened by the limitations imposed by the ancient gold standard (not having even one ideal characteristic of good money). In order to continue adding wealth, America as the world's economic leader under Bretton-Woods, ignored the limitations imposed by gold through repeated devaluations of the link to gold. The limitation imposed by gold not only threatening to stop the necessary improvements of the world's financials, but also the great march of technological advancements the world was enjoying. The problem with gold is that its supply could not keep up with the world's monetary demands. Repeated devaluations seem to be the only option. If devaluation is not performed, severe deflation will occur, just like old times. The deflation that occurred in 2009 of 0.9% in America, will never be a match to the kind of deflation possible under the old gold standard, where deflation of sometimes 25% or more will occur (Great Depression anyone?) Finally, one American President in the early 70s, made a surprise courageous act of removing the link of gold to paper money for good. Once the limitation imposed by gold was no more, economic growth exploded. The full potential of the economy can then be realized. However, free-floating paper money will require a myriad of complex management. No country, no government has ever successfully managed a free-floating paper money in the history of the planet. This was one of the largest and boldest experiments ever conducted.

With the explosion of economic growth, the government and its central bank were at a disadvantaged. They have little experience in managing the growth of paper money. It is a complex system, with subtle moves, intricate relationships that encompass everything that is happening in the world, whether it is war, calamity, riots and others. Basically, it is the behavior of people, the user of the new form of money that is creating the toughest challenge in management. As everyone already knew, human behavior is neither rational nor irrational, it can be predicted or may not, and it can make sense, or does not.

Within a few years from the free float, the new paper money experiment almost fail due to rampant inflation. Believing that the government will eventually fail in taming the money beast as previously happened to many other governments before, economic growth was affected severely, and inflation exploded. Soon after, the Federal Reserve under its chairman, Paul Volcker, finally got the hang of managing the complex system, and was successful in controlling inflation. Since then, the world's economy has grown tremendously by several orders of magnitude, and with it, came unprecedented prosperity. The money beast was finally tamed; inflation declined to very low levels and has never reached double digits ever again.

In the 1990s, a new form of money emerged. A form that supersedes even the very successful fiat paper money itself. This is a form of money that also fulfills all three ideal characteristics of good money, but did it better than paper money itself. Interestingly, the new form of money is without a physical form! Such is the evolution of money from the beginning of time; from non-existent physical form during barter trades, to various forms of physical manifestations, and then eventually back to non-physical form yet again! This superior form of money is called 'digital money'. It existed only in the memory banks of computers, presented by electrons and the 1 and 0 of the binaries. Yet this new form of money achieved superior advantages compared to paper money itself. It is extremely cheap to make (almost zero costs), it can be made and removed instantly without limitation, and it can be transferred into distant lands, half way around the world, at the speed of light. On top of that, this new form of money carries additional interesting advantages; It will not become old, never wears out and never requires replacement, and the other, it cannot be easily lost or stolen despite being carried anywhere during shopping, sporting events and other activities during the course of our daily lives (in the form of credit cards etc.).

The central banks of the world who are managing the complex economic system were elated with the ascent of this new form of money. It enabled the central banks to monitor very closely the movements of money in the economy and act before things got out of hand. Banks' balances in the banking system can be monitored every 30 seconds, instead of the usual at the end of the day or every few weeks. The fast pace of the movements of money around the world, from country to country, from bank to bank, between people during trades, presented a problem of its own. Too fast can mean big shift in the market, which can be destabilizing. The 'managers' of the economic system will need to adapt to this new technology and be prepared to manage it, by mastering the technology themselves. If the central bankers are left behind by advancement in technology, they can be caught off guard by such changes in the market and will not be able to respond in time or may even exacerbate the problem from wrong response due to obsolete data.

Since the 1990's, both paper money and digital money coexisted, and since both of this new form of money carry with them the ideal characteristics of good money, they will continue to exist for the considerable future. Despite its transformation into the new form, money still existed primarily to fulfill its original function, which is as medium of exchange and its secondary function as temporary store of value.

The hard-won success of paper and digital money is now being threatened, by none other than its very own manager and guardian— the governments and its central banks.   In their eagerness and often out of bound responses to the recent economic crisis, trendy actions such as big spending with huge debt undertaking, big bailouts with borrowed money, were taken by governments of the world to please the people, despite the damages wrought on the economy. Economists, none the wiser, cheered the move of their governments to spend big, in order to avoid painful losses; yet such actions cause grave danger to the financial system. Instead of protecting and managing the system, they may end up destroying it. This will be described in later parts of this book series.

Compound interest is not for everyone and can be bad for you.
Find out in Book 3!

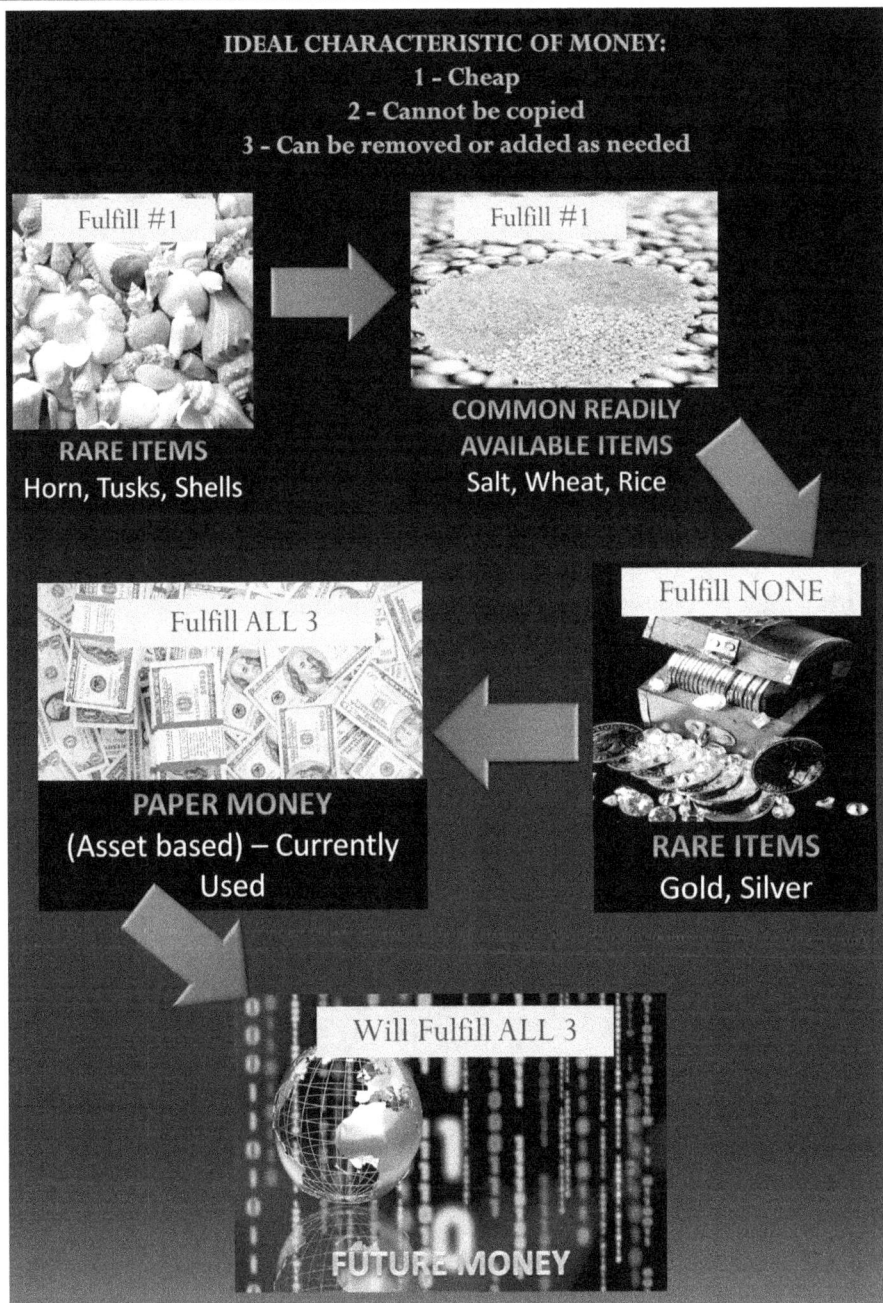

Illustration 1: Evolution and transformation of money towards the ideal money, which paper money backed by assets has already accomplished.

"MONEY IS BACKED BY DEBT" AND "MONEY OUT OF THIN AIR" EXPLAINED

*M*any people, including many economists, thought that an economy that is based on debt is fundamentally wrong. Their argument is rather simplistic. Many tried to show that debt based economy is bound to fail. They also argue that there is so much debt in the economy and that it is going to eat the country alive. They even predicted that this economy will soon crash and many other incorrect statements. One such statement is as follows:

An article found in the Internet, from Kwaves.com, stated the following:

Currently, there is about 9 trillion of US dollars in the world but a total of $32 trillion in debt. If all the US debts were repaid tomorrow, there would be not be any US dollars in the world. All the dollars in circulation today, are backed up with debts, not precious metals. Therefore, our economy today is dependent upon more debt creation.

HTTP://WWW.KWAVES.COM

MONEY IS DEBT

Illustration 2: Claims that the economy is dependent upon more debt creation is misleading.

Ouch! It is so pessimistic, but is it the truth? We beg to differ. The explanation given is too simplistic and only follows simple logic. Our experience throughout the years taught us that simply logical may not be correct all the time. This is one such case.

Another example found in the Internet, is an article written by Dr. Martenson, 'Parabolic Money Supply Growth – The End of Money'. Dr. Martenson is a respected person in the community; respected including by one of us (keep it up especially on the self preparations and being independent). However, in his article, he mentioned that money supply growth is an exponential function, hyperbolic in nature. The explosion of the debt level will continue, until the day, when it can't increase anymore just like everything else. Illustration below shows two graphs from his article.

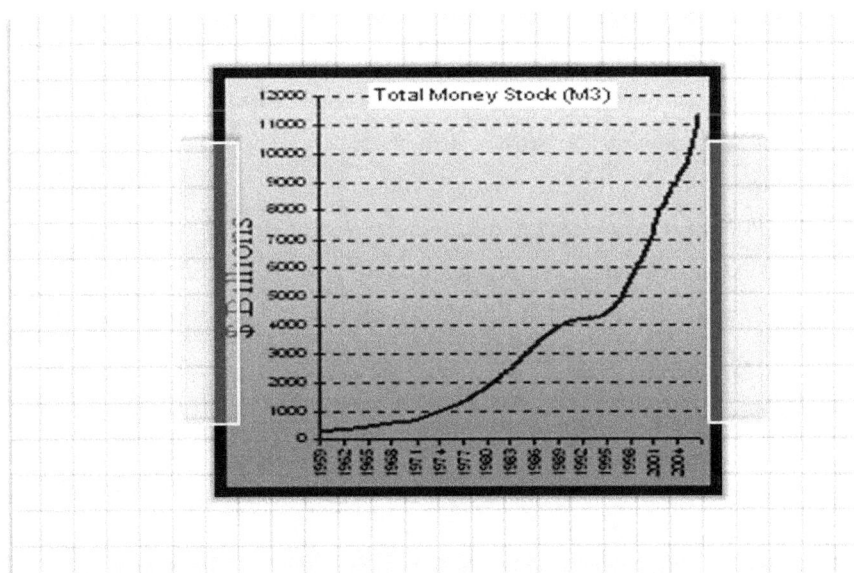

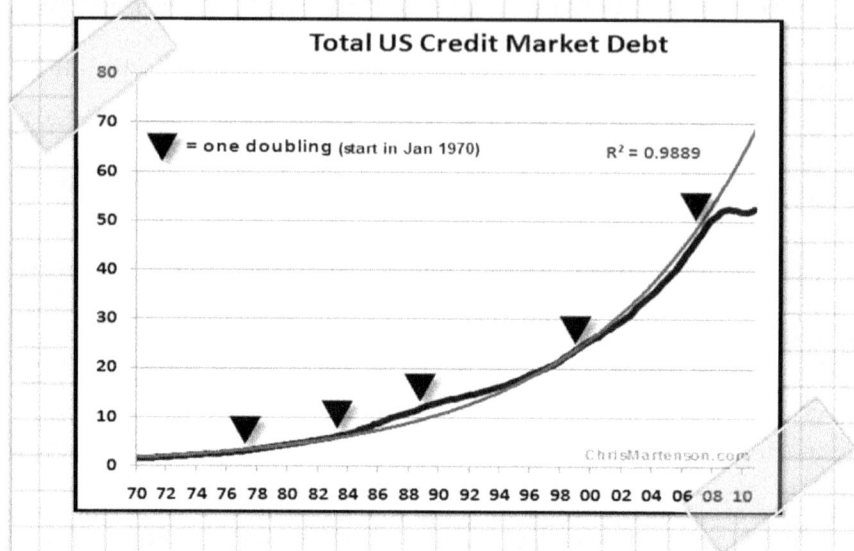

Illustration 3: Two graphs from Dr Martenson's article, Parabolic Money Supply Growth – The End of Money at ChrisMartenson.com

Dr. Martenson also wrote,

"A debt-based monetary system has a lifespan-limiting Achilles heel: as debt is created through loan origination, an obligation above and beyond this sum is also created in the form of interest. As a result, there can never be enough money to repay principal and pay interest unless debt is continually expanded. Debt-based monetary systems do not work in reverse, nor can they stand still without a liquidity buffer in the form of savings or a current account surplus. When interest charges exceed debt growth, debtors at the margin are unable to service their debt. They must begin liquidating."

Illustration 4: Quote from Dr Martenson's article, Parabolic Money Supply Growth – The End of Money at ChrisMartenson.com

He wrote further,

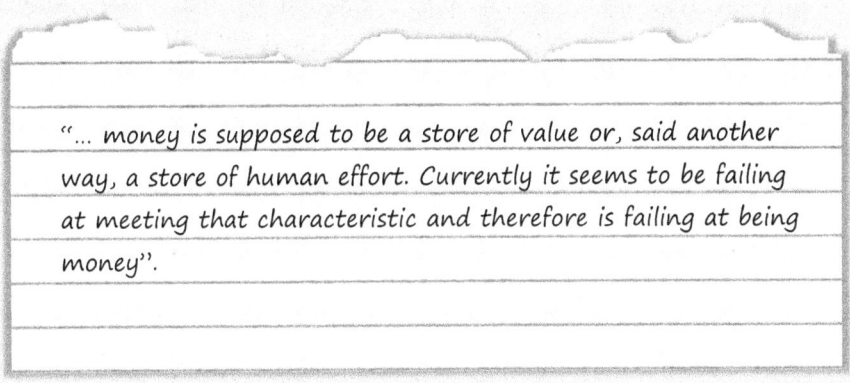

"... money is supposed to be a store of value or, said another way, a store of human effort. Currently it seems to be failing at meeting that characteristic and therefore is failing at being money".

Illustration 4: Quote from Dr Martenson's article, Parabolic Money Supply Growth – The End of Money at ChrisMartenson.com

Like so many others, Dr. Martenson said that there are not enough money in circulation to pay off all debts and its interest unless debt are allowed to be continuously expanded and several other statements such as store of human effort and the like, assuming that money is supposed to store that effort within. We however, have clear explanations on why money behave this way so read on to understand the exponential growth issue of debt and in our previous book, we already explained that money is just for temporary store of value.

In order to print money and inject the money into the economy, the money needs to be backed by something. This 'something' must be something valuable. No, gold is not valuable, as we had discussed. That 'something' is actually a real productive asset within the economy. A house or a car is far more valuable than gold, therefore our money is backed by these productive assets. For details of the discussion, refer to Lesson 1 of "Can you have your cheesecake and eat it too?" (available in Section 1 of Book 1). It was mentioned that an owner of a house could not own the house, and hold money equivalent to the house, at the same time. The fallacy created by these people (free money proponents) is that to them, someone who owns a house can issue his or her own currency, or be issued money of equivalent value and not be indebted by such an issuance. However, as was discussed earlier, this is not possible nor it is correct and fair.

When a person is issued currencies equal to the value of the house the person owned, that person will generate an additional 'wealth'. He has doubled his 'assets'; having cash and the house, which is still owned by him unencumbered. This is illogical, and since the house has no liens or claims on it, the person is still free to sell it out and run away with double the profit. He can also issues additional currencies and 'backed' such issuance to the house, yet again. And again, and again. What is there to stop him from doing it, as he owns the house indefinitely? Clearly, this has no end to it and is illogical.

Let us review the lesson again:

1. A person builds a house, which is a new asset or wealth in the economy.

2. The person does not have any hard cash and nobody will ever give him any money, unless, the house is sold or mortgaged.

3. Remember, one cannot hold the asset (the house) free of any claim or lien and money at the same time.

4. Instead of using only the house as a place to stay, the person wanted to extract the wealth locked inside the house, to do something else. However, at the same time, that person still wants to use the house as is; so, the person brings his house (title) to the bank and mortgaged it.

5. Money is issued when the asset is 'mortgaged'. Now the person has money to be used for something else, while at the same time still use the house as his home. The person has effectively doubled his command of wealth for his enjoyment. Nevertheless, clearly the house is no longer own by the person, because he had surrendered ownership of the house in return for money. This money can be used to command new wealth, but the value of wealth in the economy will still remain the same and the person, still has not double his net wealth because half of his added wealth for command is on borrowed terms.

6. Thus, the money issued to the person is backed by the asset being mortgaged. The issued money is sometimes called "debt-backed money", because it was issued from borrowing, but in truth, it is "asset-backed money" since the money was issued after the asset is swapped. The mortgaged asset cannot be used for more money issuance and is taken out of the economy; however, it still can be used in the secondary markets for swaps.

Let us review the lesson quickly in a graphical form. As usual, the illustrations are newly made but slightly altered to refresh your mind.

Illustration 6: Couple A builds a house

Illustration 7: When the house is completed, they successfully added $300,000 into the economy but they definitely don't have any cash in hand

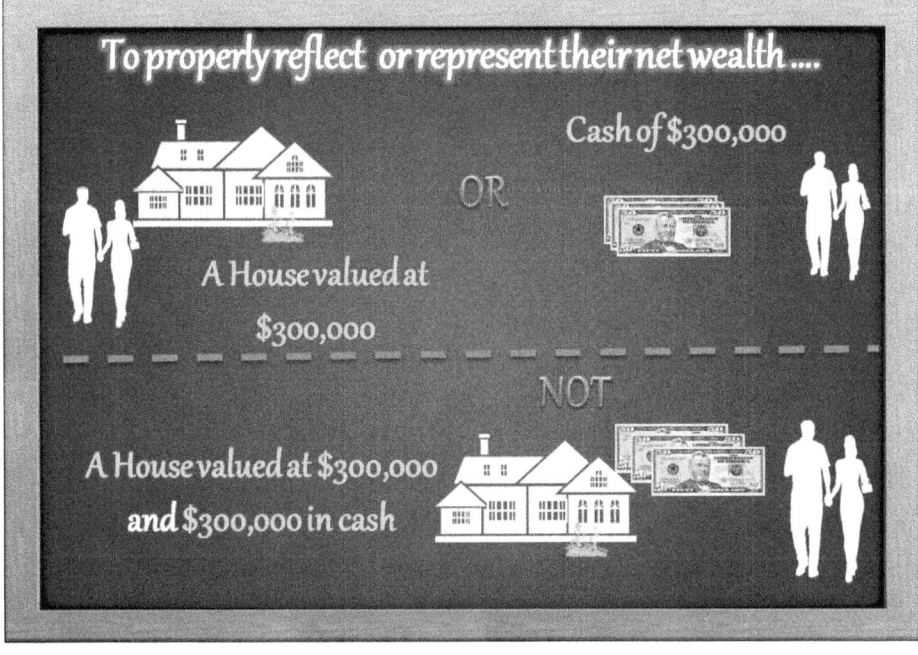

Illustration 8: Couple A's wealth is either a house valued at $300,000 or Cash of $300,000 but not both.

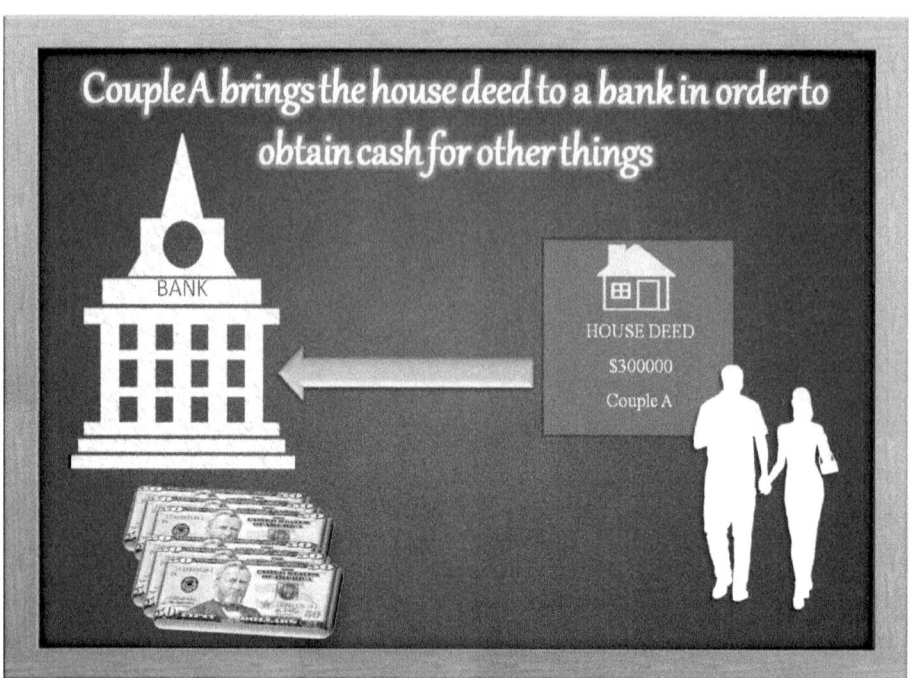

Illustration 9: Swap of asset and money occurs, where the money becomes a representation of the asset

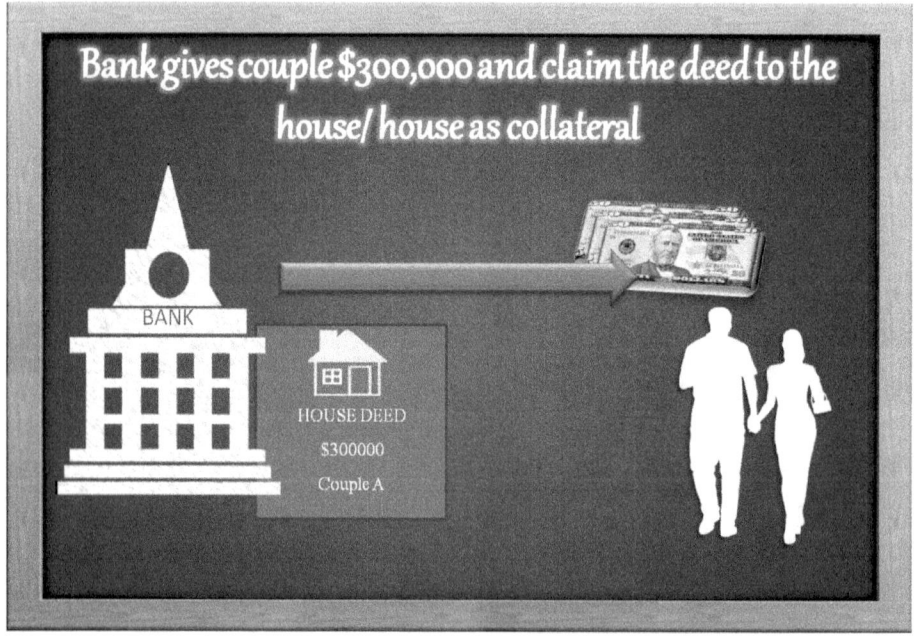

Illustration 10: Couple A is still worth $300,000 after receiving the cash and so is the bank.

Illustration 11: Paper money is backed by ASSET

Therefore, in our modern economy, an asset, such as a house, is first mortgaged, surrendering ownership of the asset to someone else, and in return is given currencies equivalent to the value of the house. The currencies issued are clearly backed by an asset, which in this case, is the house. When the statement of "backed by debt" is made, it is made in relation to the printed currency, which is backed by a debt issued, which is in turn backed by the house on which the debt is based on. Thus, there is no money created out of thin air, without backing, at any point.

Banks never create money out of thin air. Such statement is misleading. Every time a bank lends out money, it is always backed by a real asset. The bank merely exchanges the money issued with the asset mortgaged, in equal value. Looking at the deposit and the lending side of banks, every time a bank lends out money, it is always backed by a real deposit, made by someone who actually happens to have the money. Going further, this money, which is held by the depositor, was initially produced and handed to him when he sells an asset, such as a house or when he did something productive in the economy that generates wealth. Therefore, the money in question, is really truly backed by a real asset.

The consequence of this modern function of the economy is that everything seems to be backed by 'debt'. **No 'debt', no money.** In reality, there are no debts; there are only assets. Money is only issued, when it is backed by real assets. In order to issue it, the asset will need to be surrendered into the system in exchange for an equivalent amount of money. There is no slavery, no conspiracy to own or steal the world.

All of these debts can be extinguished. Just use your money to pay off the debt; it is as simple as that. The bank will transfer the ownership of the house back to you; the money issued earlier, is now extinguished. Debt based economy is really truly is, **asset-backed economy.** Read on to find more information regarding interest rates, the additional payments required to settle the debt and where that money will come from in the subsequent parts of this section.

It must be noted that a bank will not lend money, if there is no borrower. When a borrower wanted to borrow money, the borrower and the bank both are betting that the borrowed money will result in an increase in wealth in the economy and pays for itself. It is common for many people to do a job for a period of time, without any income until the job is completed. Once completed, the wealth is added into the economy. Thus, the reader must note that not all profits are immediately realized and there can be a significant time lag between the start of the work, the completion and the actual realization of the wealth or profit. Once it is added into the economy, the newly inducted asset will start producing wealth, value, into the economy. This new wealth can be used to repay the borrowed money (used to buy resources earlier).

When the earlier bet was made between the borrower and the bank, they are both counting the wealth addition capability of the new asset will be more than the loan repayments. Essentially what the bet mean is this, the value to be generated by the asset will be in excess of the loan repayments of the borrowed money, which was the economic resources and labor committed into the house in order to build it. If the value generated is less, the loan cannot be paid and the used money will be extinguished (so are the economic resources used).

Money will only be issued by banks to those who bring with them assets to be swapped, or to those who can convince the bank that their future wealth generation will be enough to pay back the issued loans plus profits for both the bank and the borrower. The money will then be taken from the always in surplus deposit side, for issuance to the borrower. When the money is running out, the bank will go to the central bank and swap the assets it is holding for fresh money. **Therefore, money is only injected into the system when it is needed.**

To answer the claim that "debt need to be continuously expanded" in order for interest to be paid (Illustration 4), one need to understand why debt is expanding in the first place. Every day, new wealth is created by wealth-generating assets, which continuously generating more and more new wealth. A factory will continue to produce things that are needed in the economy every day, and as such, it is actively adding wealth into the economy. Wealth is only destroyed when the following events occur; war, catastrophic calamities, market corrections of bubbles, obsolescence of technology and wear and tear. Thus, as wealth is expanded, money for transactions of that newly created wealth will need to expand as well. But remember, all of these assets, all of those wealth are not money. This was thoroughly explained in Book 1 – The Conundrum of Assets & Money. Thus, the expansion of debt and money in the economy is not due to the need to pay interest, it is a genuine increase due to newly created wealth.

Henceforth, interest can always be paid, unless wealth is destroyed during the events mentioned before. All money in circulation is backed by real wealth/asset and there are always surpluses of assets compared to money at all times, otherwise the money will depreciate in value.

Remember, **MONEY IS NOT WEALTH**. Money is not designed to be a store of wealth and could never be. In fact, no type of money can ever be a permanent store of value; not even when gold is used as money. The explanation is really simple, much like we cannot squeeze and store you into a box and put you away in the cupboard, we also cannot store a house into a piece of metal, or a factory into a big chunk of gold. The only way to store an asset without losing its properties and will come out exactly as it was before, is by using the 'transporter' device in Star Trek, where molecules and atoms are broken into their basic components and later can be re-sequenced to reproduce the exact same thing. Well, we're just kidding because even the 'transporter' cannot even preserve the value of the asset such as a factory. For example, the value of a similar factory in the economy continues to change over time and may even become obsolete so the factory stored in the transporter will reappear at different price level, despite keeping all of its exact properties, molecule by molecule.

Because of the reason above, which is the perfect answer to the claim in Illustration 5, paper money did not fail to be the perfect store of value because it is not designed as one. No type of money can. Our lengthy calculations and numerous simulations concluded that money existed only as a **"Temporary Store Of Value/Wealth"**. When a person receives money, it exists only for ease of transactions and for that transaction only. Money is only issued to enable transactions to take place, and since some transactions may take not days but months, money then holds the value of the wealth in question temporarily, until the transaction is finished. If someone decided to hold money longer than that, he or she must be prepared for the changes in the value of that money. To protect from the changes in value due to the impact of inflation for example, the money should be deposited, or be 'connected' to the banking system at all times to allow for automatic compensation. The money should only be withdrawn to conduct transactions and once those are completed, be returned to the banking system. We will show that this is easily done in the topic **"Shrinking Of Purchasing Power Of Paper Money Explained"** in this book. A person should not hold money in excess to what is needed for transactions because there is no need for it. Money can easily be demanded if it is needed. Hoarding money will cause trouble for the system, forcing the central bank to intervene. When you have an excess of wealth, it is normally converted into other forms of assets. The best way to store excess money is by investing into companies that add wealth into the economy for the betterment of the world via share purchase and ownership. The money is converted into a certificate of ownership of a chunk of those companies. When a person does this, he will be rewarded via an expansion of his wealth.

How does a bank produce money out of thin air as claimed by the anti-fractional reserve banking groups? There is no proof of this so far. Most banks (basically all banks) will have a loan to deposit ratio of 60% to 70% of deposit made. What it mean is that when a bank magically doles out money to someone for a requested loan, the money is actually coming from the deposit side, which is always in surplus as stated earlier. There is always more deposit than loan in any typical bank. There is however one exception— the central bank. The central bank can create money out of thin air, however two problems will appear. One is how much to print, and the other is how to distribute it fairly and widely into the economy. For the latter, the central bank such as the Fed, will only buy T-Bills issued by the government, essentially printing money for distribution and giving the government the authority to spend it. As for how much money to print, great care must be taken by the central bank, balancing many factors at once. Thus the issuance of money into the economy is basically controlled by the central bank, but the government can issue or inject money by asking the central bank to purchase its securities and bonds. We shall discuss this issue at length, so that the foundation of 'fractional reserve banking' can be properly explained.

 Since the origin of money had already been explained, we hope you will keep in your mind for good that **money is issued only when it is backed by real asset. It is better to call this process as "Asset-Backed Money issued Via Debt Instrument".** Debt-backed money phrase is coined by people who do not understand the money creation process fully. Those who do understand, have trouble in explaining this creation process to other people. In order to understand the origination of money and its propagation within the economy, please read through Lesson 2 in Book 1 of the series.

Illustration 12: Paper money is backed by assets (land, buildings, utilities, people) not debt. Debt is an instrument to distribute the money into the economy (which is turning a hard asset into a liquid asset) which is required for transactions. Of course there will always be more and more transactions in the economy as there are more and more people in the world. Money should grow in tandem with the economy.

Therefore, our money is actually backed by asset and this wealth producing assets are none other than the factories, the land, minerals, buildings, and yes, people too and everything else of value in the economy. Debt is the instrument used to fairly distribute the money into the economy and this instrument, the front face of the money creation is what people typically see and they were conditioned to assume that money is backed by debt. If they will only think one more step further, just a little bit, they will be able to see that this debt was issued when an asset is produced, making our fiat paper money, to be truly backed by real asset. So let us call it, **"Asset Backed Money Issued Via Debt Instrument"**.

From those illusions of 'mountains of debt' in the economy, a lot of "doom and gloom" writings appeared either in books published by authors, articles by bloggers in the internet, in the newspapers and even by TV hosts. They will parrot the unsustainability of these 'mountains of debt' and they will then usually go on to cite the single most popular topic — debt level of the US Federal Government. Well, we can also scare you, just like they did. Allow us to demonstrate. Let's use the National Debt of the USA as our example.

The scaring part...

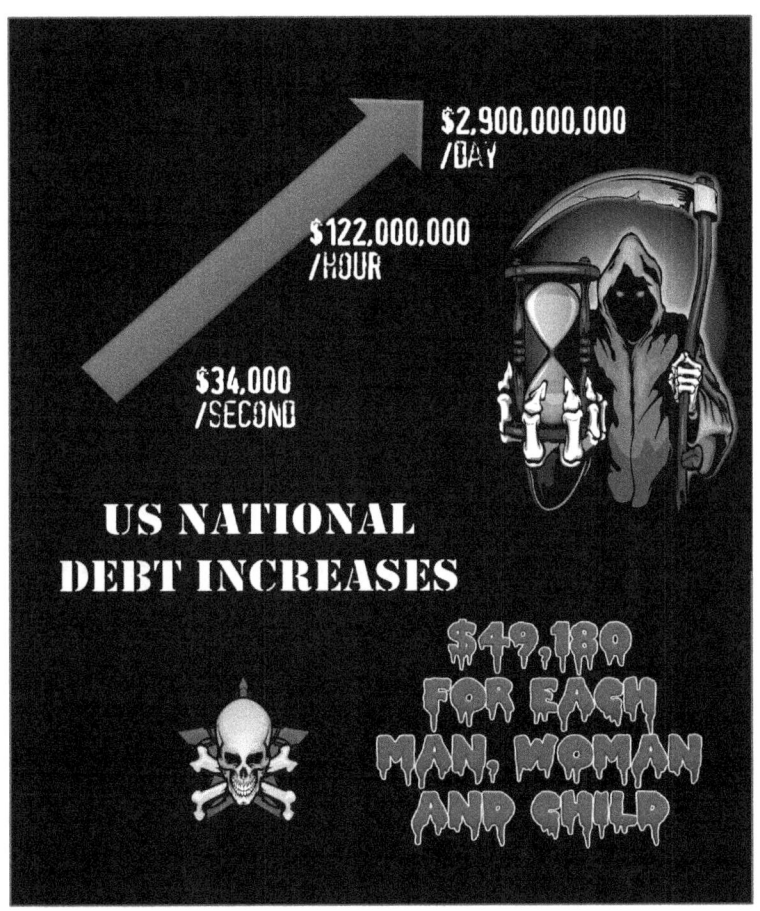

Illustration 13: The debt level of the US Federal government is fast increasing through the roof. The roof isn't your house's roof, but the reality it is so high, it is the sky itself. The debt increases by USD34,000 a second, or USD122 million an hour and in a day, a massive 2.9 billion dollars! The accumulated debt USD49,180 for each man, woman and child in the United States! It will take most of you many years just to pay off your own portion of the National Debt (which is USD49,180)

Looks creepy isn't it? But there are more! The following graphs showed the US Federal Debts and its future projected path. These kinds of graphs are what pundits like to use. Data source are from the 2012 proposed budget by the White House as well as the CBO and the Treasury.

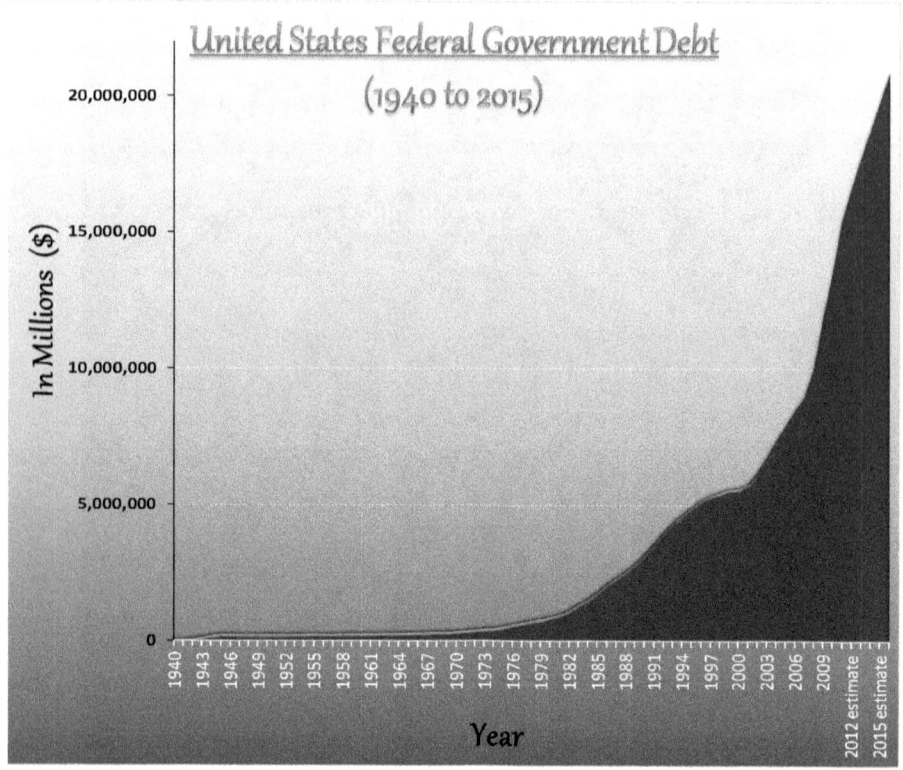

Illustration 14: Graphs shows the United States Federal Government Debt from 1940 to 2010 and Government Projection of the debt to 2015

Data Source: Monthly Statement of the Public Debt from the US Treasury

Scary that you have no idea how to pay this isn't it? It is not just you who will pay this massive debt, it is your children and their children as well! They may curse their forefathers for leaving them this massive debt.

The explosive growth of the debt as we know it, includes inflation and other factors. Let's do a correction for inflation and present the data in constant 2010 dollars.

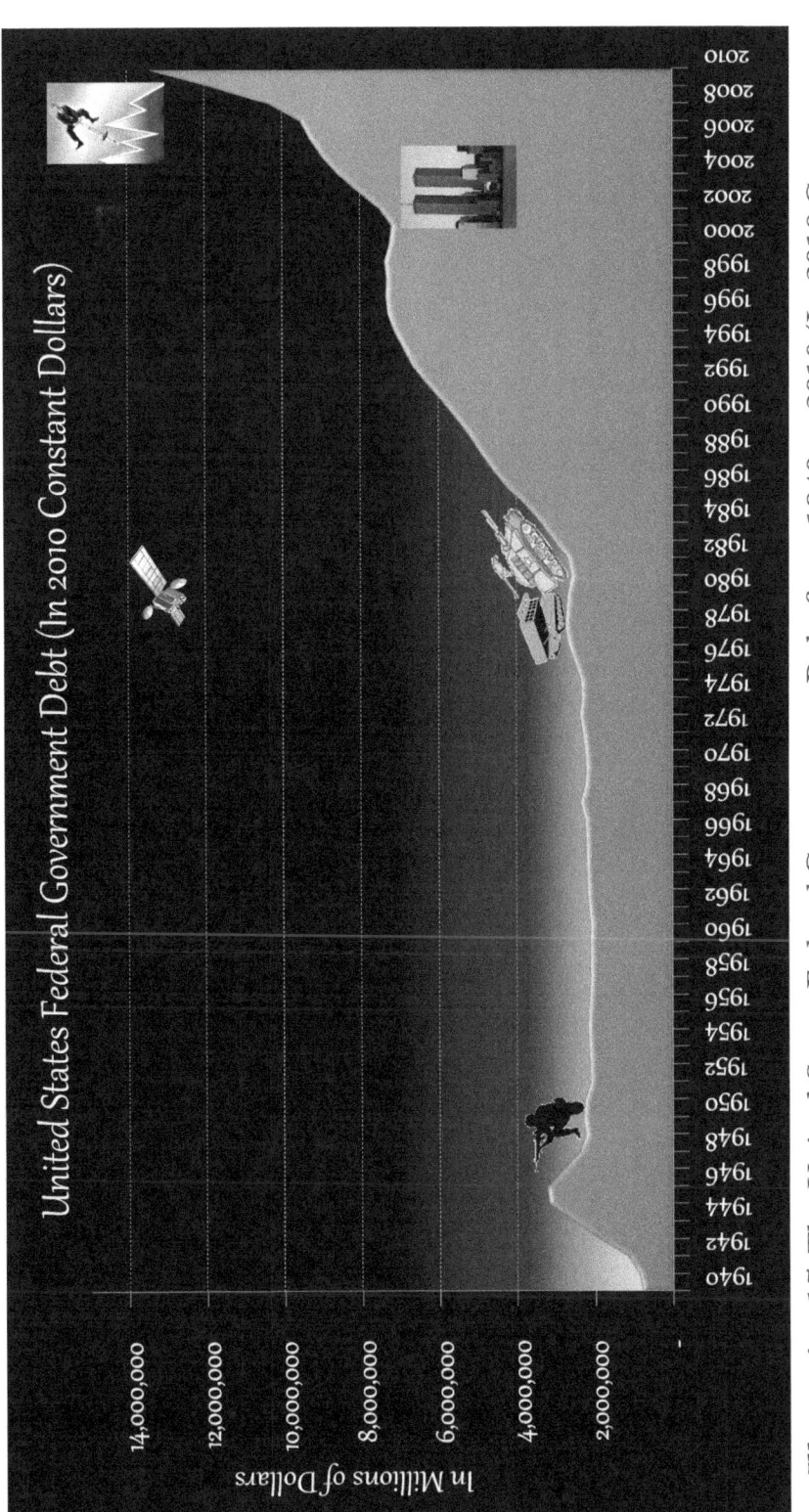

Illustration 15: The United States Federal Government Debt from 1940 to 2010 (In 2010 Constant Dollars) with Major Shocks shown

The new corrected graph revealed that from the end of WWII until the start of the Reagan years, the debt has not increased at all. It then increased explosively and then during the Clinton years, it started to decline, until Bush Jr. came into power. It then grew explosively again, unabated to this day.

Let us now see how it is projected to be in the next few years in real terms. It will scare the hell out of anyone.

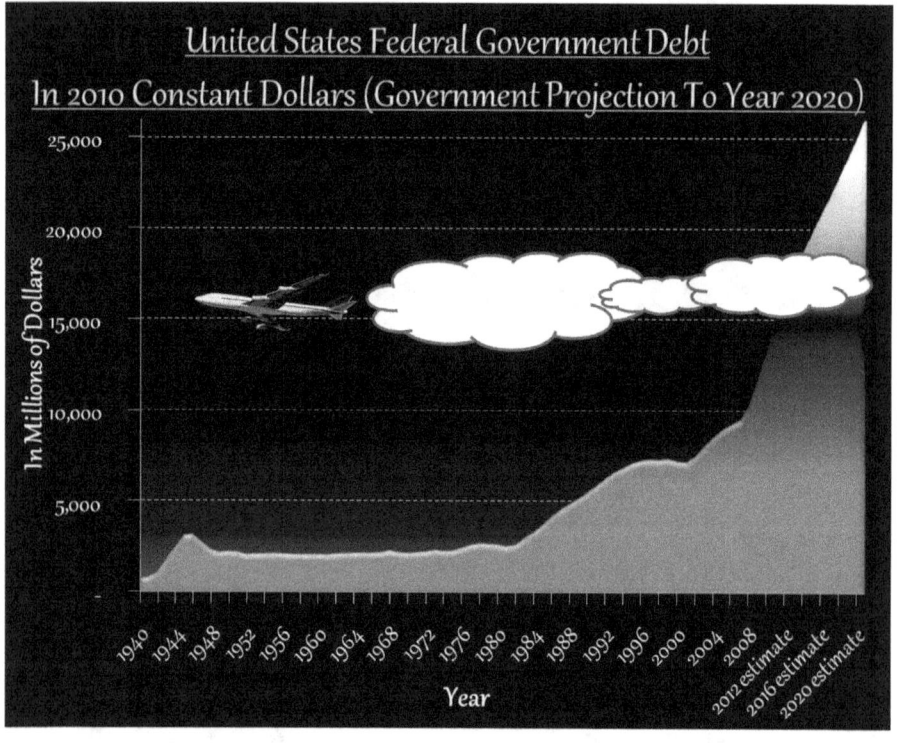

Illustration 16: The United States Federal Government Debt from 1940 to 2010 And
Government Projection Of Debt To The Year 2020
(In 2010 Constant Dollars)

Scary isn't it? Most pundits will stop here, while you are still reeling from the shock. However, there is more to the issue than that. We include just one more graph here to show how the debt grew in relation to the country's GDP. Well, this graph is not that bad, and it is still lower than during the WWII period.

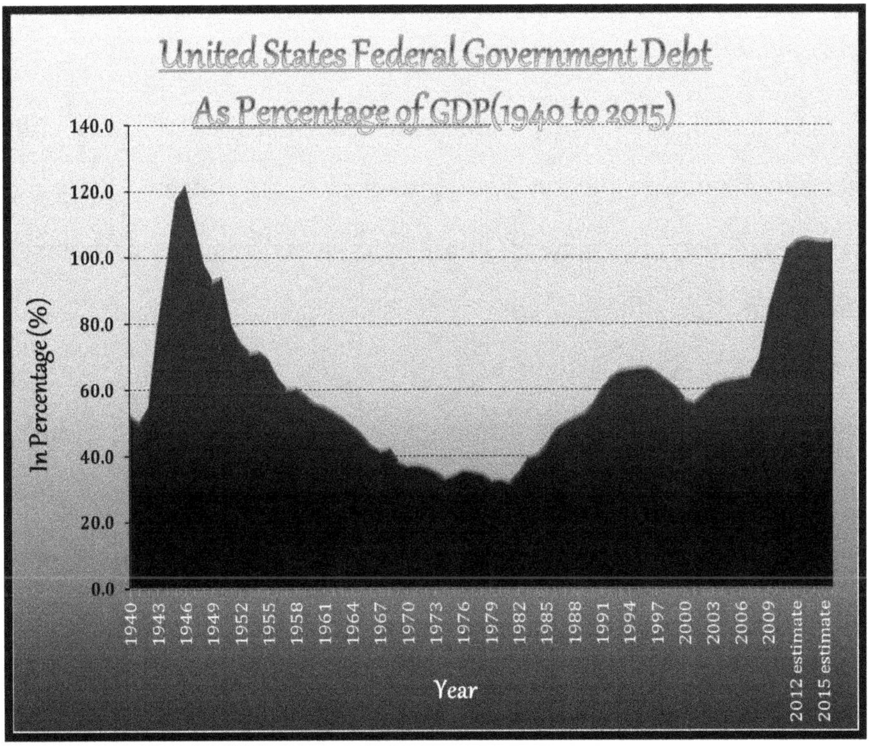

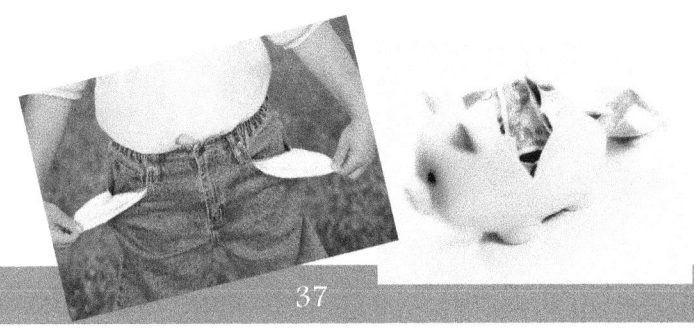

Illustration 17: Graph shows the United States Federal Government Debt As Percentage of GDP from 1940 to 2010 and Government Projection of the debt to year 2015

Enough scaring you. We want to make it a point that we can also scare you and others, and it is quite an easy task. The National Debt will be discussed in depth in **Book 3** of the series, so please read it through because we also presented a solution that is workable for everyone, to pay off the debt and build a stronger America on solid foundation. You will be surprised with the explanation there. It is not doom and gloom as has been portrayed.

Many statements only mentioned one side of the same coin. They never venture further and explain it, in its entirety. They did not explain the intricacies of the economic system, the complexity that is sometimes beyond comprehension and simple logic. This is where this book will explain how exactly the economic system function. Every economic transaction requires debt and printed currency. We already explained that printed currency can only be issued by taking out debts in **Book 1**. Some prominent people and websites go on further to state that several banks and private corporations controlled the issuance of this so called 'debt' to enslave mankind in order to steal all their wealth, yet they purportedly can print their own money out of thin air, so why the hell would they want to steal your puny amount of money?

This is simply not true!

As we have mentioned in **Section 1 of Book 1, "Central Bank or Government As Issuer of Money),** banks cannot print their own money and printing by the Central Bank can only be done by swapping of assets (asset backed) which must be issued by the Government through its Treasury.

Think about it, why would the bankers enslave people by giving **"A Lot Of Money Now"** and to be paid back later on, **"In Small Divisions Over A Very Long Time Plus Some Profits"** is considered enslaving? Did anybody put a gun to borrowers' heads and forced them to borrow? Didn't the bankers risk losing the value of their money in the event of high inflation and on top of that, if the borrowers default on the loans, they may lose all? Why would they risk losing a whole lot, for something so little?

If banks can print money out of thin air, why would they need depositors in the first place? When banks were having trouble during the recent financial crisis, **why did they not simply print money on their own and use it to bail themselves out?** Therefore it is illogical that money can simply be printed out of thin air. Wouldn't America be the super 'duper' richest country if it can print money out of thin air and need not work anymore? There are good real 'things' behind the money, backing it all the way. Just like your checkbook; whenever you issue a check, the acceptance on the check is based on the basis that there is money backing the issuance of that piece of paper (the debt instrument). After you have gone through SECTION 4 – THE BANKING SYSTEM IN ACTION in this book you will understand and will never use the misleading statement that "money is created out of thin air". The mathematical functions had proven that fractional reserve banking works and it is the fairest system of all. However, it must be noted that all systems are controlled and manipulated by human beings and as such, the performance of the system is wholly dependent on the driver.

 We must stress yet again that the **Federal Reserve is not a private bank or a cartel.** It is an entity under the government and the Chairman is appointed and answerable to the country. Even though the Fed can print money at will, history showed that it has never done so. It is always done in accordance to good economic principles. Let us contemplate the scenarios of when money is not issued in accordance to sound economic principle and the money management is left to politicians alone who are directly elected by the populists or when money is backed by commodities (gold) rather than assets of a nation.

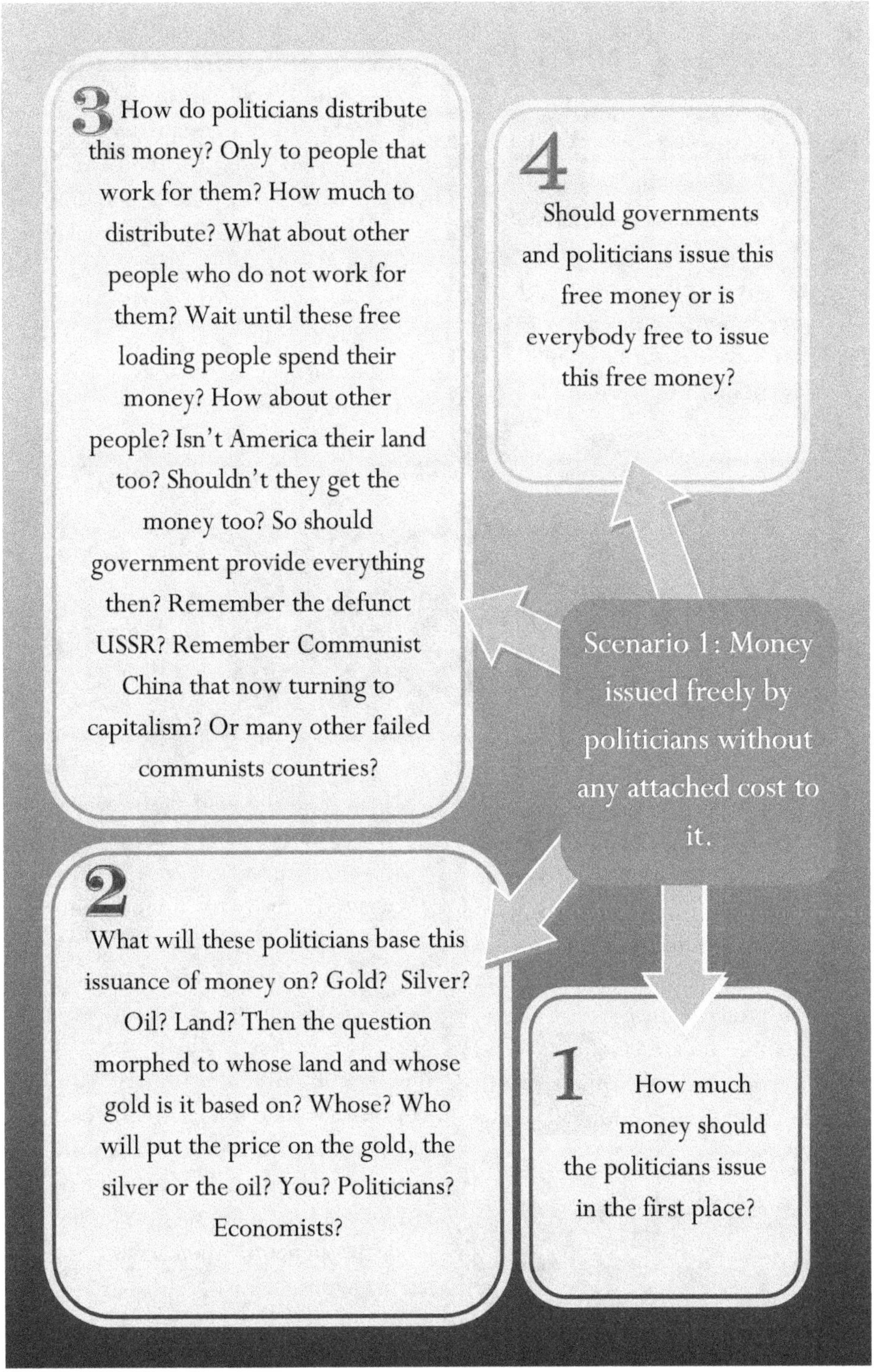

3 How do politicians distribute this money? Only to people that work for them? How much to distribute? What about other people who do not work for them? Wait until these free loading people spend their money? How about other people? Isn't America their land too? Shouldn't they get the money too? So should government provide everything then? Remember the defunct USSR? Remember Communist China that now turning to capitalism? Or many other failed communists countries?

4 Should governments and politicians issue this free money or is everybody free to issue this free money?

Scenario 1: Money issued freely by politicians without any attached cost to it.

2 What will these politicians base this issuance of money on? Gold? Silver? Oil? Land? Then the question morphed to whose land and whose gold is it based on? Whose? Who will put the price on the gold, the silver or the oil? You? Politicians? Economists?

1 How much money should the politicians issue in the first place?

Illustration 18: Scenario #1—When money is used freely by politicians with no cost attached

1 Who controls gold? Gold is mined and most are mined by corporations and not governments. Should gold then be illegal to be mined, except by the government?

2 Should gold in raw forms, other than its monetary form be made illegal to be owned by individuals in the economy because they can use it to make counterfeits? How would this be enforced and at what cost? How about those countries without any gold deposit? How can they "buy" their money?

Scenario 2:
Physical gold money or
gold backed money

3 Gold as money has been tried and failed. At that time the entire wealth of the world was only a fraction of today's wealth and gold could not keep up then. How can gold keep up now? Devalue wealth? Inflate Gold? Would anybody even want their wealth deflated to accommodate gold? Would you?

4 If all the gold in the whole wide world (already mined) is melted and then distributed equally to all inhabitants of this world, then each and every person would get a minuscule amount, not enough even to buy a 3D TV. And we will be stuck at this wealth level until more gold can be found or less people live in this world. So it is probably not the bankers or Rothschild that want to kill off many people, seems like the gold proponents themselves for having a motive for it.

Illustration 19: Scenario #2—When gold money is used or gold backed paper money

So which scenario would you choose?

For Scenario 1, what these misguided 'freedom fighters' parroting free money is actually parroting communism whether consciously or not. Back then, the communist citizens pretended to work, and the government pretended to give them real money. Nobody can own anything and everyone is on the payroll of government. Their economies failed. China realized this and they turn to capitalism but still pretended to be communist. We had gone through the question whether the government is the issuer of money and whether it is issued at no interest and free thoroughly in our simulations of the economic system and we concluded the followings:

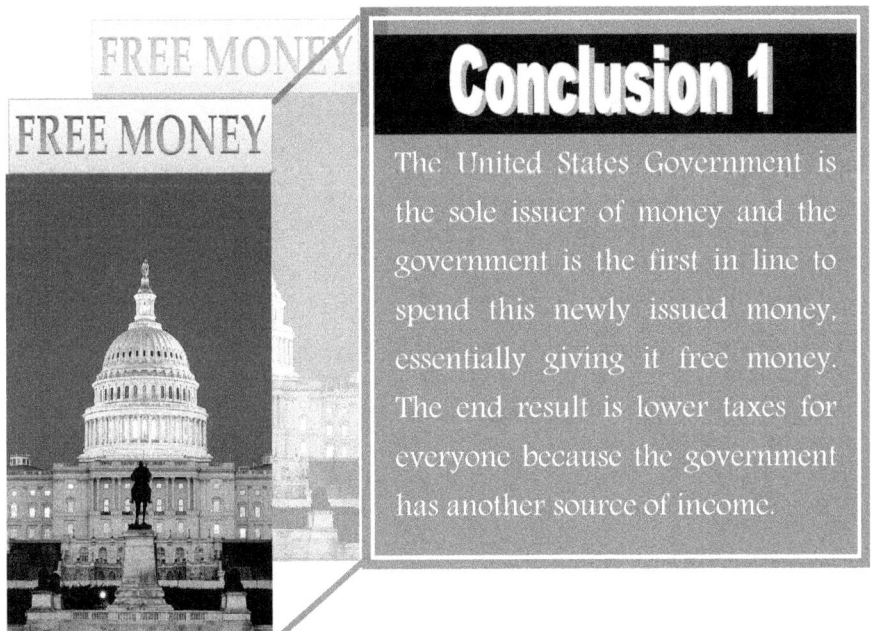

Conclusion 1

The United States Government is the sole issuer of money and the government is the first in line to spend this newly issued money, essentially giving it free money. The end result is lower taxes for everyone because the government has another source of income.

Illustration 20: Conclusion #1 on "Free Money" issued by the current USA government

Conclusion 2

The issuance of this money via the debt instrument is free and at no cost to the government because all of the interest payable to the Fed on the so called 'debt' is returned to the government and relabeled as 'profits'. In 2010, the Federal Reserve returned USD 89,000,000,000.00 (89 billion dollars) of profits to its only shareholder, the United States Government. This totally negate the interest payable on the so called 'mountains of debt' that is due to the money supply issuance.

Illustration 21: Conclusion #2 on "Free Money" issued by the current USA government

Contrary to what populists said that government must print their own money without any need for debts (assets actually) with proper governance, history had proven multiple times that such socialism never works and all countries who adopted them has failed or now in a very bad shape. Some countries can sustain this silly giving for extended period by plundering their natural resources. Free market will work as each individual has a choice

in participating. Banks are just another component of the economic system that distributes money that is printed by the government. Banks also have to charge for the services they give everyone (voluntary acceptance in accepting their services-nobody forcing consumers at gunpoint to accept these services) because they have to pay salaries, rents, buildings, consumables and so forth. There are also many banks to choose from. They do not monopolize the market because banks that are not reliable with bad services will definitely get less and less business and eventually fail. The Federal Deposit Insurance Corporation (FDIC) introduced by the government actually covered sizable sums of deposits, guaranteeing all depositors. Anything exceeding the covered amount is not covered and should be allowed to liquidate and be eliminated from the system. This is a very basic form of capitalism. We urge you to think twice of where you put your money. Don't just look at the returns, but look at the strength of the bank itself. This is absolutely essential if your savings exceeded the insurance coverage limit.

In bad times, people tend to blame something that they can't put a face on but as usual, it is never themselves. For example, as house prices continued to go up above and beyond the affordability level of most people and with loans that they couldn't possibly afford, many Americans continue buying homes, even houses that they knew they could not afford. Is it greed of profiting from the house appreciation or is it because of fear that house prices will continue to go up or is it because they follow those "Property GURUs" that said, "Real Estate will always go up and up!" which is a very misleading statement! So who is exactly to be blamed? Ultimately, the blame fell upon each and every one who participated in that crazy bubble blowing period. All bubbles will eventually burst, that is why, knowledge is the most important weapon in navigating the economic system and your own personal finance. Not money, not gold and certainly not greed. As we have said in **Book 1, Greed Is Not Good!** Forget Gordon Gecko. He was not correct then and was not correct now.

Now that you have understood the real meaning of asset, the real meaning of debt and then the real, absolutely true meaning of "debt-backed money" which is in fact "asset back money via debt instrument", we can now easily explain why or how there are only 9 trillion dollars of money, to 32 trillion dollars of debt. Money is only a medium of exchange, it does not have to be in similar value to asset, wealth or debt. Money can be used repeatedly to pay for things, and similarly the same money can be used to pay many loans repeatedly over and over. It is like tokens in the arcade center. To pay the 32 trillion debt mentioned by kwaves.com article in Illustration 2, is really easy. Withdraw 9 trillion of money from the banks, pay off the loan of 32 trillion by paying the banks, so the balance becomes $32 - 9 = 23$ trillion.

Money in the banks is now back to 9 trillion of course. Then withdraw the same 9 trillion, and pay off the remaining 23 trillion. Repeat the steps until all debts are paid off. This is how debts are being paid in the economy because to have that much debt, is to have at least that same amount in wealth (there are much more wealth than debt typically, and they do not openly tell you how much). Wealth is discussed thoroughly in **Book 3**. To prove these payment cycles are possible, look in **"Lesson 6 – Loan Repayments in Fractional Reserve Banking"**.

In **Book 3** of this series, we shall discuss the importance of good financial education. Please read through it to prepare yourself for the world and thus, allowing you a great peace of mind while pursuing your dreams, all in a safe and confident manner, knowing that you actually do good for society.

Why the US Federal Government is bleeding money? Is it simply due to reckless spending or some other reason?

Find out in Book 3.

EXPONENTIAL GROWTH EXPLAINED

$\mathcal{T}$his is an interesting topic, one that will blow the economists hats off. Let us start with looking at the 'famous' bacteria population growth chart.

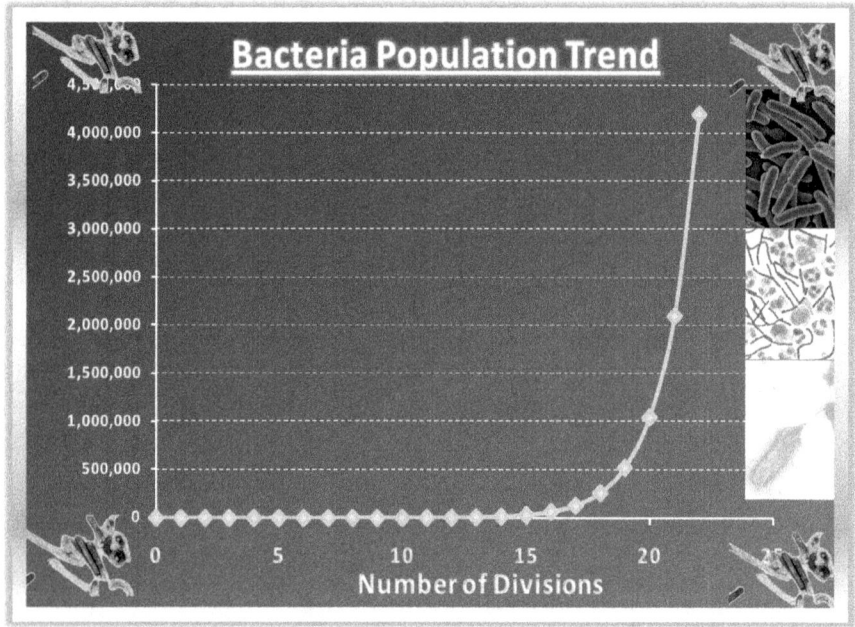

Illustration 22: Bacteria Population Growth Is Exponential!

In this chart, bacteria population growth over several divisions is shown. As you can see, this is the typical exponential function mentioned by many 'experts' which they used to back their proclamation of the impending doom of the economic system. In this chart, bacteria will double during each division, growing exponentially beyond imagination. Now let us check out the chart for human population growth and compare it to that of bacteria.

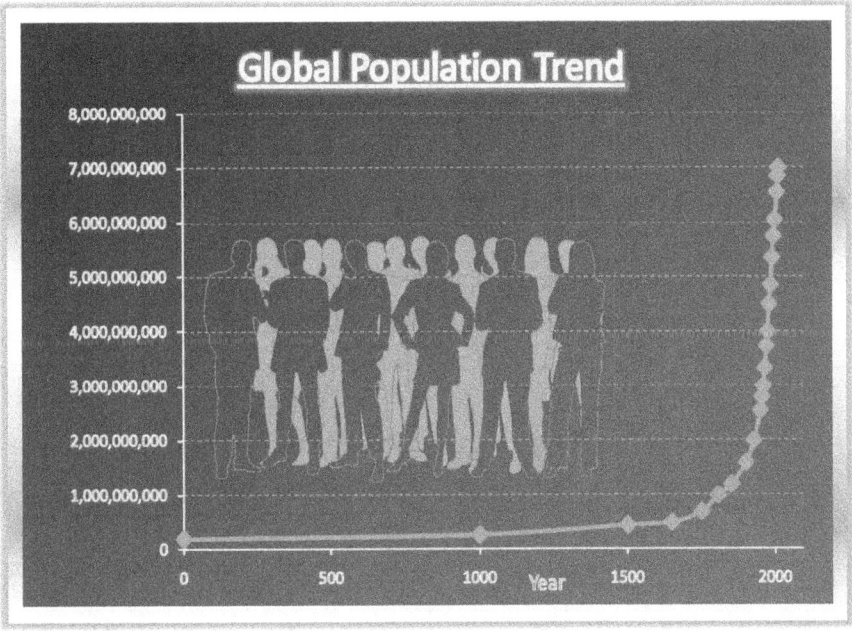

Illustration 23 : Global Human Population Growth Trend Is Also Exponential!

Both charts are showing a similar exponential trend! In fact if the charts are switched, it will be impossible to tell which is which. Both of them are indeed exponential functions. Why you might ask? The answer is that we humans, just like the bacteria, also double ourselves every generation or so. When you get married and have four children, you will double the human population for that generation. If you have three children instead, that's 50% increase and if you have only two, you will not cause any increase at all. If you have more than four children, then that is more than double. The minor difference between the growth of bacteria and humans is the time taken for successive new generations to grow up where bacteria are measured in minutes while humans are measured in years.

If human population growth is indeed exponential, then how about our economic growth? Since every person will generate his or her own monetary activities, is it logical to assume that our economic growth will also be exponential? The answer is yes, and this is proven from the charts shown by those economic 'experts' who claimed our monetary growth is exploding exponentially. There is a perfectly logical explanation for this phenomenon. The economist and those experts do not realize it though. The very fact that human population growth is exponential, will push the economy to exhibit a similar trend. On top of the exponentially growing population, there are two other factors directly contribute to the exponential growth of the economy; Inflation and Productivity. Both can skew the rate of increases, far higher. But for America, there is one other special contributing factor— the USA economy is the dominant economy on the planet, and the US Dollar is the de facto worldwide currency. The demand for this currency will skew the monetary base or the money supply, since it is used by an unknown number of users worldwide (It will tend to show higher money usage and demand by the internal US population). We hardly see economists correct their data for US Dollars demand abroad, therefore care must be taken in digesting data presented by them in this regard.

Before we proceed, let us check out the chart for linear increases, which is not exponential. Those economists and certain 'experts' think everything should grow linearly over time, especially things that are related to money, debt and the economy. But consistent linear growth is entirely impossible for reasons we are about to show you.

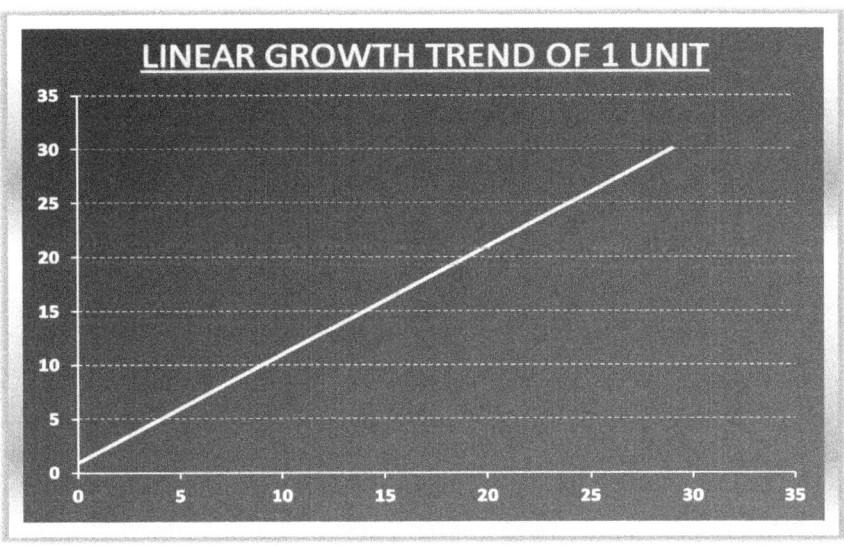

Illustration 24 : Constant Linear Growth Trend Graph. Each cycle, the same amount of increase is added. No fix yearly percent increase is calculable because the value goes to zero as the cycle or year progresses.

As you can see, linear growth is the same amount of increment, every time, on every cycle. In the example above, the rate of increase is one unit per cycle. No surprises here, it is just constant and steady growth, the same amount every time. An example of things that are linear in growth is your age. Every year, you will age by a year, not more and not less. It does not matter how old or how big you are, the amount of incremental increase is the same throughout.

Let us now turn our attention to exponential charts, starting by a regular and continuous 3% annual growth rate. Let say you put in one dollar in CD (Fixed Deposits) earning an annual return of 3%.

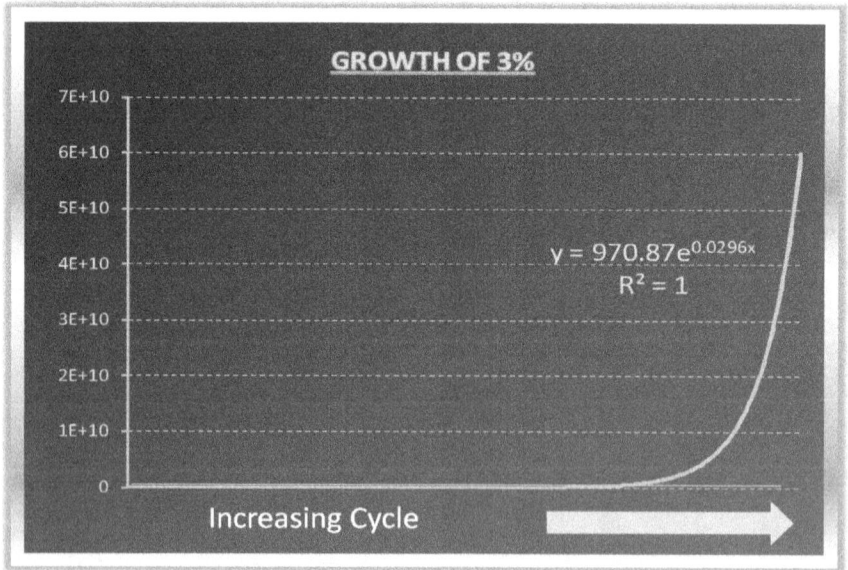

Illustration 25: A Constant 3% Growth Per Cycle Will Result In An Exponential Growth Trend

An increase of 3% per annum will result in the parameter to increase exponentially. From the chart above, the trend line fit is showing e0.0296, which is basically a 3% compound increase. Now let us see what will happen if a smaller increase of only 1% per annum is used.

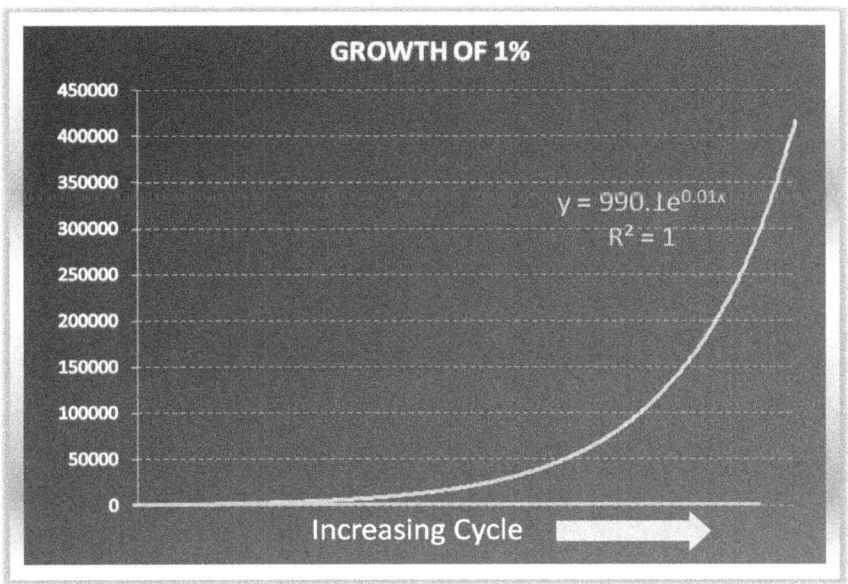

Illustration 26: A Constant 1% Growth Per Cycle Will Also Give Rise To Exponential Growth Trend

Interestingly, even a 1% per annum increase every year, will result in an exponentially growing line.

Well, let's try an even more extreme value, one that is less than 1.

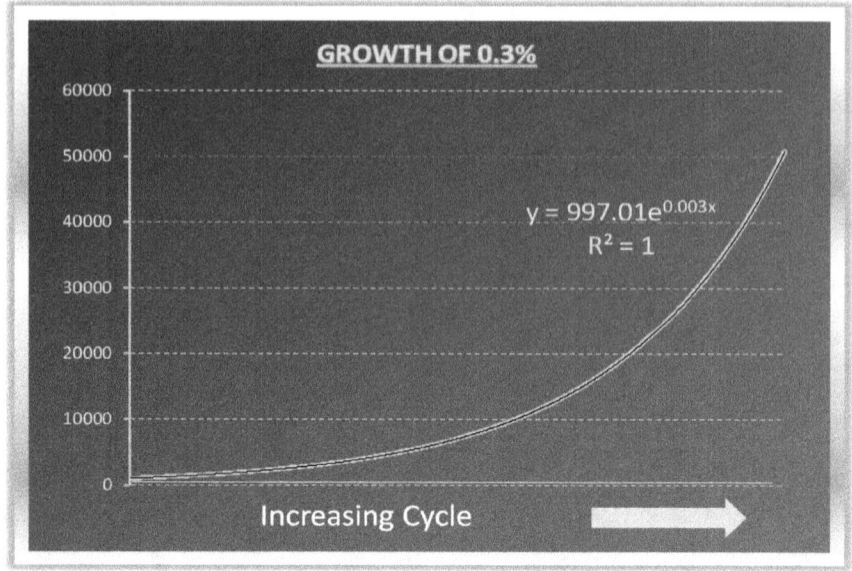

Illustration 27: A Constant 0.3% Growth Per Cycle Will STILL Give Rise To Exponential Growth Trend

It is still an exponential function! Actually it does not matter what percentage it is, whether it is 10% or 0.3%, as long as it is a percentage of a parameter, compounded over time, will result in an exponential function. Any parameter that is to be grown, or be increased using 'percentage', will result in an exponential function. All engineers should know this fact, as well as many other regular folks, however not those economic 'experts'. Somehow, it does not stick to them. They harped on the exponential functions, exploding money growth and so on, yet they had missed the point.

 The point is, it is supposed to be exponential!

Now let us turn our attention to the chart of United States GDP since 1792.

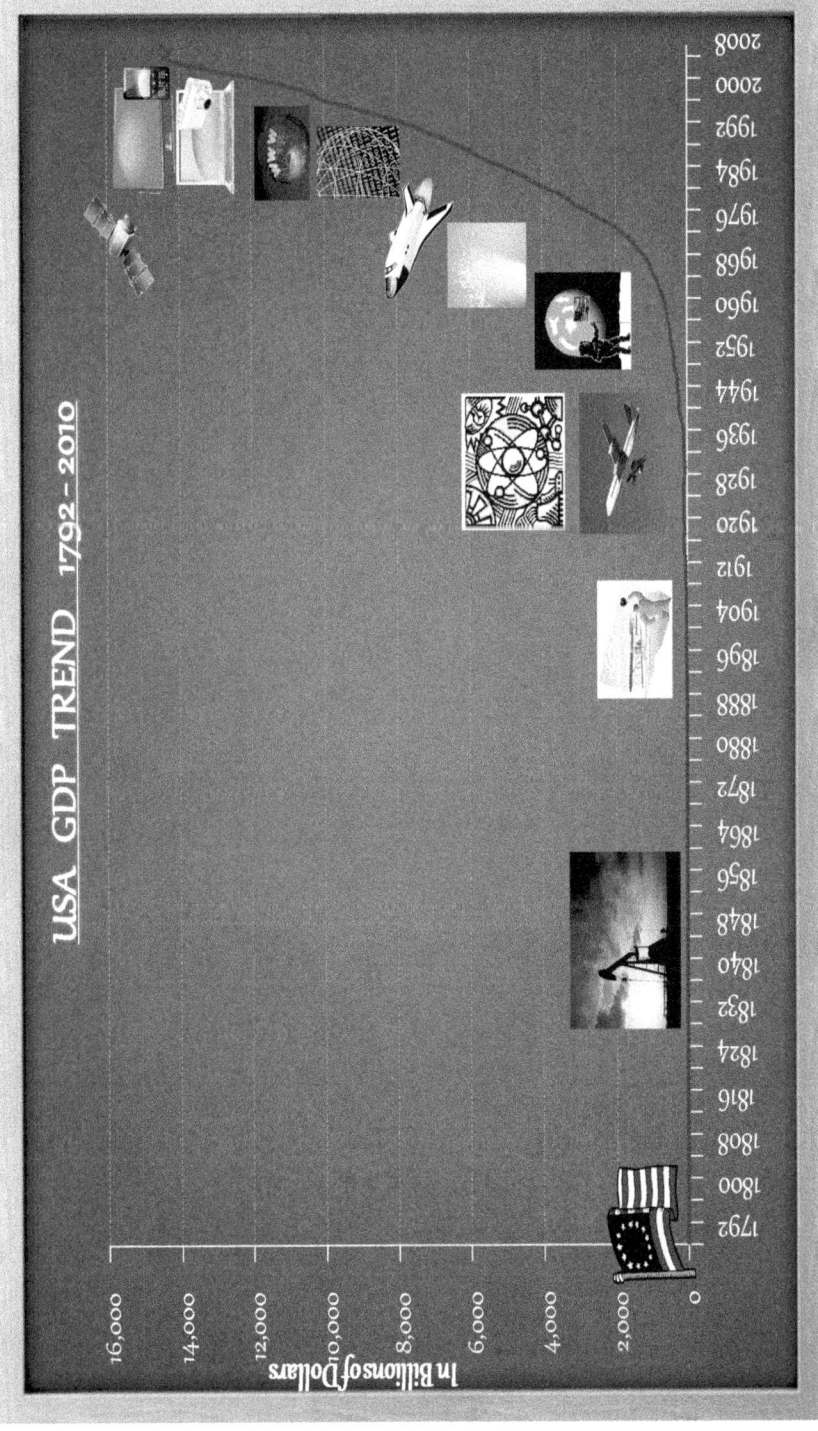

Illustration 28: USA GDP Trend Over The Period Of 213 Years Is Exponential Too!

As you can see in Illustration 28, this US GDP chart is an exponential function. The reason for the exponential nature is of course, due to population growth and productivity, coupled with inflation.

We inserted some pictures of major discoveries and technological advancements during the period. We can conclude that the pace of scientific discoveries and other advancements of the human race, accelerate according to the exponential growth trend. Since we (the authors) is from a heavily technical background, we would like to inform the reader that the compounding effects of multiple technological breakthroughs are truly massive. When the internet was first commissioned, it was just a simple network. But today, the internet has grown tremendously, connecting billions of devices. It also spawned many other advancements and possibilities such as online shopping, online banking and whole new industries, residing fully in the virtual world. Just a few years ago, it will take you hours and hours to queue up and pay all your bills. Today, you can settle all of your bills in mere minutes, without even travelling. The increase in efficiency is enormous. Imagine saving three hours of your time, which can be used for other purposes.

The graph of the USA GDP were packed with pictures,

especially towards the end, as the pace of advancement accelerates. However there is no space to insert more pictures at the end, with shorter time span but more discoveries. The exponential growth of the GDP of America is therefore justified and realistic.

In the following exercise, we will try to isolate the effects of inflation, productivity and population growth, on this GDP numbers. First we shall pick a shorter period to focus our attention on, let's pick the 1980 to 2010 period. The following chart showed the close up of the GDP for that period.

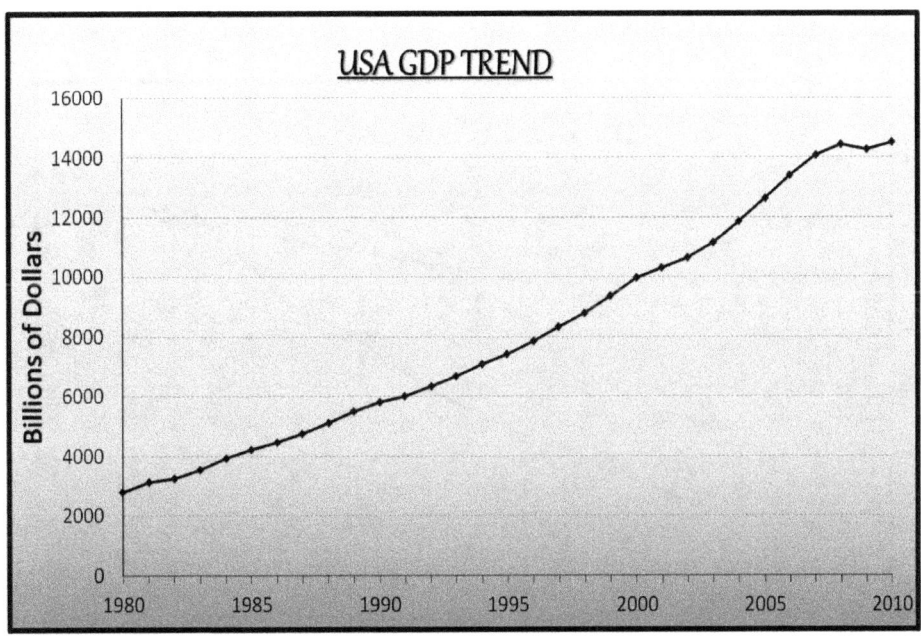

Illustration 29: Graphs shows United States Gross Domestic Products Trend From 1979 To 2010

The USA GDP trend that was shown earlier (Illustration 29) is an exponential chart, however, the steepness of the curve is rather subtle due to the shorter time span. If you notice, this is one way where the economic 'experts' will try to do their magic in trying to confuse you. Shorter time span can mask the true exponential function, showing an almost linear graph to untrained eyes. Now we know, that all of our economic charts relating to population, will be exponential, no matter what. Economists and the 'experts' can manipulate the time period to show otherwise.

Now let's superimpose the population growth trend during the period inside this GDP chart.

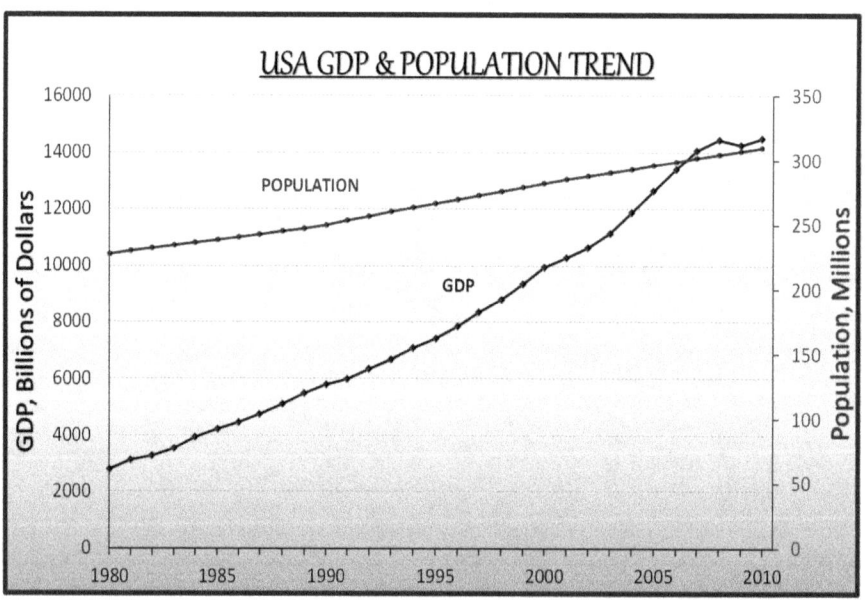

Illustration 30 : Graph shows USA GDP & USA Population Trend From 1980 To 2010.
GDP is growing faster than population growth as it should.

Now you can see that the population growth trend line is almost a straight linear line. Don't be mistaken like the 'experts' who can't distinguish between an exponential function and a linear function, because as we had shown earlier, the population growth trend is no doubt, is an exponential function. Due to the graph's much shorter time span, the steepness of the exponential curve is not easily seen. From both trends in the chart, the rate of increase of GDP is much higher than the population growth rate. This is typically shown side by side or in the same chart by our friendly economists, and they will then harp that the rate of increase is exponential, exploding beyond belief and so on. It's a pyramid, a ponzi scheme and many other terms. Let us assure you, that is really not the case. If the Fed is inflating the economy or the money supply exponentially (which we now know is suppose to be normal, so let's reword our sentence); If the Fed is inflating the economy or the money supply in a higher exponential function with a steeper curve than the prevailing exponential rate of the population growth, then we can surely find the facts to support it. **So far, we did not find such supporting facts.** The Fed actually injected money as necessary and not purposely to keep the 'pyramid' scheme going as they claimed. Every dollar of injection is well justified all these years, even during the financial crisis of 2008. Their supposed steep exponential curve of money growth is not corrected for inflation and productivity growth. Now let us correct the GDP data for inflation rate, which had skewed the rate of increase of the GDP.

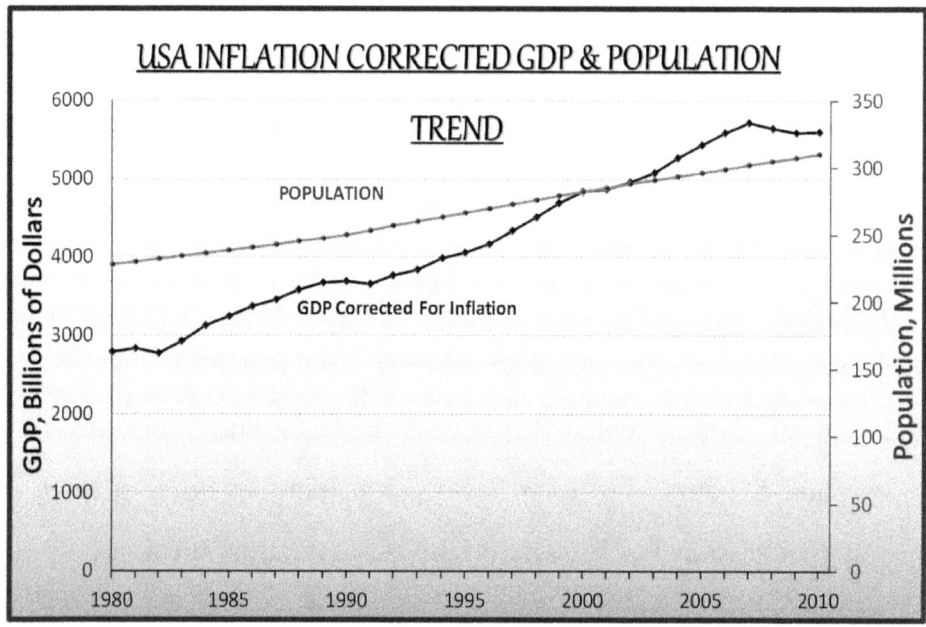

Illustration 31 : Graph shows USA Inflation Corrected GDP & Population Trend From 1980 To 2010. When corrected for inflation, the GDP growth is flatter.

The rate of increase of the GDP is now less steep and approaching the rate of population growth after inflation rate correction is applied.

Now let us correct for the other source of GDP increases skewness— productivity growth.

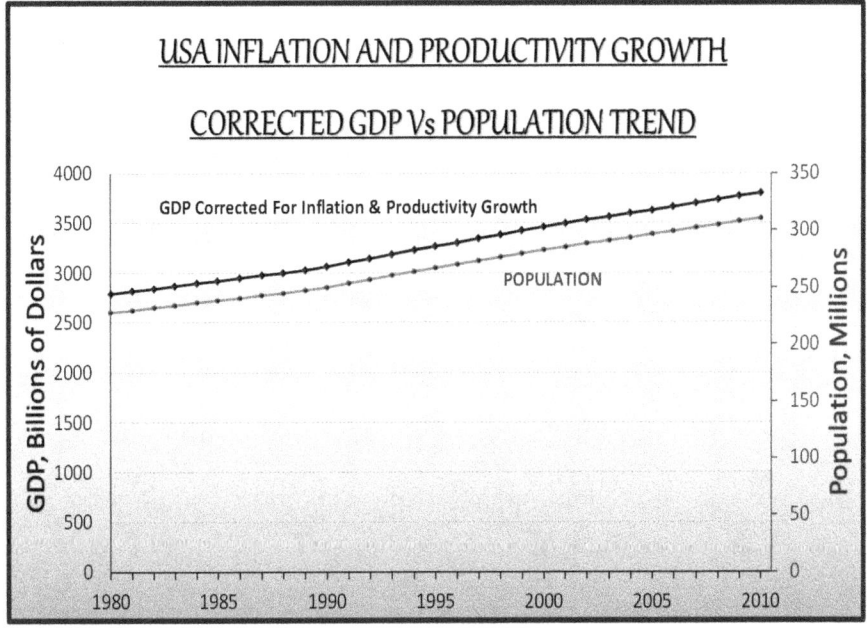

Illustration 32 : Graph shows Inflation & Productivity Growth
Corrected USA GDP & Population Trend.
Both graphs grew exactly in tandem. This proved that GDP is related
to productivity, population and inflation.

Voila! Now you can see that the rate of increase of the GDP with the absent of inflation and productivity growth, mirrors the rate of increase of the population exactly. There is no 'explosion' or anything, and since we already knew that population growth trend is actually exponential in the long term, then the GDP growth is also exponential. No surprises there. The data is obtained from various sources such as the BEA and the Federal Reserve and for productivity growth, the data is obtained once inflation and population growth is filtered out. Afterwards, it is compared to standard productivity growth data such as from the

Bureau of Labor Statistics and others which are scattered all over the place (there is no consolidated productivity growth trend chart for the whole country). As it turns out, it is not easy to measure this parameter, however we are able to confirm that the productivity growth are averaging around 1.3% over the period, close to other productivity improvement data.

The following illustration will show that in the absence of other factors, the GDP will typically follows the growth of the population, which by itself, is an exponential function. This GDP is shown in the chart as 'GDP Base'. The second line is the 'GDP Base + Inflation'. This line shows the impact to GDP growth when inflation is factored in. The exponential function of the original GDP Base has become a steeper exponential function. The third line will show the impact to GDP growth when inflation and productivity are both factored in. This is the typical GDP figures we are seeing and published by the Fed and economists.

Until now, economists still do not know the answer of whether government deficit spending is inflationary or not. Find out in Book 3 of the series!

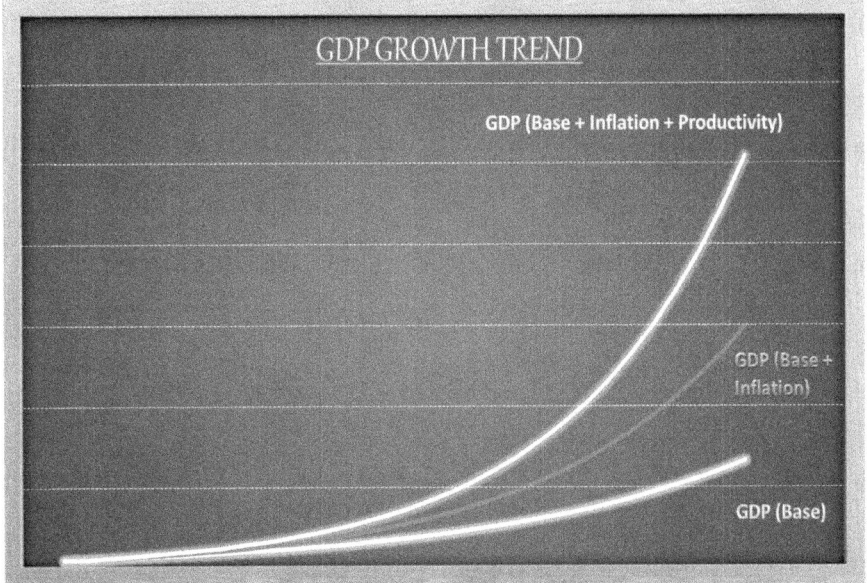

GDP GROWTH TREND

GDP (Base + Inflation + Productivity)

GDP (Base + Inflation)

GDP (Base)

Illustration 33 : Graph shows United States Gross Domestic Products Trend From 1979 To 2010.
As shown earlier, GDP (Base) will grow at least in tandem with population growth. The high level of GDP growth over the years is due to productivity gains and inflation.

To conclude;

GDP growth is exponential in nature. Factors affecting GDP growth such as population growth trend, inflation and productivity are all exponential in nature as well.

Thus, exponential GDP growth is not a problem and is to be expected. In fact if it is not growing exponentially, something is wrong because the economy is not performing as it should.

Now let us turn our attention to another popularly attacked

parameter, the monetary base of the banking system. The growth of the monetary base frequently becomes the stalking point of the anti Fed and the anti paper money groups. They as usual harped that the monetary base growth is exponential and made many other wrong accusations. We had demonstrated that the growth of any part of the economic parameter where there is some sort of dependence to the growth of the population as a whole, would indeed be exponential. The growth of the monetary base is no exception to this, as we shall present below. To those who do not know what monetary base is, it is the amount of reserves of all banks, whether it is in their vault or in the Federal Reserve System. Economists sometimes called it 'high powered' money due to its ability to be used for lending expansion in several orders of magnitude from its base.

The following is the chart of the monetary base of the United States since 1980 until the mid 2011.

Do you think the poor is poor because the rich took theirs? Find out in Book 3.

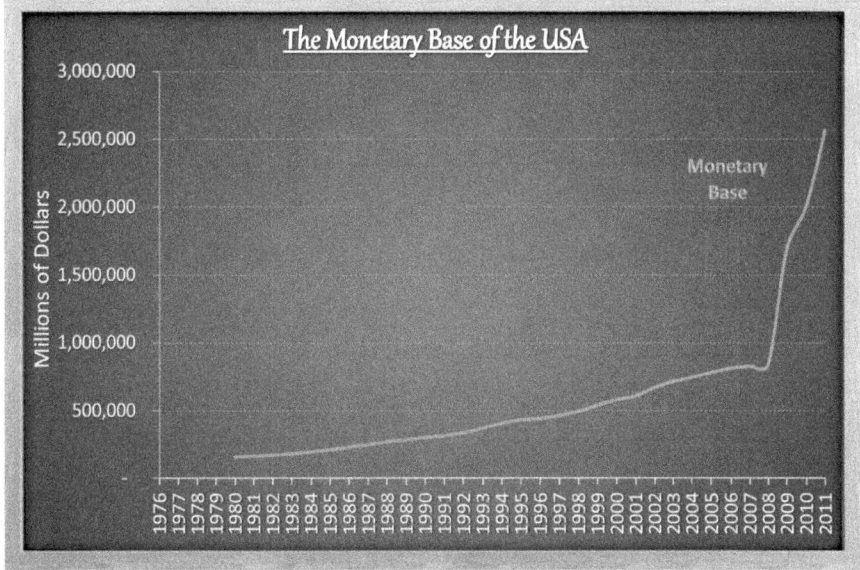

Illustration 34 : Graph shows the United States Monetary Base Trend From 1979 To 2010

The very large increase towards the end was due to the Great Financial Crisis of 2008 where the Federal Reserve injected massive amount of liquidity into the banking system. The unit of this graph is in millions of dollars, thus in 2006, it was 812 billion dollars.

Due to the large increase in 2009 onwards, we have to omit these data in order to compare whether the growth of the monetary base will follow the general population increases or not and then to check whether the amount of dollars per person also increases as well (or not!). As usual, any crisis, whether it is financial, natural calamities or war will have an impact on the economy as well as the monetary base.

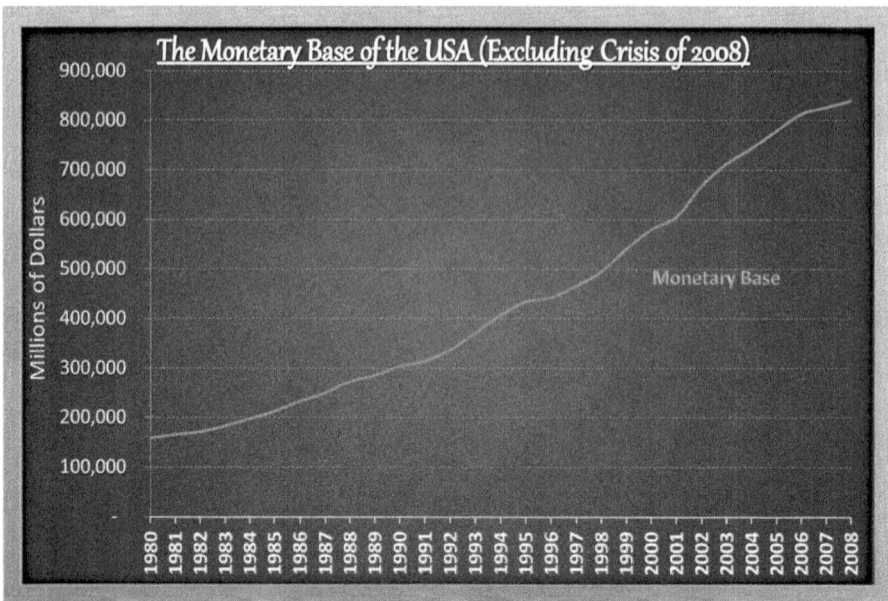

Illustration 35: Graph shows the United States Monetary Base
Trend From 1979 To 2008

Now let's insert the population increases of the United States
over the same period into this same graph.

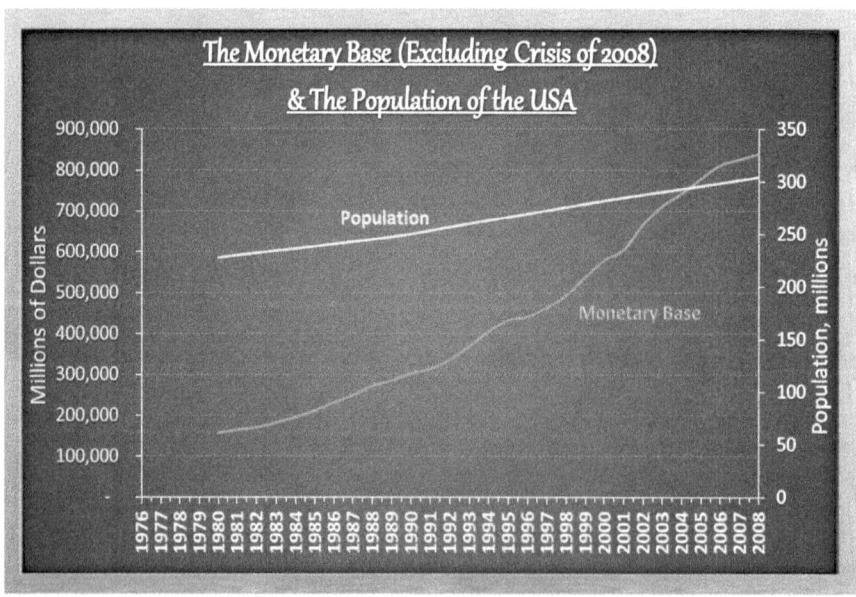

Illustration 36: Graph shows United States Monetary Base Vs
Population Trend From 1979 To 2008

Looks like the monetary base is growing faster than population growth, just like the GDP trend was earlier. Again, this very chart will be used by the doom and gloom club, to scare you. Let's filter out inflation and see how the graph will actually look.

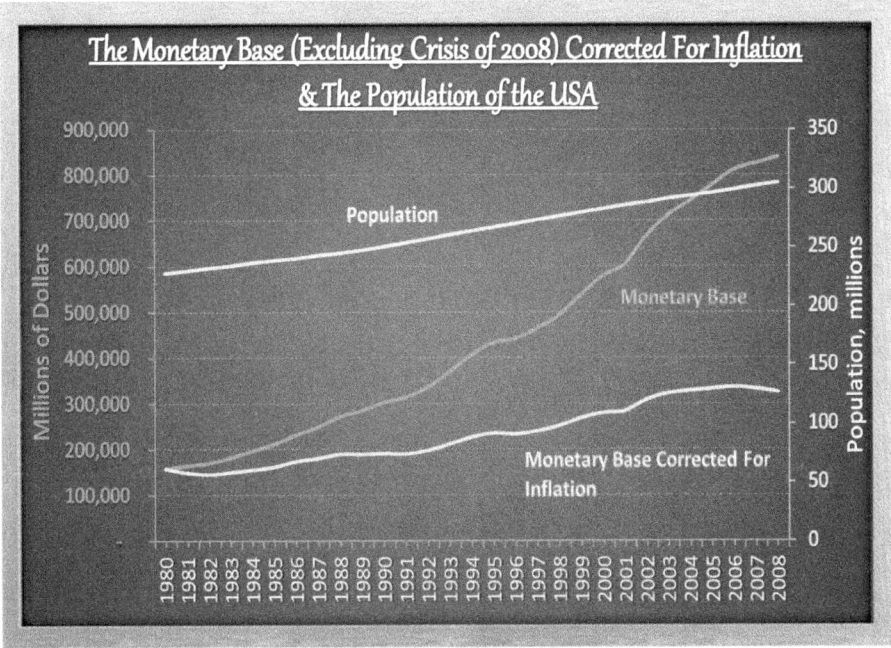

Illustration 37: Graph shows the United States Monetary Base And Monetary Base When Corrected For Inflation Vs Population Trend From 1979 To 2008

When inflation is taken into account, the growth of the monetary base is much less spectacular. Instead of ending at 812 billion dollars in 2008, it only goes up to 325 billion dollars. The increase of the monetary base now matched the increase in the population, and it definitely did not grow faster than the growth of the population. It grows in tandem with increases of the population because each additional person born will increase the monetary demand, and when they enter the working age, the demand will be even higher. Every additional person in the economy will require money for his or her day to day activities. When an expatriate or an immigrant enter the country, whether the person is working or not, monetary demand will increase. **It is not true that the monetary base is inflated in order to ensure debts can always be paid as claimed by them.** Inflation occurs for different reasons altogether.

It is possible to be more precise in our numbers' presentation. Let's present our data in terms of dollar per person instead, which are shown in the following series of graphs. Ideally, the amount of money per person should stay rather constant, i.e. a graph with a flat straight line because your currency need is not going to change if everything else remains the same (this may not be true if the period is sufficiently long, though).

The chart on the next page does not show that fact.

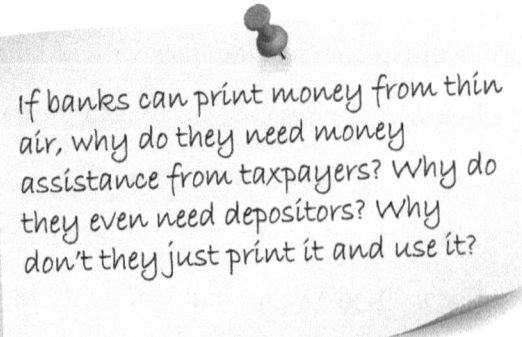

If banks can print money from thin air, why do they need money assistance from taxpayers? Why do they even need depositors? Why don't they just print it and use it?

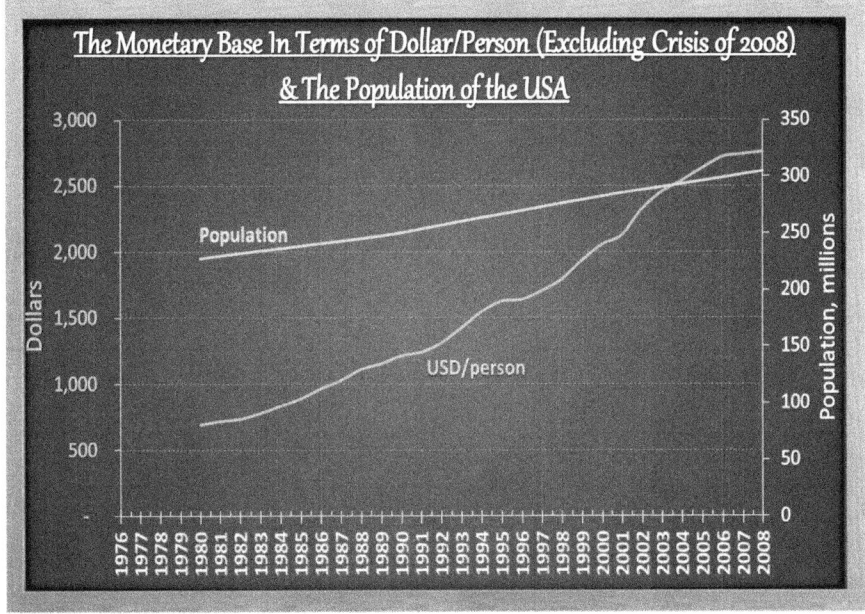

Illustration 38 : Graph shows the United States Monetary Base In Dollar Per Person Vs Population Trend From 1979 To 2008.

From 1980, the amount of currency per person, increase steadily from 625 dollars per person, to 2,700 dollars per person. This showed a large increase in the monetary base in the 30-year period. It grew by 330% compared to the growth of the population of 29%. As you are already aware, a large part of this increase is due to inflation.

Now, let's filter out the effect of inflation on the monetary

base, which is shown in the chart on the next page.

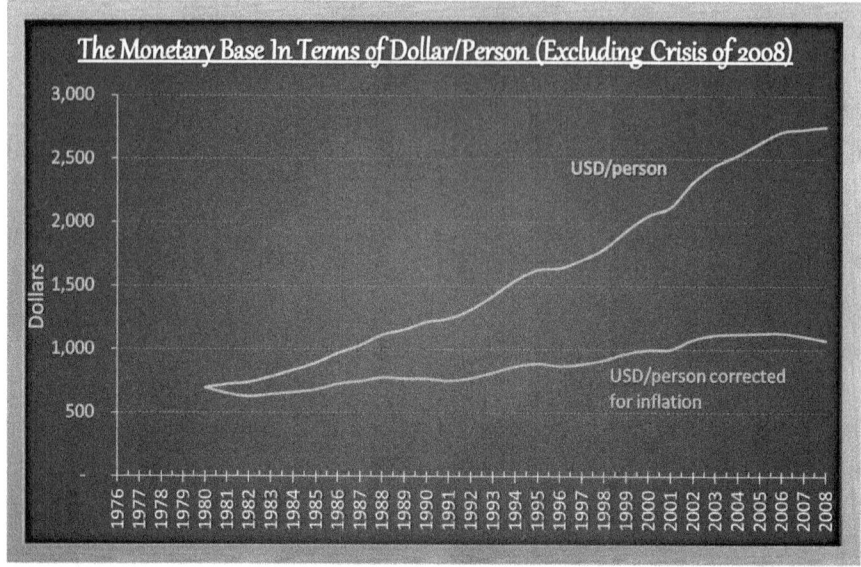

Illustration 39 : Graph shows the Monetary Base In Dollar Per Person When Corrected For Inflation From 1979 To 2008

As shown earlier, the increase is mostly due to population growth, so the monetary base simply follows in tandem. Nevertheless, we actually expect the data to show a rather flat trend without any growth because the monetary base is already divided by the total population of the United States, regardless of how many new person is born or enter the country. **There were several periods where the monetary base actually declined, which obliterate the argument made by certain groups of people that the monetary base simply goes up and up and never comes down.**

The graph looks similar to the previous graph (Illustration 37), except the unit is different. Here, the graph shows the monetary base per person and that monetary base per person corrected for inflation. Instead of growing to 2,700 dollars per person in 2008, it actually only grew to 1,060 dollars per person (a gain of 69%) when corrected for inflation.

In order to find out why the **use** of US dollar increases per person, it is necessary for us to study who are the **users** of the currency. As it turns out, it is not only Americans in America that use the dollar, but many other foreigners in foreign countries use the dollar too. Well, this does not surprise us, because the dollar is the world's reserve currency of choice. **We found that the figures run into hundreds of billions of dollars; all are held overseas.** In fact, our data sourced from the Fed showed that there are more dollars residing overseas, than in America itself! Believe it or not, some countries adopted the dollar as their de-facto currency, because it is simply easier or because their own currency is too unreliable (mismanagement leading to high inflation). The fact that a lot of US Dollars are residing offshore, make it extra difficult for the Federal Reserve to manage the currency, to which a lot of credit must be given to them for their excellent management work.

The dollar is also the currency of choice for international trades. These trades are between countries that don't even use the dollar (in their countries) because they have their own national currencies. For example, when South Korea trades with Vietnam, they don't even use their Vietnamese Dong or the Korean Won between them but preferring the US Dollar instead. The Dollar is also used as international reserves of central banks of many countries. The Federal Reserve estimated that currently, up to 72% of the US dollars is held overseas and usually does not return to America. This distorts our data significantly. Therefore a correction on the amount of dollars held overseas is necessary and presented in the next graph.

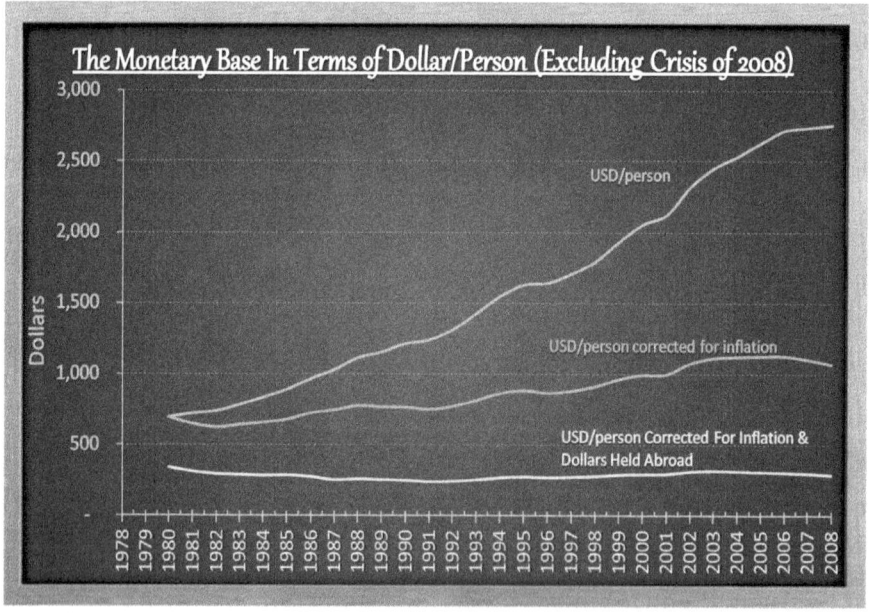

Illustration 40: Graph shows The Monetary Base In Dollars Per Person Corrected For Inflation & Currencies Held Abroad From 1979 To 2008.
Note that, monetary demand actually has not increased at all per person in the USA.

When corrected for inflation and the amount of dollars held overseas, the monetary base per person data trended flat with a slight downward bias. **Again, we have destroyed their claim that the monetary base increases too much whenever paper currency is used as money, and gold is a must to prevent it. It is absolutely not true.**

In 2008, the Great Financial Crisis was already occurring in full swing. The economy went into a big correction, and the excesses of the economy were being shed. The correction however, caused a total freeze of lending, especially inter-banks. The Federal Reserve stepped in to prevent a total collapse of the banking system. The Fed provided ample liquidity and this is reflected in the monetary base. Despite the large injection by the Fed, little of this extra liquidity is being utilized by the banking system, even until today. The hesitation to lend by banks triggered a breakdown of all the usual links between the monetary base and the general money in circulation in the form of loans and savings, and other financial instruments. As loans are being paid, and few new ones are issued, the actual financial money in the general economy was shrinking, and was shrinking fast. The Fed countered this effect in concert with the Federal Government who spent massively into the economy, buying a large chunk of the distressed financial assets and consumed the production of the economy like a drunken sailor. We shall discuss further in **Book 3** of the **259 TRILLION VS. 5 TRILLION SERIES** (look for **"SHOULD GOVERNMENTS SPEND HEAVILY DURING RECESSIONS?"**).

Thus, the hype on exponential growth and so forth, from some economists and parroted by misinformed people is just something that is actually perfectly normal. It should behave that way. **So remember, all economic functions that are dependent upon population or productivity parameters are exponential in nature.** To close out this issue, we will show in the following illustration how an exponential chart when taken at a short period and then 're-graphed' will look similar to a linear graph.

So be careful!

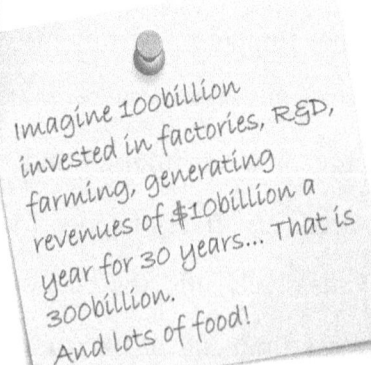

Diversion of resources in acquiring and storing gold is tremendous. 100 billion dollars spent is such a terrible loss to a small and medium country, they will end up poor

Imagine 100billion invested in factories, R&D, farming, generating revenues of $10billion a year for 30 years.... That is 300billion.
And lots of food!

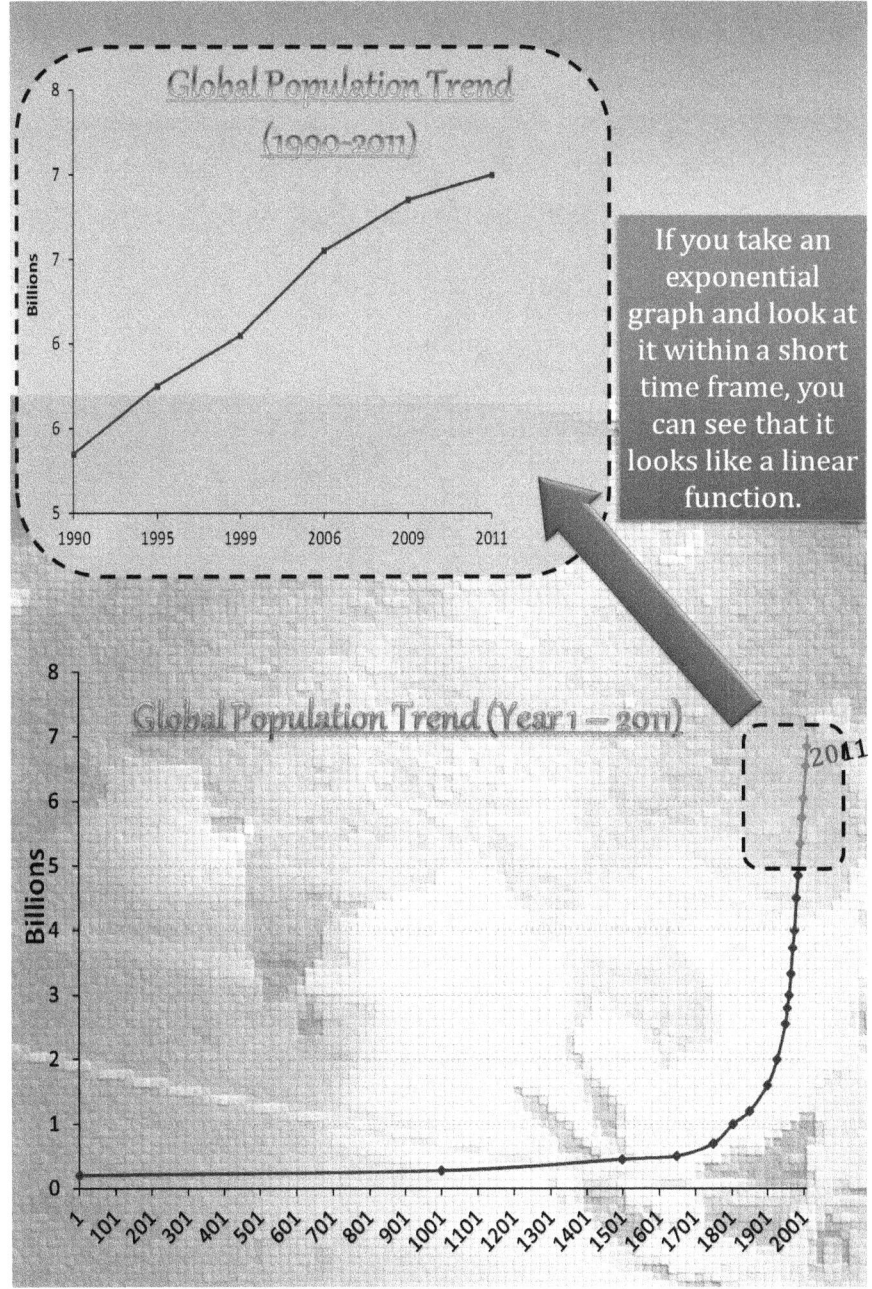

If you take an exponential graph and look at it within a short time frame, you can see that it looks like a linear function.

Illustration 41: All economic functions that are dependent on populations or productivity are exponential in nature.

SHRINKING OF PURCHASING POWER OF PAPER
MONEY EXPLAINED

Gold proponents routinely mentioned that the purchasing power of the dollar is continuously shrinking. According to them, all of the fiat currencies of the world is experiencing the same phenomenon by virtue that paper money is worthless papers and bound to return to its intrinsic value, which is practically zero. They are only partly right; this is a common phenomenon, due to inflation. But, not all currencies are experiencing inflation all the time. For example, the Japanese Yen has increased in value over many years, and the holders of Yen are able to buy more with the same amount of Yen. Although the gold proponents are 'partly' right that paper money is continuously losing its value, they are not correct again as usual, because they fail to mention that the inflation phenomenon is completely negated by adjustments in the incomes of the economic participants. For example, households' incomes had kept pace of inflation all these years, spanning multi decades and in fact as of 2010, there is a real net increase in households' incomes. The American Institute of Economic Research mentioned in their study that the US dollar had lost 30% of its purchasing power since 1990. Despite this seemingly large loss in purchasing power, more dollars are being obtained by US households than before, increasing their incomes to compensate, and then some more. American households can buy more than ever before, despite the losses in the value of their money.

Data from the Census Bureau showed that the median incomes of US workers had risen even if adjusted for the increase in CPI. What it means is that compared to say in 1967, the median incomes of Americans had risen by 23% up to 2010.

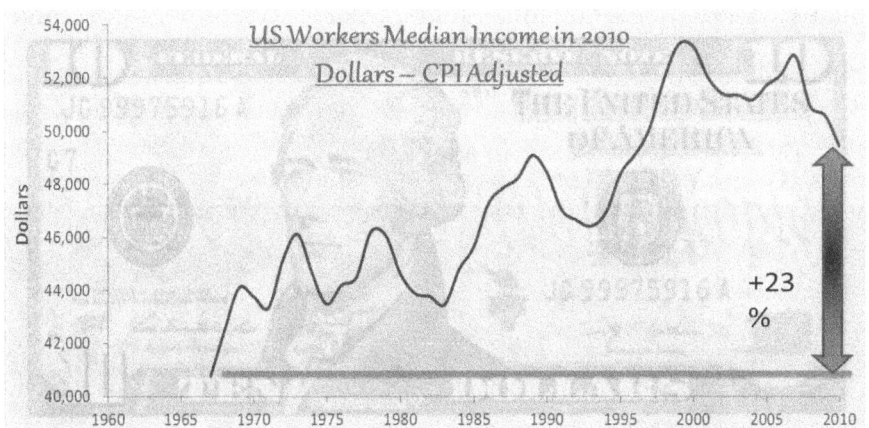

Illustration 38 : US Workers Median Income in Constant 2010 Dollars Shows An Increase in Median Income of 23% in 2010 Compared to 1967 Which Peaked In Year 1999

This is a real increase, signaling that today's workers enjoy better standard of living and can afford more, compared to workers from 40 years ago. The economic performance goes up and down, but overall, the workers did better than before.

During price stability period, none of the population segment will lose anything due to inflation. All inflationary expectations were already factored in. Price stability is defined as the slow rate of change of inflation from year to year. Therefore, price instability is defined as high rate of change of inflation from year to year. For example inflation rate of 2% a year, every year, is considered a stable period while inflation of 5% every year, is also considered as a stable period. Price instability period is when the inflation rate from the previous year of +2% suddenly increases to +7% this year. With such sudden large increase (or decrease), many economic participants will be unable to adjust in time, and they will lose incomes in real terms.

Let us show you better in a table below:

	Period of Price Stability (Inflation Rate - Rate Of Change LESS Than 5% year to year)	Period of Price Instability (Inflation Rate – Rate Of Change MORE Than 5% year to year)
Salaried Employees	No Impact Most employees incomes are adjusted for inflation	Impacted Most employees incomes are adjusted for inflation, but slow
Self Employed	No Impact Most Self Employed incomes are readily adjustable for inflation because they set their own price	Minimal Impact Most Self Employed incomes are readily adjustable for inflation because they set their own price
Pensioned Retirees	No Impact Most retirees incomes such as Social Security are indexed for inflation	Impacted Most retirees incomes such as Social Security are indexed for inflation, but slow to change

	Period of Price Stability (Inflation Rate - Rate Of Change LESS Than 5% year to year)	Period of Price Instability (Inflation Rate – Rate Of Change MORE Than 5% year to year)
Banks With Fixed Loans	No Impact	Impacted
	Inflationary expectations were already incorporated into loans calculations	No returns or negative returns are possible because there is no mean to adjust returns
Banks With Variable Rate Loans	No Impact	No Impact
	Lending rates is adjusted automatically	Lending rates is adjusted automatically
General Businesses	No Impact	No Impact
	Selling prices can be adjusted as needed	Selling prices can be adjusted as needed
Bond Holders With Fixed Returns	No Impact	Impacted
	Inflationary expectations were already incorporated into returns calculations	No returns or negative returns are possible because there is no mean to adjust returns
Bond Holders With Variable Returns	No Impact	No Impact
	Returns are automatically adjusted for inflation	Returns are automatically adjusted for inflation

Illustration 43: Table shows the Impact of Inflations On Various Groups Of People during price stability and instability.

As you can see, nobody will be impacted if the inflation rate is stable and known. Not even bondholders will be affected. We do not understand why these people continue to harp on the falling purchasing power of paper money, yet everything that they wanted to buy then or now, they can still buy. If their grandfather can buy a TV then, today they can also buy a TV; in fact, they can buy a bigger, slimmer, lighter and brighter set— a much better TV in every aspect with the same or lower price. They can buy more of it because of their higher incomes in real terms.

When there is a sudden change in the inflation rate and the rate of change is significant (in excess of $\pm 5\%$), several groups of the economic participants will be affected. For example, those who lend their money to others at a fixed interest rate, will lose because the increase in inflation shrinks their returns. In fact they may lose money altogether. Because the loan interest rate is fixed, there is no recourse for the lenders. They may even go bankrupt just because of one mistake.

The main mandate and goal of the Federal Reserve is to maintain price stability; ensuring that none of the economic participants lose. Certain groups claim that the Federal Reserve does not manage inflation well, it failed to eliminate inflation altogether. Some even say the Fed is the reason there is inflation in the first place. These claims are certainly amusing to us. In our opinion, the Fed has done a wonderful job maintaining price stability, even during the Great Financial Crisis of 2008. For example, if the dollar is still linked and backed by gold, with the more than doubling of the price of gold (from USD650 to USD1,400), will surely result in a crash and burn of the US economy, and not to mention the economies of the rest of the world.

We also would like to make it very clear to everyone that prices of 3 years ago, 10 years ago, 20 years ago, 50 years ago or whatever it is in the **PAST**, matter not to all of us. **Only today's prices mattered**. Only current prices are important and relevant to all of us. What the prices were before in the past does not matter to us and does not affect us whatsoever. When economists and these 'experts' compare today's prices with 20 years ago, they will portray it as bad, and bad and more bad. This is very misleading.

The first thing is, from the past to the present, does any group of the economic participants lost money? Has there been a period of price instability? Did they manage to adjust? These are the questions that mattered. To answer these questions, we need not look further, today's situation will explain whether certain segment of the economic participants lost or whether they did well.

The second thing is, can today's economic participants still muster the same purchasing power they once did before? Or perhaps, better than they had before? What your grandpa can buy 50 years ago with his money does not matter much to you today. As long as each segment of the economic participants adjusted and no segment has lost, you are bound to be well compensated and maybe even can buy more than what your grandpa once did. When we study the change in inflation rates spanning over decades, we found that no group were truly impacted by changes in the inflation rates. Prices were rather stable. Bondholders were the only loser in the late 70s; however, who's in their right mind would give someone else their money, for fixed returns, for the next 20 or 30 years? We wouldn't. It is like seeking trouble and trouble will certainly find you. The rest of the population did not lose any money or much money, and the standard of living grew significantly, even during that period of high inflation.

The world that existed 30 years ago is far different from the world today. The economic needs, and the economic constraints also differ significantly. The labor force was different as well. The nation's focus was different, the technological level was different, and so on. In short, it is impossible to compare exactly then, and now, even if all kinds of corrections are made. Remember, what you can buy with your money today, is the more important thing, not what it can buy a hundred years ago, because such comparison can be misleading. Even the consumer price index is subjected to big weight reallocations due to introduction of new items such as computers, mobile phones recently and many others will be added in the future. Old and obsolete items will be removed from the index. As the period of comparison grows longer, such as 50 years or longer, the difference will be even greater. Your needs and your grandfather's needs differ significantly, therefore what he used his money for then, may not be comparable to your own uses, today.

The third thing is, if you think about it, can your Grandpa or anyone else who was a rich millionaire or even a famous billionaire, living in 1940s, use their money to travel out to space? Or would their $500 buy them that smart Android phone or that thin 60inch wide 3D LCD TVs? What does it mean having all that money when you can't do what you want to do because it is not available yet? Why doesn't the economist who harped on the "loss of the purchasing power of the dollar" do any comparisons on these prices? We wonder how they will compare a sleek, thin, light, portable and advance smartphone with the equivalent item in the 1940s. The fact is, there is no real comparison with what we have today.

Everyone prefers to have higher and higher incomes all the time. The drive for more is ingrained and is part of human nature. The drive for ever more, ever-higher salary, for ever-higher consumption is so human, it is one of the major driving force of our inflationary environment. Even the central bank is not immune from its effects; hence we are seeing central bankers took advantage of the increase in the population to pump in slightly more money than they are suppose to. This is not bad however, as it provide the feeling of continuous improvements, of ever-higher salary for employees, ever-higher revenue for businesses and ever-higher incomes for the rest of the economic participants. There are no losers, just winners. Central banks tend to inject a little bit more money than actually needed causing a slight inflationary bias, rather than keeping money exactly as it should, in order to have just enough safety margin and to allow the economy to grow properly without constraint. Keeping money too tight will be too restrictive for growth, as was experienced years before, during the gold standard. The decline of the currency if it is over a very long period (30 years or more) is considered insignificant and will not impact anyone in the economy other than giddy economists and historians.

As we wrote earlier, comparing what a dollar can buy 70 years ago with what it can buy today is very misleading. All of the money in the world 30 years ago will not buy you an internet access, online shopping, computers etc. So would you want to be in your Grandpa times or now? You can't keep looking back in some sweet areas and wanting more of them, times have changed. In our 3rd book of the series, we will examine more on incomes, classes of incomes and will answer one very interesting question, **'where did the middle class disappeared to?'** We guarantee that you'll be shocked to learn where they have gone to! Nevertheless, it will come as a relief, so read on!

We shall also discuss inflation at length in two separate parts in this book series, you will be amazed by what you will discover! So keep on reading. After digesting all of our inflation and deflation writings thoroughly in this three books series, we hope you will then keep all of these possibilities in your mind whenever the economists or even we ourselves present to you information involving comparisons with past data.

Central banks need to use inflation to administer proper dosage of new money into the system. Otherwise they won't be able to match the needs of the economy, whenever new wealth is created and whenever the economic participants want to transact the newly created wealth with each other. It is dangerous to allow deflation from occurring, as it can feed on itself (this is according to the central banks, however this may not be true in most cases). Central banks also typically monitor the amount of money borrowed by member banks from them. If persistent borrowings occur, it signals that the central bank can continue to inject money into the economy. When central banks overshot their money injection, inflation may follow.

Interestingly, according to a recent study conducted by Venessa Wong (and Business Week), the cost of buying a pound of coffee in 1980 was $8.38 in 2010 dollars. The 2010 price? It's only $3.70! The price of the world's most favorite drink? Declined by more than 55%! The price of Coca-Cola in the 80's was $3.35 in 2010 dollars, and its current price is hovering only around $1.51. This represents a decrease of 54% for the cost of buying a 2-liter bottle today, compared to the year 1980. There are many other goods and services in the economy which had actually decreased in prices; it is not true that prices of goods and services always go up, allegedly due to the shrinking purchasing power of paper money. But what about those that actually went up? We found they did so because of their limitation in supply, and higher demands. It was not due to the shrinking of the purchasing power of paper money. An example we can cite here is gold's price and other commodities, which went up significantly due to supply limitations, as well as higher world demand.

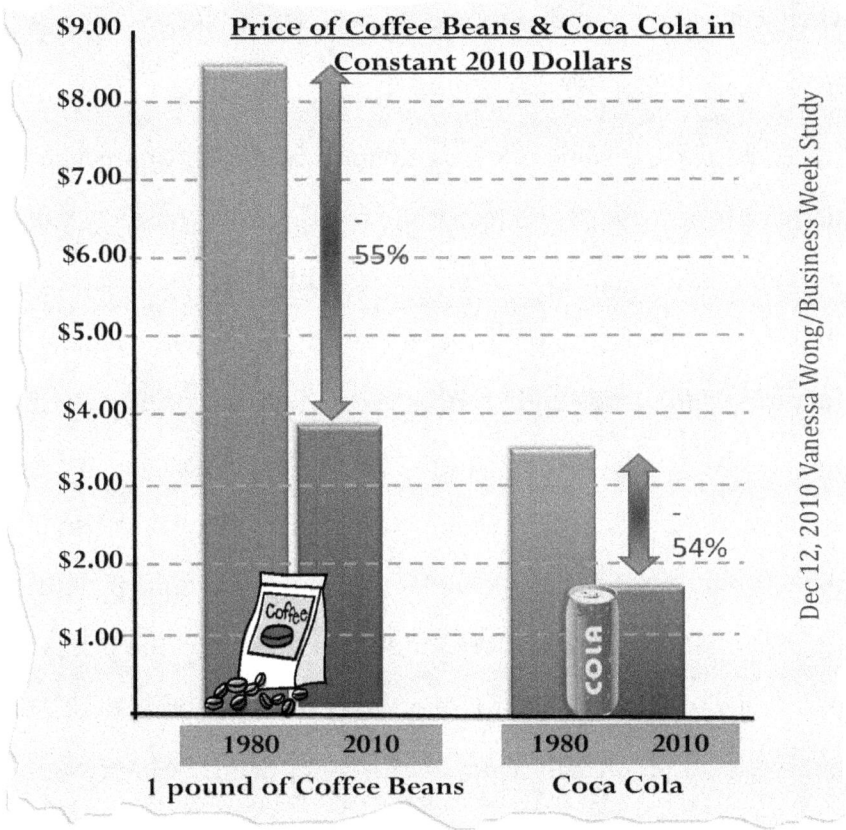

Illustration 44 : Price comparisons of two popular items in constant 2010 Dollars.

Our study won't be complete without checking for house prices. The median value of a house in the USA in 1980 is $166,946 in 2010 dollars, while the value it is hovering currently, is $172,600, in today's dollars. That represents an increase of only 3.4%. This showed there is hardly any devaluation in the dollar's purchasing power. It was widely reported that the new post millennium houses are bigger in size, with extra rooms and more attached 'accessories'. Perhaps, there is probably no increase at all when correcting for these factors and may in fact be cheaper compared to those old days.

Looks like the value of paper money has actually appreciate in many respect while seems to decline in others. If we solely focus on the price of each good or service within the economy and not thinking of the value of the paper money itself, we will realize that the price of all goods and services go up and down with varying degree, due to myriad of reasons. Some of the reasons are the supply and demand, due to competition or changes in consumer focus, advancement in technology making certain products, obsolete and many others. We found that generally, the prices of food items typically went up, due to supply limitations (weather and population growth were big factors) while the prices of newer and 'hotter' items such as electronics, declined tremendously in price despite getting more advance. When the CPI data is released by the government, it will show that OVERALL, and on average, the sums of the prices of all goods and services may show a slight increase. Inside the CPI, we know for a fact that some components such as food items may increase and others such as communications and TVs may decline.

The CPI is a weighted average of all of its components such as food, communications, apparels, transport—which supposed to mirror the typical consumer spending pattern. But in most cases and with most consumers, their consumption patterns actually differ greatly and wildly than the 'standard' typical consumer. No two individuals are similar in the country and no two families are similar as well. The CPI also cannot mirror the patterns of retirees, teenagers, rural folks, a middle class worker who is also studying, and many more. The list will be endless. In fact, the only time the CPI is valid for comparison is when the weighted average model and spending patterns match an actual living and breathing consumer in the economy— exactly. Well, good luck with that. Consumers don't buy shoes every month, some do not buy mobile phones every year, don't have the same number of children and other dissimilar needs.

Therefore, great care must be used when the CPI (the inflation data) is used for comparison purposes, between economic participants, and especially so if the comparison is for long period of time spanning decades.

Gold proponents and other economists and financial advisors forgot to show their customers, readers and clients the following facts: 500 dollars of paper money back in 1880, if divided evenly into several forms of investments and safekeeping will end up amazingly different in values today. Let's start with choosing the investment type for each of the 500 dollars as shown in the table in Illustration 45.

Initial Investment	Type of Investment
$100	Put under mattress and pillow
$100	Savings Account (other short term assets)
$100	Long term assets (CDs and bonds)
$100	Shares in broad S&P companies in the stock market
$100	Physical gold

Illustration 45: Different types of an initial investment of USD100 in 1880

After more than a hundred and thirty years, each of the five, 100-dollar investment will end up as shown in the table and graph on the next page.

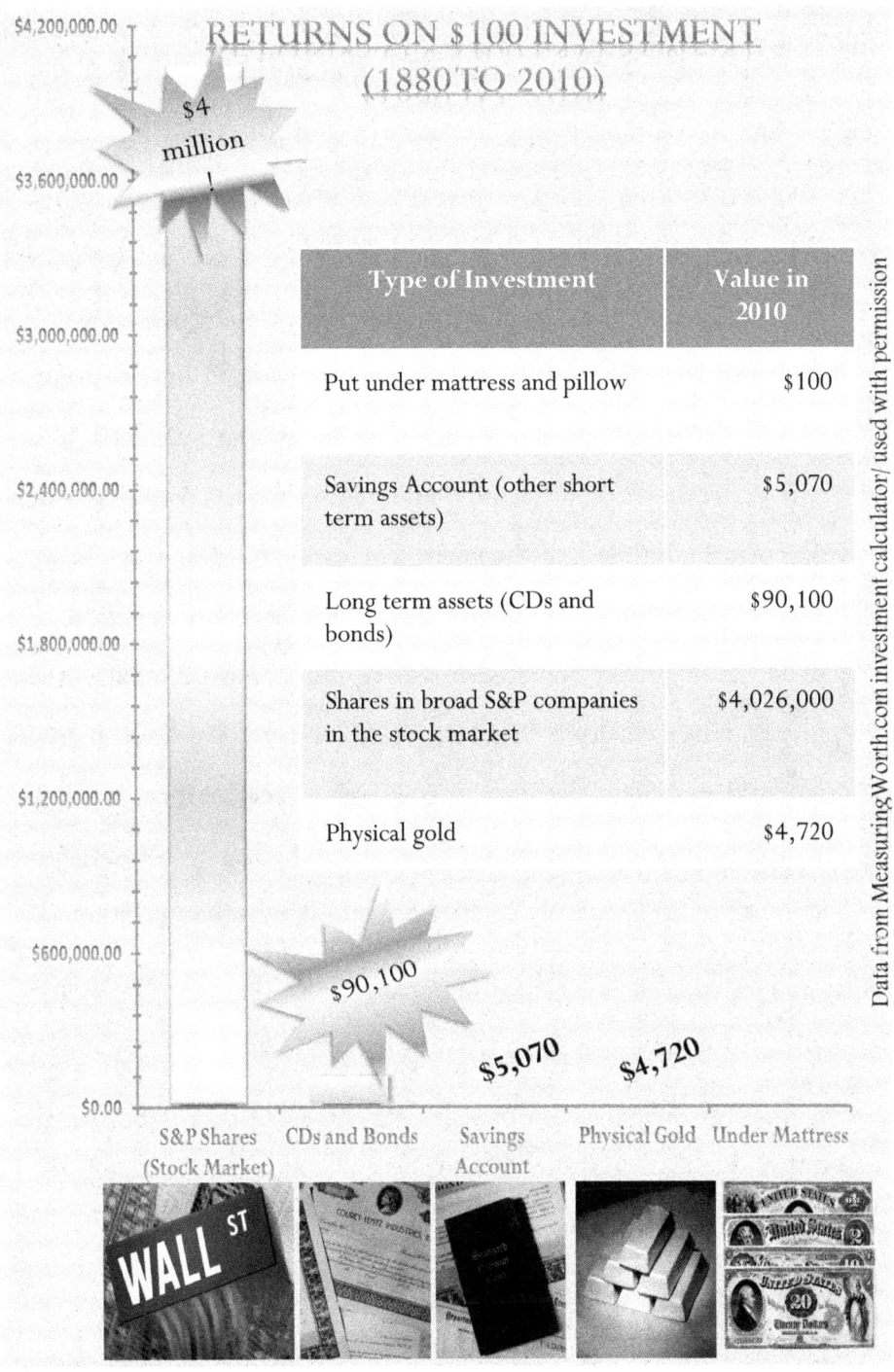

Data from MeasuringWorth.com investment calculator/ used with permission

RETURNS ON $100 INVESTMENT (1880 TO 2010)

Type of Investment	Value in 2010
Put under mattress and pillow	$100
Savings Account (other short term assets)	$5,070
Long term assets (CDs and bonds)	$90,100
Shares in broad S&P companies in the stock market	$4,026,000
Physical gold	$4,720

Illustration 46 : Returns of an initial investment of USD100 in 2010

Such a big difference in the final outcome of the money! It is clear that investing in the stock market will bring the most value to the 100 dollars despite several large declines in the stock market including several crashes. If stocks are too risky for your taste, the CDs (FD) and bonds also did well. There was hardly a difference between gold, and money put away in a savings account. However most of the increase in the value of gold occurred rather recently, only after the year 2007 where the value of gold doubled. If the recent rise of the last few years is not taken into account, the increase in value of physical gold will be halved, leaving a very large gap even to the money invested in the 'puny' savings account. That's USD2,300 for the physical gold compared to USD5,070 for the USD100 in the savings account. This fact also conveniently showed that money in savings accounts would be largely protected from the wrath of inflation.

The 'worst' is the $100 money left under the mattress, which is still —a hundred dollars. That hundred dollars, will buy much less than in 1880. In 1880, a hundred dollars then, can buy in today's dollars, goods and services worth more than $2,200 (according to MeasuringWorth.com calculator).

We initially thought that paper money under the mattress had lost, well how else can its value be higher than a hundred, if that is what is written all over the paper? Gold will then be able to crawl out from being the dead last, to the second last spot, by beating paper money until someone told us that old paper money, is worth a lot more than the face value because it is a piece of valuable antique! So we decided to check it out and we found that, the $100 note may possibly fetch an astounding $195,000 with art dealers! (The rare 1880 $1 legal tender in mint condition could fetch $1,995 and having 100 pieces of these will yield $195,000 —from rmcurrency.com).

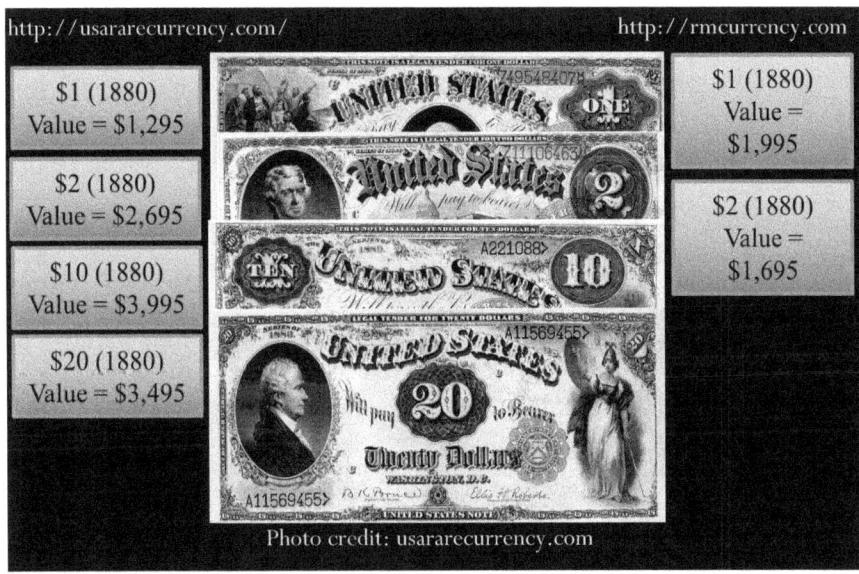

Illustration 47 : Antique Currency Prices from usararecurrency.com and rmcurrency.com

There you have it, the truth about money and gold. **All of the other type of investments beat the crap out of physical gold** stored under the pillow, which would only worth less than $5,000. Who said paper money is worthless, or will be, even under the pillow for a hundred plus years? Loss of purchasing power of paper currencies will be duly compensated, and if the money is well invested, it will grow more than inflation itself, netting profits for the owners. We shall explain in more detail why this loss is occurring, however not all currencies are losing their value continuously. For instance, the Japanese Yen has been appreciating in value in the past decade.

The simple lesson here is, if all of the paper money are continuously connected to the economic and the banking system, those money will be corrected or compensated in value automatically and none of the holders will lose. If the money is removed from the system and stored under pillows, the face value will be frozen in time and may lose (or gain) value depending on inflation (or deflation) levels. The disconnected money will never be similar to the other paper currencies within the rest of the economic system anymore, therefore only store them under your pillow or mattress if you intend to make it as a piece of antique to be collected by your children's children!

[Photo credit: usrarecurrency.com]

Illustration 48: 1880 US Legal Tender Note

What is the real reason for Japan's malaise and its failure to exit from its 'balance sheet recession' as predicted by "classic economist" back in 2006? Find out in Book 3

Hours worked by Americans has been steadily declining giving more free time to..uh, well, spend money.

REMOVAL OF THE GOLD STANDARD ALLOWS FOR STABLE AND THRIVING ECONOMY

*P*rior to the abandonment of the gold standard (and other metallic standard) to free floating paper currency, the world experienced frequent economic recessions followed by resurging growth, then inflation and finally deflation. The cycle repeats itself many times, which became unacceptable and ruinous to the economic participants. In the 1880s, in the United States, a group of ordinary people, called themselves the **Farmer's Alliance**, embarked on an extraordinary mission. To replace the gold standard, the source of their economic ruins. The mission was taken over by other influential groups and morphed into something more coherent with a credible and winnable plan, and the gold standard was finally replaced in part with the creation of the Fed. However it was not a full removal of gold, it is a hybrid system where gold is used to back up all money. The good part is the creation of a central bank was finally realized. The rather hybrid system was finally replaced in full only (and belatedly) in 1974 and the world has totally abandoned the gold standard for good.

Our great grandfathers fought long and hard for the removal of the source of their problem— gold, and their history should be a required reading for anyone who is re-proposing the gold standard.

Let's analyze the United States economic performance from 1790 to 2011 and see how the economy fared under the gold standard and under the fiat money standard. There were a total of 47 recessions in the US since 1790 (a period of about 220 years). This represents an average of 2.25 recessions every 10 years, which is pretty frequent. After the gold standard was abandoned in 1973-74, the US experienced only 6 recessions, which averaged out to be almost half of the previous rate. The recessions were also shorter and shallower than before. The trend showed greater stability despite the increasingly complex world finance, interlinked economies and faster communication. It is highly doubtful that using gold as the sole basis for currencies will enable the world to enjoy the unprecedented prosperity and growth that was experienced for 37 years until today.

Data from the National Bureau of Economic Research, also showed similar trend towards higher stability after the abandonment of gold standard in the US. The data is from the year 1854 until 2009, which showed that the **incidence for recessions halved after the free floating currency regime is used.**

These are clear proofs that the removal of the antiquated gold standard resulted in better living standard, fairer and more stable economy. Additionally, when we investigate the inflation trend prior to the collapse of Bretton Woods in the early 1970s, we saw that there were many severe swings in the inflation trend for all countries of the world. For the USA economy, the swings from inflation, to deflation and back, were frequent and severe. The economy swings from high inflation, to high deflation, and back, repeatedly (53 times in 234 years). The swings are often violent and in quick successions. There were 44 times where inflation exceeded 5% (or can be reworded as 44 years with inflation exceeding 5%) and there were 57 times or years where deflation exceeded 2%. Multiple large swings occurred, from a high of 30% inflation to a deflation of 20% also occurred. All of these periods exceeded the 'price stability' concept we presented earlier where the rate of change of inflation, not steady low inflation itself, is the one that is important and will greatly affect many economic participants. For example, a consistent and steady inflation of 5% per annum is not damaging to anyone, but the rate of change of inflation in any direction (up or down) exceeding 5%, will. The inflation data obtained starts from the year 1775, all the way to 2010. Amazingly, after the year 1974 when the gold standard was totally removed, there was **only one swing** albeit a small one, from inflation to deflation which did not even exceed 1%.

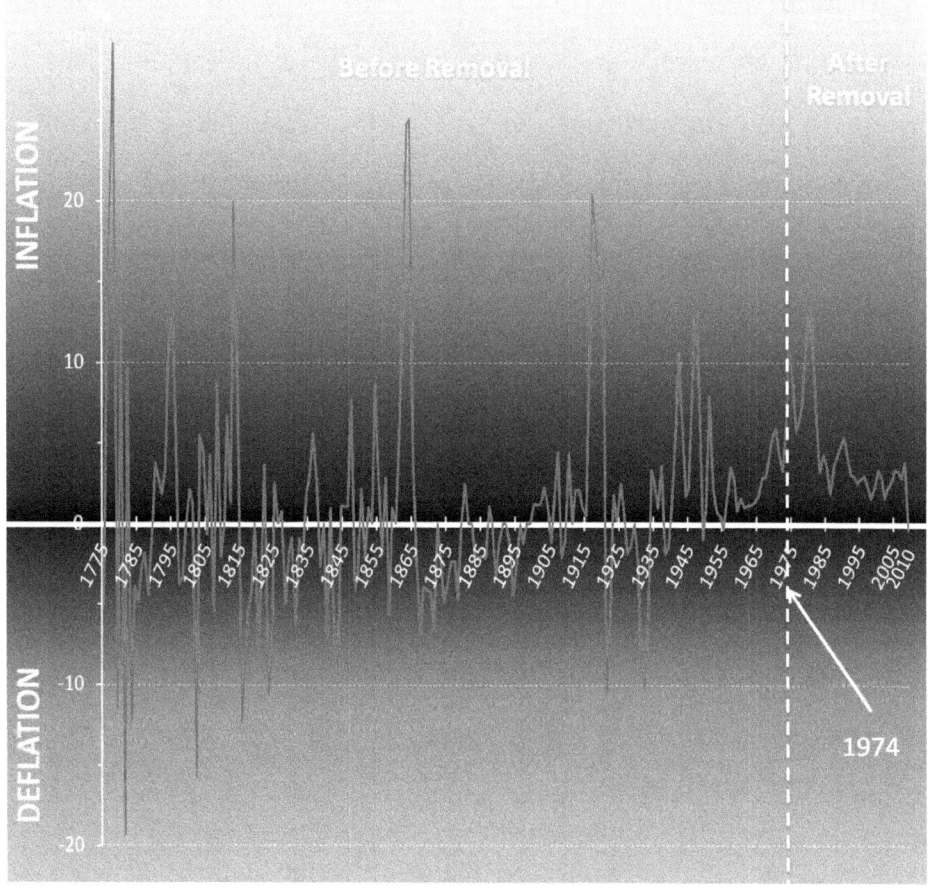

Illustration 49: Graph shows US Inflation & Deflation Rate in Percentage
From Year 1775 to 2009

The post 1974 period was initially the period where the Federal Reserve and the whole country had to learn the hard way in managing the newly freed economy and the inflation rates increased to high levels, until the Federal Reserve able to muster enough courage to face the threat of inflation head on. Thereafter, the inflation rate declined to low levels, and in fact, went down to very low levels and stays there until today. This was a great achievement in part of the Federal Reserve, and deserved to be commended. There was no inflation rate higher than 5% since 1983 until today and there were only one deflationary period recorded, which is in 2009. The Fed has achieved the dream of smoothing out the impact of the economic cycles. The difference between the two periods (before and after Bretton Woods collapsed) is large, that replacing paper currency and drift back to the old gold standard is not practical and downright scary due to the persistent swings between inflation and deflation. Every time a swing occurs, certain groups of the economic participants will lose and they typically represent the bulk of the total economic participants.

Calculating the swings' frequency rate, there were 2.6 swings from inflation to deflation or vice versa, per 10 years, compared to only 0.3 swing per 10 years, after Bretton Woods (there is only one swing in the whole 35-year period which occurred in 2009). This is a massive reduction largely to the credit of paper currencies and the improved money management by central banks the world over.

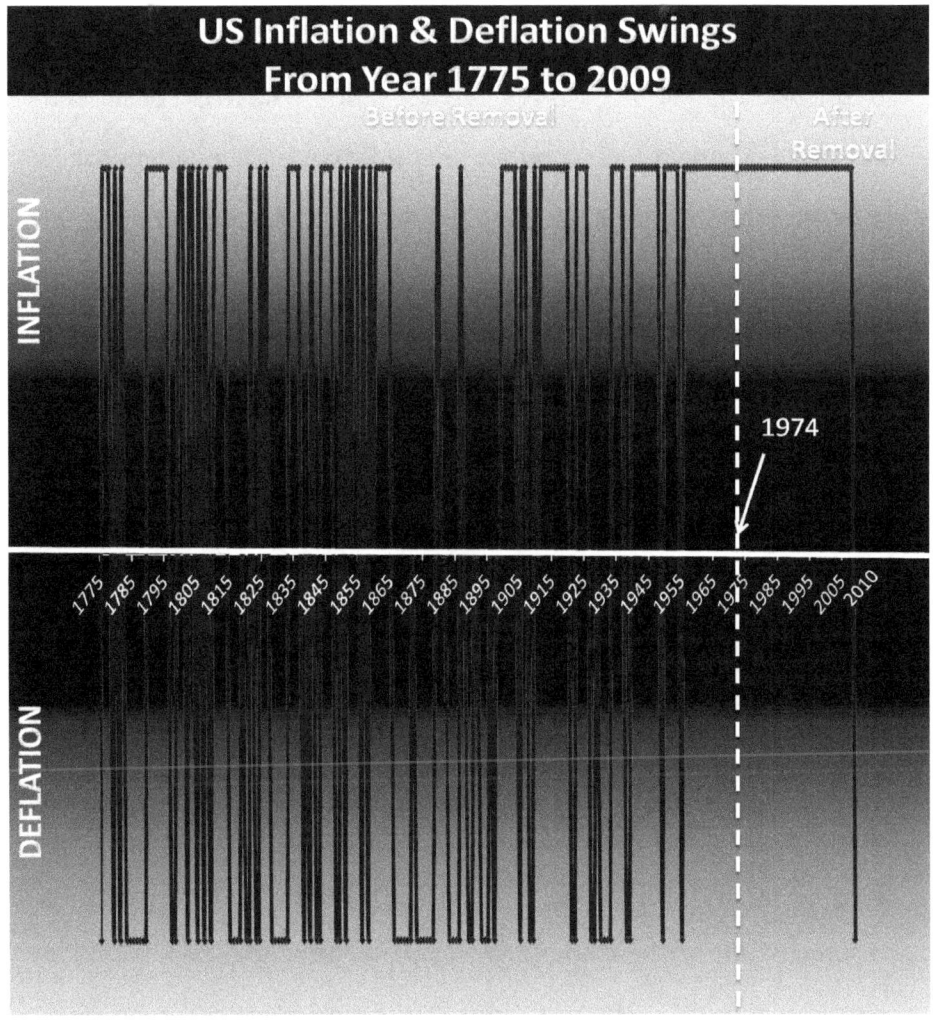

Illustration 50: Graph shows US Inflation & Deflation Swings From Year 1775 to 2009.
Notice the absence of swings since the removal of the gold standard until the 2008 Economic Crisis , where the first swing occurred in 2009

Now, let us look at Great Britain, which was the previous world's superpower, the data obtained is from a much longer period, 1265 until 2009. It showed similar trends, there were 308 large swings between inflation to deflation, back and forth repeatedly and violently during that period. This represents a frequency rate of 4.3 swings per 10 years, which is considered extreme. There is little wonder why gold and other metals were 'despised' during such period. Britain experienced inflation in excess of 5% a year for a total of 207 times (or 207 years) and experienced deflationary period of 2% or more, far longer, at 258 times (or 258 years). How torturous! What 'price stability' under gold and other standards purported by those gold bugs? Imagine living during such times. Today we have no idea how terrible it would be because the worst inflation or deflation period we went through is actually very mild in comparison. The people of Britain had managed several times to replace the gold standard with others, even with sticks (which was the most stable period they ever had then and was highly successful), but their successive Kings relented to the gold bugs once more and the torture resumed. All of these tough living were prior to 1974. Similar trend occurred in Britain after 1974 where the swing only occurred once in 2009.

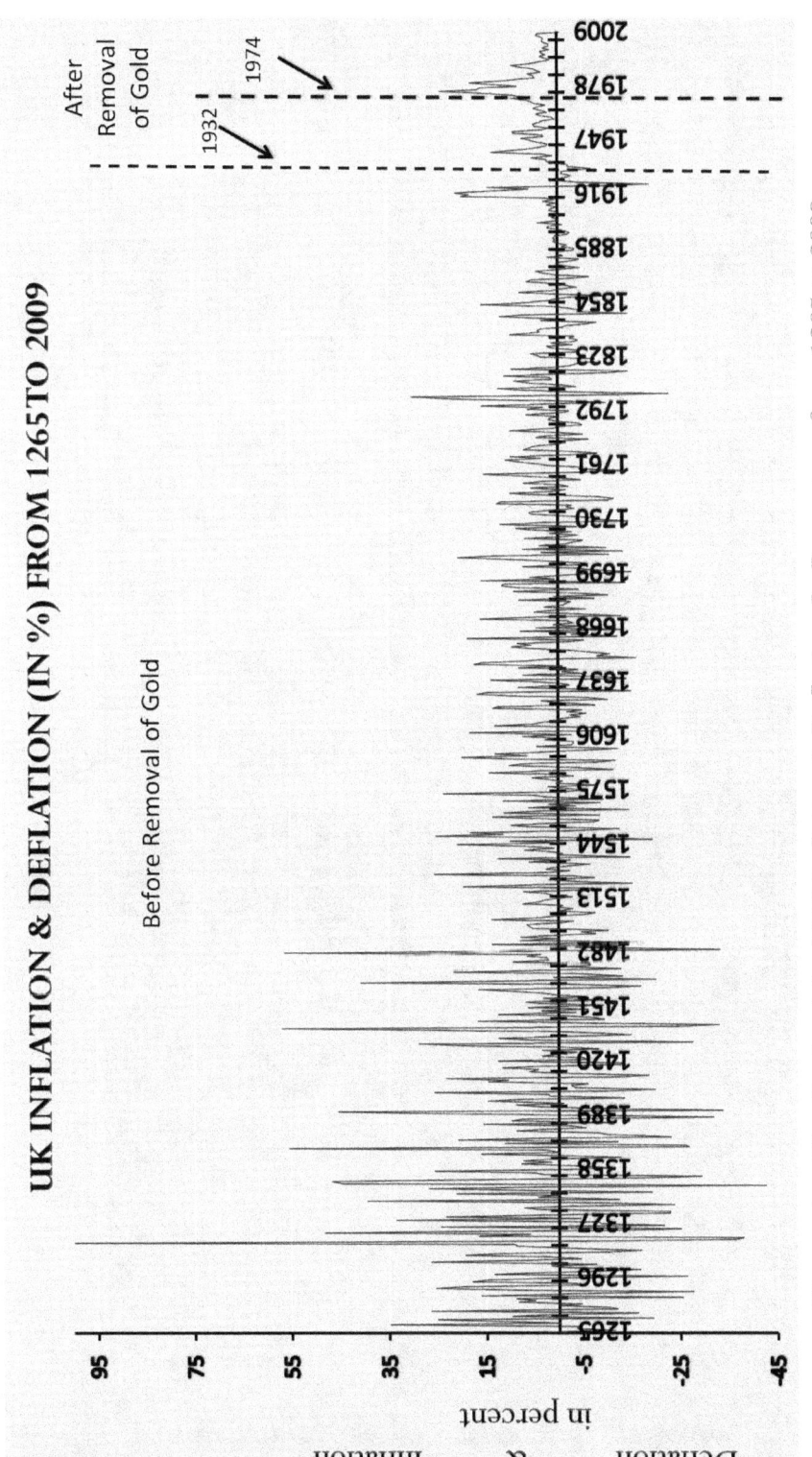

Illustration 51 : England And UK Inflation & Deflation In Percentage from 1265 to 2009

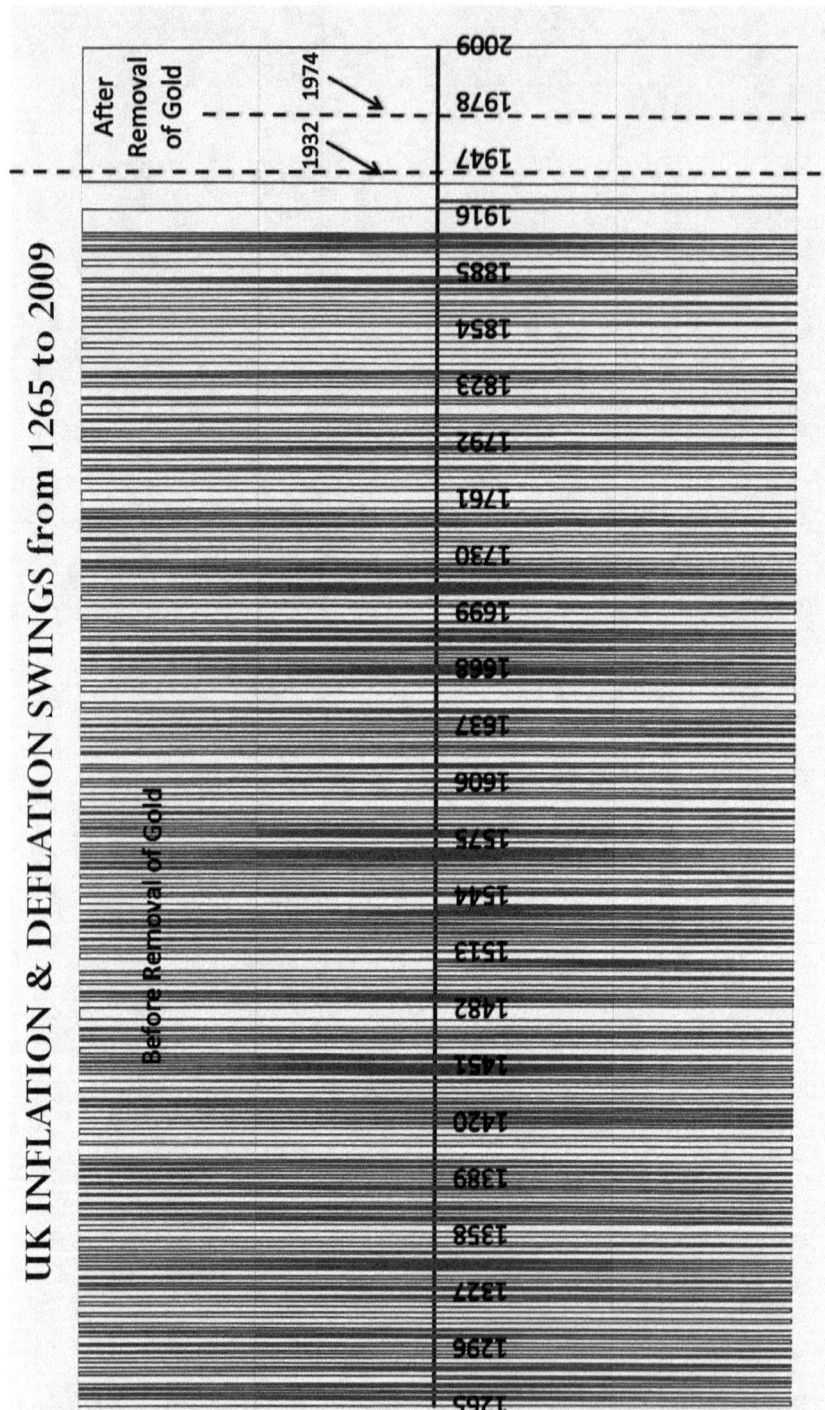

Illustration 52 : Graph shows England And UK Inflation & Deflation Swings from 1265 to 2009

Britain was a special case that they dropped the gold standard earlier than America did, back in 1931, at the height of the Great Depression. However after that, they decided to peg their currency to the US Dollar, until March of 1973 when Bretton Woods was abandoned by the United States resulting in all currencies of the world to be freely floated. Each country's currency was then determined by the strength of their own economy and no longer be subjected to forces beyond their control.

This fact showed that violent swings stopped once gold and other standards are abandoned in favor of paper currency. The other thing the data signify is that the creation of the Federal Reserve back in 1913 had managed to prevent violent swings between high inflation and high deflation down to only once. This is a commendable feat indeed, despite several major wars during the period.

Reinhart and Rogoff's empirical study of banking crises in 66 countries between 1800 and 2008, shows that banking crises were frequent in both advanced and emerging economies. For example, since 1800 there were 13 banking crises in the USA, 12 in the U.K., and 15 in France. On top of these so-called banking crises, there were perhaps hundreds of isolated episodes of 'bank run' throughout the period, where many savers lost their hard-earned savings. This is during the period of the gold standard and other standards. Thus, it is not paper based money that culminated the various banking crises and bank runs, but rather banks as a business model tend to fail if managed badly, especially if they are not supervised. Banks are not non-profit or social institutions and they must be viewed just like any other businesses in the economy. Their primary purpose is to make money for their owners by providing services that people need and want. It is imperative that savers choose wisely their banks to minimize risk to themselves. Remember, knowledge is power. We shall discuss more about banks in later part of this book including understanding their loan and deposit business and the extent of leverage.

The duration of recessions in America were typically longer before the creation of the Federal Reserve and before the abandonment of the gold standard. In 1974, the USA experienced the longest economic expansion since World War II, a duration of **only four years.** There was no similar expansion during the gold standard period. The abandonment of gold standard and the creation of paper money backed by the wealth of the nation made this achievement possible. In the 90s, the four-year record was broken with the **longest economic expansion in history.** The economy expanded continuously for more than 120 months, or 10 years. Millions of people from all income levels were lifted to higher level and almost 20 trillion dollars of new wealth were created, essentially doubling the gross wealth of America. If the gold standard is still in place then, the world surely will be in severe deflation with negative economic growth and lower prosperity. Imagine the losses in productivity, technological advancements such as the Internet with its instant communication and information at our fingertips may not materialize and the loss of the economic potential of the economy and therefore of human civilization as a whole. Imagine if the economy, no, the country actually, lost 10 trillion dollars or more of wealth due to loss of economic potential. If the whole world enters into deflation and negative economic growth during that period due to the restrictions of the gold standard, the losses will be many trillions more. People will be impoverished and large scale wars may result just like WW1 and WW2.

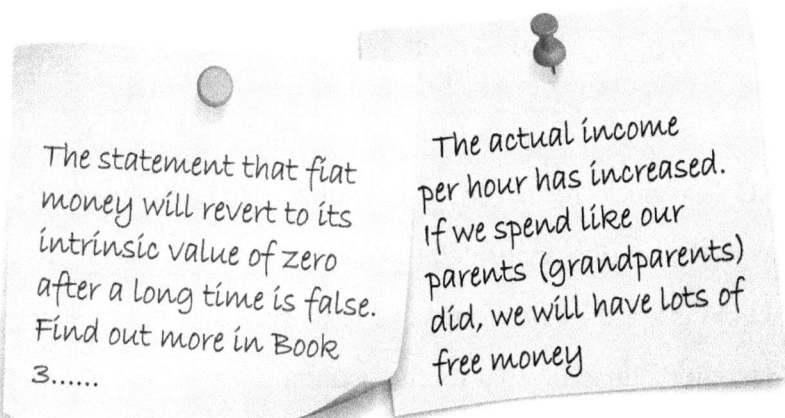

The statement that fiat money will revert to its intrinsic value of zero after a long time is false. Find out more in Book 3......

The actual income per hour has increased. If we spend like our parents (grandparents) did, we will have lots of free money

From the book, "Secrets Of The Temple", by William Greider regarding the gold standard,

"Whatever its virtues, the gold standard did not guarantee stable prices. Price stability under the gold standard, contrary to what its advocates have perennially claimed, was actually a rare and temporary condition that usually lasted no more than a couple of years. The historical record clearly demonstrated this, yet modern politicians and economists who espoused the gold standard .... persisted in distorting the actual experience of the past. Typically, they alluded to the nineteenth century as a halcyon time of orderly growth and stable prices, when money's value was anchored by gold. ..... gold advocates liked to point out that the price level in the United States in 1800 was almost precisely the same more than a century later—when the gold standard was permanently abandoned. This left out what happened to prices in between. The observation was narrowly correct, but fatuous—equivalent to suggesting that an airplane mainly flew on the ground, since, after all, it began and ended its flight at ground level."

Illustration 53: A Passage From
William Greider's Book, Secrets of The Temple

Gold proponents never really want you to look at past history, how gold actually performed. We have shown in a simple way that gold is not the best money due to its very own nature as a rare commodity. Imagine that as the economy grows, the amount of gold needed will be more, but the supply of gold is limited and dependent on the amount of new gold discovered. The mismatch will always be bad for the economy. Gold usage also diverted critical and scarce resources away into useless endeavors, blowing up mountains and polluting the planet with dangerous and toxic chemicals just so you can trade using it. Gold bugs typically care not about the planet, only their shiny metals count. Remember in Book 1 when we stated that the cost to produce $100,000 of gold money will be $81,250 leaving only $18,750 left for consumption. Of course that money went to the gold bugs and their honchos. Did you remember how much it will cost the government to print a piece of paper currency with a face value of $100,000? It's 8.9 cents.

In the following drawing, we show that the economy is having just enough gold for all transactions. However as the economy grows, many new assets or wealth are added into the economy so the amount of gold needed is more, yet the supply is not keeping pace. Transactions will have constraints from proceeding and economic growth will falter. The end result is none other than deflation.

If gold has no value of its own, much like paper dollars, produced only when needed, then it can be used as money and as a medium of exchange. When paper dollars are given out in exchange for the house, the paper dollars will represent the house and the paper dollars value, is essentially backed by the house in question. This simple example showed that it will lead to problems should a commodity of which nobody really has any control on the supply or anything of value, is used as money. One of the problems is that when gold's supply cannot keep up with the economic demands, new transactions of newly created wealth cannot proceed, deflation will occur and no one can do anything about it.

Thus, paper money is the most ideal choice in a modern economy.

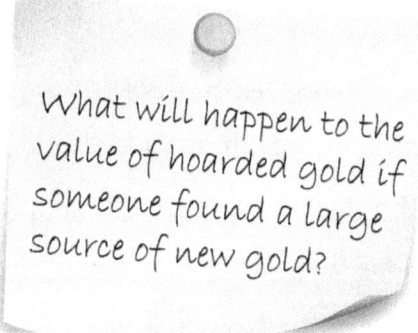

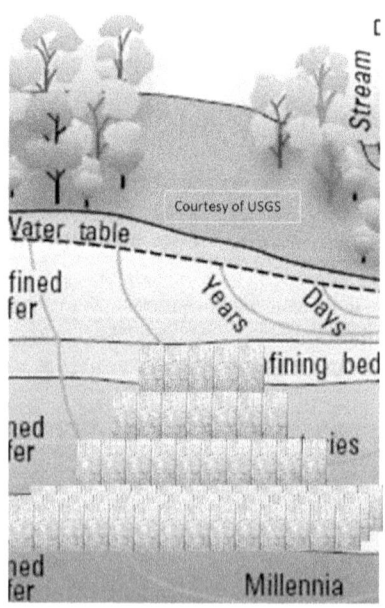

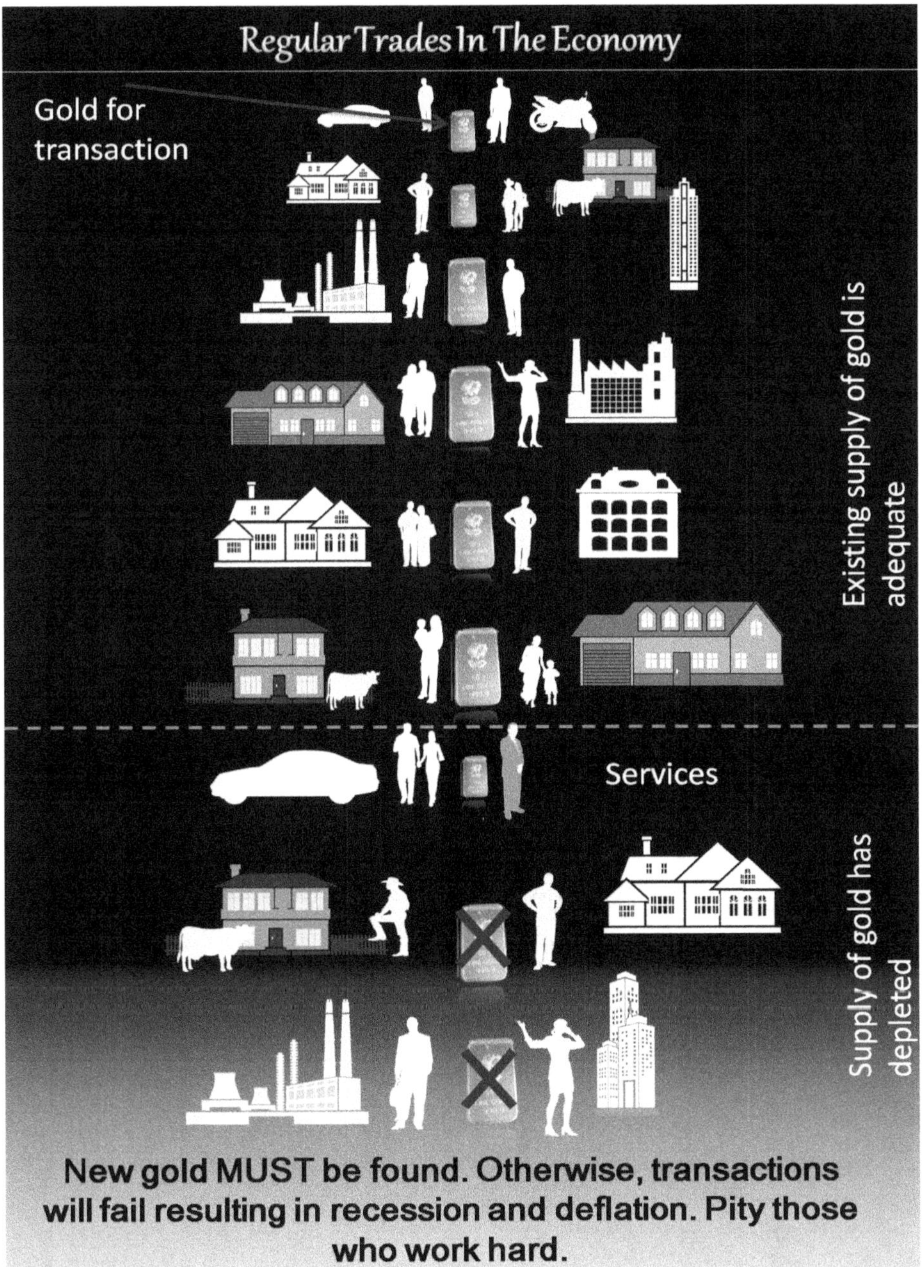

Regular Trades In The Economy

Gold for transaction

Existing supply of gold is adequate

Services

Supply of gold has depleted

New gold MUST be found. Otherwise, transactions will fail resulting in recession and deflation. Pity those who work hard.

Illustration 54: Gold supply easily depleted even during normal economic transactions. It is not easily added into the economy as it has to be found and the supply is controlled by others (other countries/companies).

END OF SECTION 3

Federal Reserve Marriner S. Eccles Building in Washington D.C.

The Federal Reserve is headquartered in this 1935 building, which is renamed in the honor of Marriner S. Eccles in the 1970s, an American banker from Utah who has never studied economics or attended college, but saw the problem with the economic system. He is one of the proposer of the FDIC, reform of the central master bank known as the Fed, tax redistribution, minimum wage law, unemployment insurance and many more. He was one of the architect of Roosevelt's New

Deal and the president chose him to serve as the Fed Chairman in the early 1930s to carry out the proposed reforms. He served as Chairman for 14 years and was one of the highly celebrated Fed Chairman who has restored the credibility of the Fed.

Photo of building is courtesy of Wiki Media Commons by AgnosticPreachersKid.
Photo of Mr. Eccles is sourced from Library Of Congress, taken by Harris & Ewing

SECTION 4:

THE BANKING SYSTEM IN ACTION

INTRODUCTION TO THE BANKING SYSTEM

*S*uppose a bank lends you USD300,000 for your house. You are to payback the bank USD400,000. Now where does the extra USD100,000 will come from? Suppose that in an economy the size of just a few houses, when the bank lends money to three house owners for example, all to be paid back plus interest, will there be enough money in the economy to pay back the loans plus the interest/profit, because originally only USD900,000 are printed for the three mortgaged houses? This is one issue where many economists failed to answer properly and where most anti modern banking system harp on. They argued that there is not enough money in the economy for the participants to pay off their debts, and these participants will need to borrow ever more, to pay off their loans. This statement is misleading and did not explain the full workings of the monetary and banking system.

An article from the internet (hazariba.com), vehemently says the following:

http://www.hazariba.com

"Suppose Bank XYZ creates Dirhams 100,000 and supplies it at an interest rate of 10% per annum to several ..... a combined sum of Dirhams 110,000 is due on all borrowers to repay to the loaning bank. But the money available in the economy is only Dirhams 100,000 as the bank is only supplier of money, so from where the rest 10,000 would come that is the difference in the borrowers intake and total repayment amount...... from NOWHERE. Yes, that is right from nowhere because that money does not exist in the economy. ....but as per loan agreements - these borrowers collectively have to pay back 110,000. How is that possible? There is no way. Don't you believe, it is 100% like this - no less. This is cheating and criminal foul play.

So what will happen, at least one or more of these borrowers would default on their loan(s) and would lose their personal assets.... The money creator has designed a mechanism that would force few of the borrowers each year to default so that the bank could forfeit the security assets and gain wealth by foul play."

Illustration 55: A wrong view that shows a complete lack of understanding of our banking system as a whole.

Such strong words and condemnation of the banking system. Yet our economy is thriving; and had thrived for hundreds of years. Millions of people had benefited tremendously from their relationship with their banks, and still, banks are no way richer than they were before. The shareholders do however, but then so are the shareholders of every other companies on the planet.

Interest charges existed long before paper money was first used, in fact since time immemorial—when the first commercial lending took place. Paper money is their chosen scapegoat forgetting the fact that even under other monetary standard such as gold, interest exists.

What will happen in the economy is that when loans are being paid, the supply of money will diminish, making day to day trades more expensive and difficult, on top of new monetary demand from the daily addition of new wealth. This contraction can be dangerous and must be carefully monitored by the central bank. As the debts are being paid, there will be less and less money in circulation, deflation may occur unless new loans are issued into the economy. This occurred in 2009 when a large percentage of the economic participants paid their loans and did not take new ones. The central bank constantly monitors monetary conditions especially for such a sign, and ensures that enough money is always in circulation, enough liquidity at all times.

The claim by the website is not true because once the banks made their profit, the profit will be paid to others, such as the government in the form of taxes, suppliers of the banks for services provided and the shareholders of the banks. The money is returned into the general economy and shortage of money mentioned by the website will not occur. This poorly and misdirected claim by the website will be further answered as you go through this section.

In 2008 and 2009, during the Great Financial Crisis, the Federal Reserve was forced to inject trillions of dollars into the banking system due to collapsing money supply as millions of people and businesses started to pay off their loans simultaneously. The courageous act of the Fed under Ben Bernanke has averted a crash in the general economy, not just in the United States, but the world at large.

How does the central bank inject money into the economy to counter the effects of everyone paying off their loans en masse? Surely the central bank cannot give money away for free as it is unfair to others. For example if the same Ron Pele (in Book 1) is only sleeping in his USD300,000 home every day and paying his loan only by using his original mortgage money, he will soon run out of money and still owe USD150,000 or so to the bank. Does the central bank now need to step in to give away money to Ron Pele? Certainly not, not according to any economic principle.

Basically as long as the house owner work and continue to generate value or wealth into the general economy, he or she will be paid for the work performed, either in cash or by another type of asset. This way, he can continue to pay his loan until maturity.

Now let's change the situation to that if Ron Pele is actually working hard and continue to pay his loan, just like millions of other economic participants. They generate plenty of new wealth making themselves and the country richer. What will happen to the money supply? Overtime there will be more and more wealth per person, but with the same amount of money in circulation. The central bank will inject money into the economy to ensure there is no shortage from this wealth additions.

How does the central bank inject money into the system? When money in circulation per person is not enough for daily transactions, commercial banks will start to hold more assets, but less debt. At one point, commercial banks can no longer issue loans out, even if new would be borrowers bring in additional assets as collateral because there is no more cash money available for lending. The banks will go to the central bank and ask for additional money, in exchange for the assets they held. The central bank will only issue money if it is backed by real assets. What thin air? NO SUCH THING. This way, the central bank knows exactly how much money is needed in the economy and will be able to maintain the liquidity requirements. If banks within the economy consistently borrow from the Fed, the Fed will know that the economy is short of cash, that it has outgrown the cash amount in circulation, and therefore the central bank can proceed to inject cash via other means such as giving money to, well— the government.

It is totally untrue that banks will want to bankrupt its borrowers. In fact, theoretically, if there is not enough money in circulation and the borrowers could not repay their loans, the bank can repossess their collateral, but do the borrowers lose? Actually, they do not. They already obtained equivalent money for their collateral already (it is as good as already been sold off), therefore what's there to be lost? If they use the borrowed money to buy properties and then collateralized those to the bank, losing it means that they will only lose a small portion of their money. When the bank sells their properties out, they could get reimbursement for any extra amount from the sale. Further, assuming that a portion of the borrowers went bankrupt and stopped payments to the bank, there will be excess money in circulation for other purposes. This will result in inflation, as now with the same amount of goods and services, more money are in circulation. The bank will be paid with inflated currency by the remaining borrowers, essentially losing out from its supposed earlier gains. So, why would the bank want its customers to go bankrupt? That will destroy wealth, and nobody benefits, especially the bank itself.

The following series of drawings clearly explains this "no money lost" situation, which is hyped by silly economists and politicians alike for political mileage by mislabeling them as "lost of family homes – lost of hundreds of thousands of dollars hit family hard" or simply as "where would the family stays after losing their homes?".

In reality, there is no loss for the family, except during one instance. We illustrate the facts and the truth behind it, in the series of drawings below:

Illustration 56: How can anybody buys a house without money?

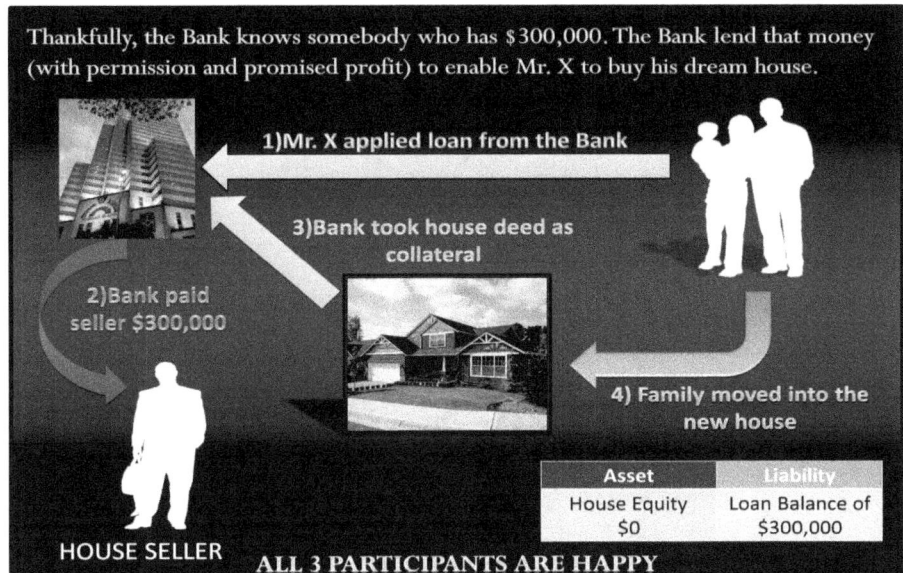

Thankfully, the Bank knows somebody who has $300,000. The Bank lend that money (with permission and promised profit) to enable Mr. X to buy his dream house.

1)Mr. X applied loan from the Bank

3)Bank took house deed as collateral

2)Bank paid seller $300,000

4) Family moved into the new house

Asset	Liability
House Equity $0	Loan Balance of $300,000

HOUSE SELLER ALL 3 PARTICIPANTS ARE HAPPY

Illustration 57: Borrowing the needed $300,000 and using the house as collateral, they got their dream home.

After 12 payments.....

Regular monthly loan payments

Asset	Liability
House Equity is $290,000	Owed To Depositors $290,000

Asset	Liability
House Equity is $10,000	Loan Balance of $290,000

Notes:

1. House is freely used by the family despite the house is not totally theirs. Bank has no use for this asset except to back the earlier issuance of money.

2. House equity owned by the family increases with each payments and is accumulated into the house. Subsequently, with each payments, bank's liability (what it owed to depositors) decreases.

3. Interest payments are not counted into house payments because house is freely used by the family (using other people's money), thus it is fair for them to pay "rental" to these owners.

Illustration 58: Bank is short on cash because it gave away money as loan, however it will count the loan's collateral as its asset. Loan balance decreases and their equity increases with each payment.

However, after a year, Mr. X loses his job and could not make any more payments.

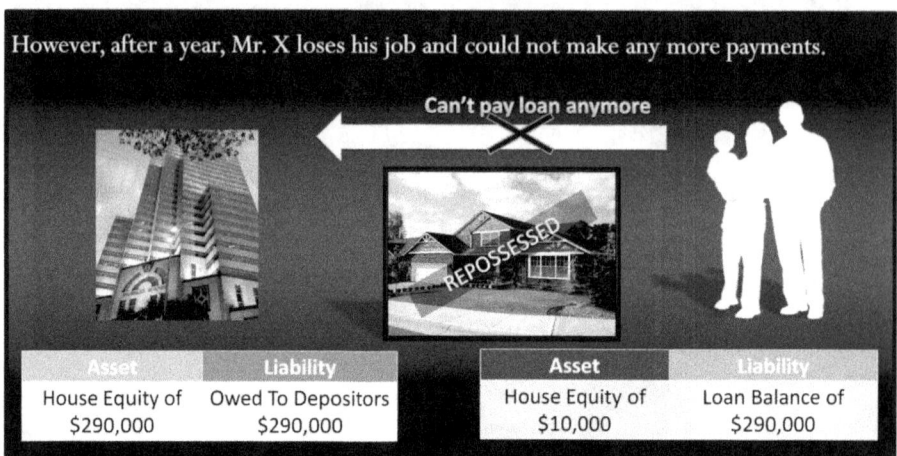

Asset	Liability		Asset	Liability
House Equity of $290,000	Owed To Depositors $290,000		House Equity of $10,000	Loan Balance of $290,000

Note: Bank repossesses the house because Bank has liabilities to the original owner of the money. It has to get back the cash from this hard asset. The only way to do it is to sell the house. One has to remember, the house is not fully owned by Mr. X as long as even $1 is owed to somebody else. However, Bank legally must return all the sale proceeds above the loan amount (minus fees) to Mr. X.

Illustration 59: The family came upon a rough patch and were unable to service their monthly payments anymore. After several missing payments, the Bank forecloses and repossesses their house.

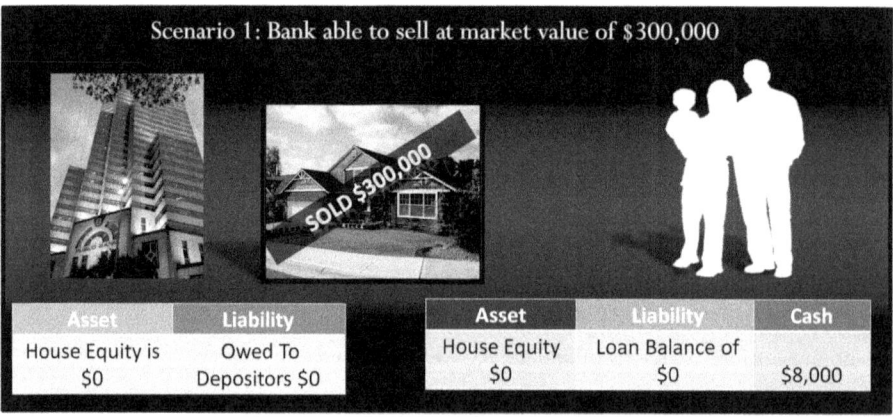

Scenario 1: Bank able to sell at market value of $300,000

Asset	Liability		Asset	Liability	Cash
House Equity is $0	Owed To Depositors $0		House Equity $0	Loan Balance of $0	$8,000

Note: The bank sells the house and obtained $300,000. The outstanding loan of the family is extinguished, with some extra money due to the equity of $10,000. Money paid to interest is not a loss, as Mr. X would have to paid rents regularly if he did not buy a house. These interest payments should be considered similar to rents when calculating loss. The family did not lose $300,000 at all.

Illustration 60: The family loses some cash from the house equities for fees but their debt to the Bank is eliminated. In all, they barely lose any money and were able to live in a good home.

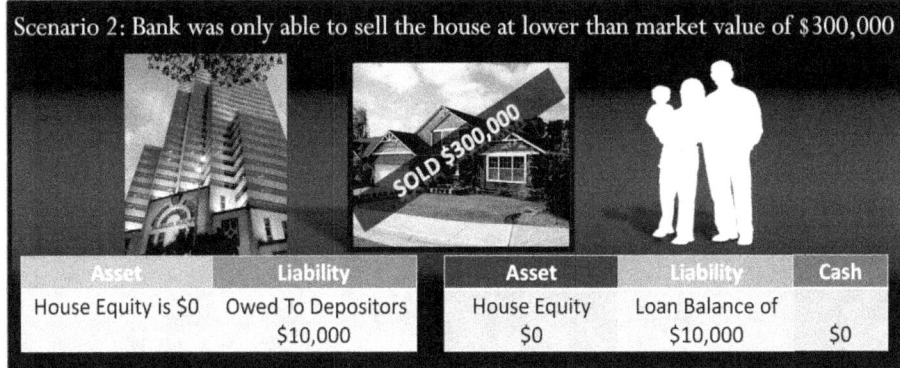

Scenario 2: Bank was only able to sell the house at lower than market value of $300,000

Asset	Liability	Asset	Liability	Cash
House Equity is $0	Owed To Depositors $10,000	House Equity $0	Loan Balance of $10,000	$0

Notes:

1. Bank owed its depositors $10,000 because the house value has dropped. It needs to repay this loss from its own money. It will try to recover this from the family.

2. Family lost all equities in the house, which is $10,000 plus the remaining debt of $10,000. This is the trap of no money down, but legally there is a way out.

3. These loses are not the Bank's fault but the norm because hard asset fluctuates in prices due to market forces.

4. The family however, could stay on during the repossession period (usually taken many months) – rent free.

Illustration 61 : Family still did not lose $300,000. Bank lost its money too. These are risk associated with doing business when payments are being made by future incomes. Thus, risk must be compensated. If however, the house market value has increased by 6%, then the family would gain. The Bank would return all money above loan amount (net fees).

What if one day gold can be easily manufactured, just like diamonds are today?
Do gold bugs even know there are already several ways to turn lead into gold ... today ? Only thing is, it is still difficult .. But one day ...

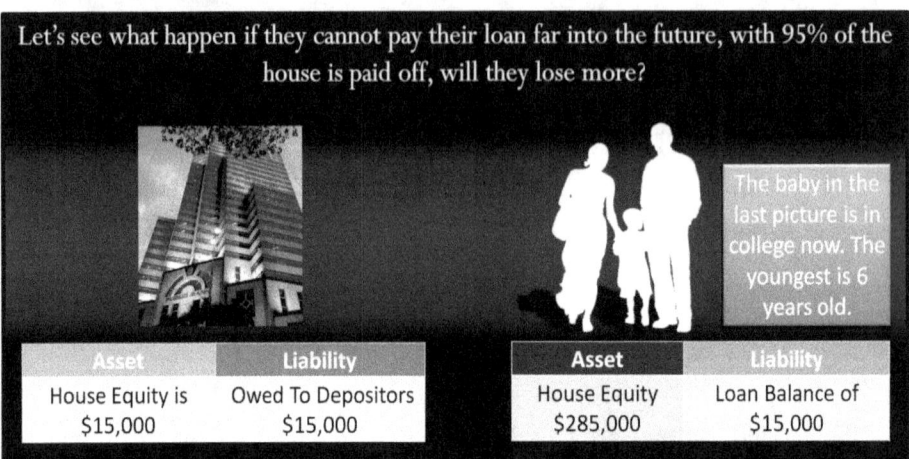

Let's see what happen if they cannot pay their loan far into the future, with 95% of the house is paid off, will they lose more?

The baby in the last picture is in college now. The youngest is 6 years old.

Asset	Liability
House Equity is $15,000	Owed To Depositors $15,000

Asset	Liability
House Equity $285,000	Loan Balance of $15,000

Notes: As you can see, the house is now nearly owned by Mr. X. He only owes $15,000 to the bank. Will he lose all his money and the house too? As hyped by many pundits, banks is said to love bankrupting people and make profit on it. Is that really true?

Illustration 62: What happen to the family if they hit that rough patch way into the future, say after 95% of the house is already paid off? Will the family lose significantly?

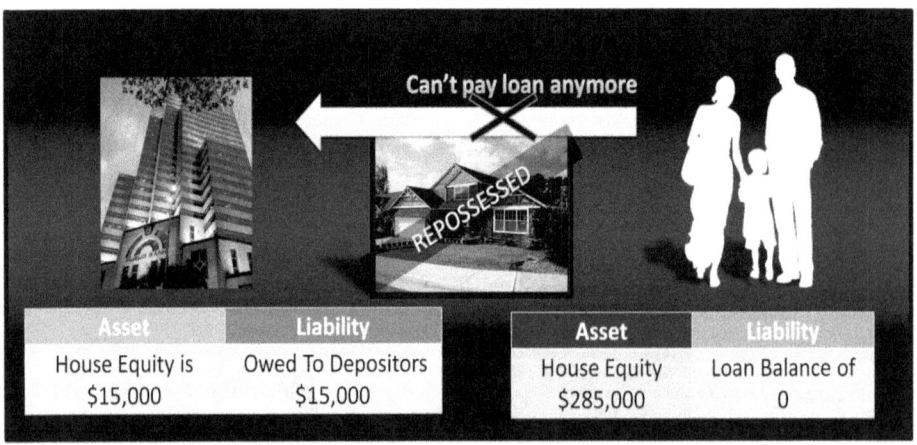

Can't pay loan anymore

REPOSSESSED

Asset	Liability
House Equity is $15,000	Owed To Depositors $15,000

Asset	Liability
House Equity $285,000	Loan Balance of 0

Illustration 63: However, after paying 95% of the mortgage, they came upon a rough patch and were unable to service their monthly payments anymore. After several missing payments, the Bank forecloses and repossesses their house.

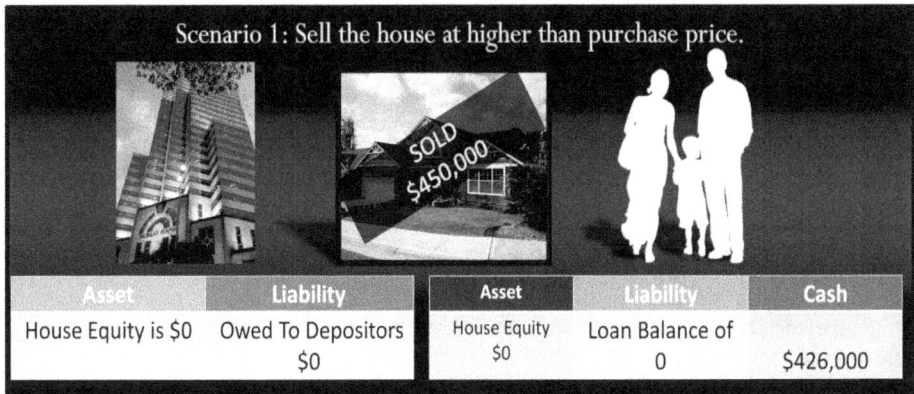

Scenario 1: Sell the house at higher than purchase price.

Asset	Liability	Asset	Liability	Cash
House Equity is $0	Owed To Depositors $0	House Equity $0	Loan Balance of 0	$426,000

Notes:

1. Bank repossesses the house, but can legally get $15,000 at most (plus some fees) from the foreclosure. The Bank needs to liquidate the house and get their money. Legally, they must sell the house at market value and are not allowed to liquidate it at very low price.

2. Money from the sale proceeds will be returned to the family, as the family still owes 95% of the house.

3. The Bank does not get the whole house and definitely cannot stay in the house!

4. $450,000 - $15,000 – 2% fees = $426,000

5. Average house increase in value of about 50% (after 23 years).

6. Bank recovered its money but do not make any additional profits because they don't profit from foreclosure as the house they have to sell still belongs to the owner and they can only legally claim loan dues (lawyers probably get more profit from foreclosures than banks) .

7. Owner netted $426,000 from the sale of the house. Did the owner lose? Of course not.

Illustration 64: Even if the family had paid 95% of the loan and lost their house , if the market value of the house have increased, they would not lose any money. In fact, they actually saved at least USD 105,000 in rentals plus any gains in the house's value –it's the spread between rental and interest).

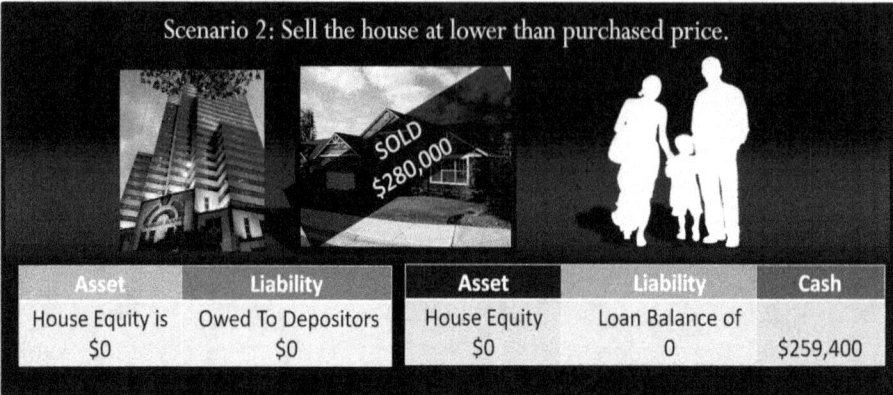

Asset	Liability	Asset	Liability	Cash
House Equity is $0	Owed To Depositors $0	House Equity $0	Loan Balance of 0	$259,400

Notes:

1. $280,000 - $15,000 – 2% fees = $259,400

2. Did family lose $300,000? The answer is still a big NO. If the house is sold at lower than purchased price, the family would lose some money. But they still get a lot back from the sale of the house.

3. Bank recovered its money but do not make any additional profits because they don't profit from foreclosure as the house they have to sell still belongs to the owner and they can only legally claim loan dues (lawyers tends to get more profit from foreclosures than banks).

4. They did managed to stay in the house for decades, saving rental fees of hundreds of thousands of dollars

Illustration 65: What will the bank do with the house? A bank cannot squeeze in and stay in a house! The house must be sold at market value. The family at this point has eliminated their debt to the bank, while collecting $259,400 in cash. They can purchase a cheaper home, outright!

As shown in the illustrations above, banks do not make money from making its borrowers go bankrupt. Furthermore, owing the banks money for purchasing a house does not make someone go bankrupt. The statements that banks purposely and menacingly dupe borrowers and exist to take the people's hard-earned money are really misleading and just to create shock value.

Many losses and foreclosures occur because people are greedy, always wanting things beyond their reach and getting them by shortcuts. When home values are skyrocketing, people did not stop and think the basic questions:

 Are the property prices already beyond "sane" figures that "sane" people would pay for?

Is this something that they can afford (loan repayments as a percentage of income)?

What will happen if they fall ill or lose their jobs?

Will the house generate more value for them compared to what they pay it for?

One must remember, in dealing with property related 'losses' (if foreclosure occurs), the only relevant factor that is immensely important (other factors are irrelevant) is the house's market value. If the property value stays the same as the original price or goes slightly above, then loses would be negligible (or none whatsoever, depending on the difference between rents and interests payment). If however, the market value of that property goes way below, then both borrower and lender will experience significant losses. Banks will suffer the same fate because their cash is backed by an inflated asset (looks good on paper but worth less) and recovering money from borrowers who have no money are always a loss making act.

If one borrows $300,000 to buy a house at 5% interest to be paid in an even spread for 25 years, the interest total would be around $226,000. Rental for a $300,000 house is usually around $1,200 a month. So if renting, in 25 years, the person would have paid $360,000 in rentals. By buying the house, he would have saved $134,000 in rentals. After deducting the associated costs of owning a house (property taxes, repairs etc.), he would still have saved money (maybe about $30,000). Any payments made toward the principals of the loan will turn into equity in the house, which belongs to him. So, if the house is repossessed at any moment in time, the equity is still his. The final amount received would depend on the selling price of the house. If he is prudent and bought the house at a good price (not inflated like at the height of the property bubble), then he would not lose any money. However, if he were one of the "poorly misguided souls" that bought houses during the height of the bubble, then he would lose a lot of money, would end up losing all of the equities, and still owes the bank. These losses or gains are all stemming out of variations of property prices, which have nothing to do with banks. Whether a house is a good investment or not, find out in Book 3 of the series (look for "Rent vs. Buy").

No matter how you slice and dice it, it is not the bank's fault if a person could not pay his loan due to unfortunate incidents in life. Good banks will even work out a plan in dealing with rough patches. For example, they would reduce the interest rate or suspend monthly payments during a layoff or illness. Some banks would deduct built up equities as monthly payments and stretch the payments out. Banks usually want to avoid foreclosures. Loss of jobs, illnesses and so forth are not in the power of the banks, contrary to some beliefs that banks are very powerful and control the world or even acting as the proxy of Satan itself.

One question that people need to ask themselves is, if there are no lenders, how could they buy a house at this instance, using their future incomes? Another question is, are there any lenders who would lend people money to be paid in the future (knowing there are many uncertainties in life) if there is no profit? Would you give your money freely, no strings attached? If you will not, then of course nobody else's would. Donations and charities are an entirely different matter than parting with money you would want to use in the future.

Therefore it is clear that there are no losses involved for people who are in foreclosures when they fail to pay their monthly payments as long as the house price is above the purchase price. If the price is lower, there bound to be losses, which can be contra out with the cost of rentals. This potential gain or loss, is SOLELY due to market forces of supply and demand, which dictates the current price of the day for the house and has nothing to do with the mortgage or the bank. Thus, we have disproved the claim that banks are in the business of bankrupting people in order to make more money. We had shown that banks also lose money if they extend loans on bad quality houses (over-inflated prices) and lo and behold, banks certainly cannot print money out of thin air to cover these loses, otherwise they would have already. Not even the mighty central bank can do anything (everyone loses when an asset depreciates in value).

An important entity in the banking system is the central bank (the Federal Reserve). The most important role of the central bank is to maintain price stability. In essence, it must ensure deflation is not occurring as the economy grows due to not enough money in circulation. The other side of the coin is, if too much money is injected, inflation can occur and erode the value of existing money in circulation. Thus the central bank must find the right balance, which is to ensure there is adequate money in circulation for the economy to function properly. For that reason, now we can understand why the inflation (or deflation) data are very critical for a central bank, and they monitor it like a hawk. The central bank also continuously monitors the balances of depository and lending institutions and will act to inject or remove money when the situation warrants it.

Now to the question on how the central bank injects money into circulation, a.k.a. "printing money out of thin air". It does so by ONLY buying government securities (Treasury Notes as in the USA). This purchase of securities by the Federal Reserve with newly printed money will give free money to the federal government, which in turn will spend it. The interest earned by the Federal Reserve on this T-Bill (paid by the government) it is holding, will be returned to the government at the end of the year. This is basically what Quantitative Easing is about, which is the other name for printing money out of thin air. At any other time when the central bank is buying other kinds of securities from any other banks (e.g. from the overnight loans or from the discount windows), it will demand collaterals to back the securities. This will not give a similar increase in the money supply, as is the injection via government securities because it will only use money that is already in its reserve and will not print new money.

All of the currency issued by the Fed is now backed by the T-Bills, which is in turn backed by nothing else, other than the 'Full Faith Of the US Gov'. The interest incurred by the government for the T-Bills payable to the central bank (Fed) will eventually end up back into the other pocket of the government. It is much like a zero-sum game, where the government will pay the central bank the interests of the T-Bills, and then the money appears in the balance sheet of the Fed, without any caveat on it, which will later be returned, back to the government, the owner of the Federal Reserve. This is one explanation why the debt of the US government to the central bank remains low over time and will always be manageable. We do not consider this debt of the government to the Fed as a debt per se; it is just a statement on how much money is issued into the economy. Paying off this debt hardly creates any inflation and it is not a problem for the government to pay it off. The government needs to conduct this operation quickly, by paying the Federal Reserve and demands the profit from the balance sheet of the Fed, be repatriated back into the treasury account right away. It is easy to do and does not cost anything. Currently the Fed is holding more than two trillion dollars of government securities, to which the government, is paying interest on. The interest collected by the Fed, will be returned to the government via the Treasury, as most or all of the Fed's profit is returned to the Treasury anyway. In FY2010, the Fed returned to the US Treasury a record total of USD89 Billion, making it by far the most profitable bank in the world.

The central bank also monitors the demand for money from the balances of depository institutions in the Federal Reserve

System. When there is a decrease in the balances, there has been an increase in demand. The Fed may start buying Treasury securities to increase the supply of money in the economy. Frankly speaking, the Fed can also print the cash and distribute it, most likely directly to the government. We had explained this relationship between the central bank, the government and the people (the economy) in Book 1 of this 259 Trillion Vs 5 trillion series (look for "Money Origination And Propagation Simulation").

Another common lie being parroted by bank bashers is that there are not enough money in circulation to pay for all outstanding loans and interest in the economy. Please go through the fractional reserve banking simulation to get the complete picture, but for the moment, apart from our answer in "Money Is Backed By Debt", the simple factor contributing to the recirculation of money back into the system is as follows:

"When a borrower pays a loan to the bank, normally the principal plus interest, it seems that there is not enough money in circulation to pay for it. However, when a bank is being paid, the interest portion is actually used by the bank to cover its operating expenses such as rents, hardware etc. and the leftover if any, will be the profit for the bank. This profit is then given to its shareholders who are the owners of the bank who will promptly redeposit the money into the bank or spending it into the economy. This will result in the 'extra' money taken out of circulation earlier will be immediately released back into the system. Therefore there is no continuously draining of money out of circulation occurring even if there is an element of "interest" for loans".

This may well explain why the Islamic Banking system adopts the same principle, whereby 'interest' is rephrased as 'profit' and it works exactly the same. It is unclear and murky to those Islamic 'experts' and scholars who are still arguing about the prevention of usury for the past 1,400 years. It may take them a few thousand more years to solve this issue unless they upgrade their economic knowledge before they start to debate the issue. For us, it is clear that the payment of interest or profit, is a must for equitable profit and risk sharing between lenders and borrowers. The amount of profit or interest chargeable must be in accordance to the wealth generation potential, otherwise there will be a mismatch and injustices will occur. Charging the borrower more than originally agreed is also an injustice to the borrower and is the essence of the prevention dictated by God. We will discuss on 'interest' later on but first we shall explain further the role of the central bank, by first unraveling the workings of the modern Fractional Reserve Banking.

MISLEADING EXAMPLE COMMONLY USED BY ANTI FRACTIONAL RESERVE BANKING SYSTEM GROUPS

*T*he following is one of the most common misconception about fractional reserve banking system. It is always said as creating money out of nothing, without anything backing such creations, and the bank holds little money and lend out many times their actual deposits.

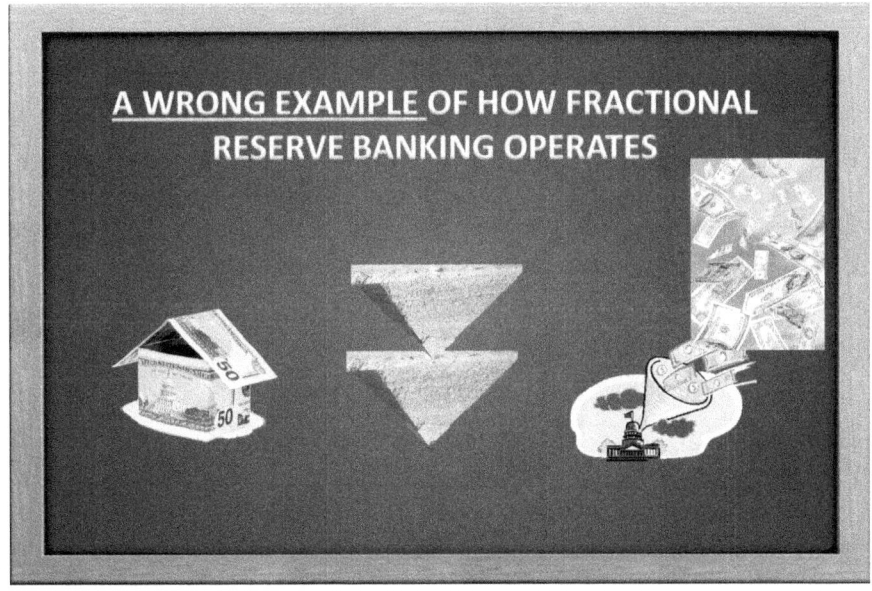

Illustration 66: The following examples and illustrations will show one of the main misleading statement on how fractional reserve banking operates.

By using an approximate 10% fractional reserve ratio requirement, let's start with :

Step 1: A depositor deposits $100 with a bank.

> The Total Reserves: $100,
> Total Loans: $0,
> Total Money Supply: $100

Step 2: The bank holds $10 for its reserves and lends the other $90.

> Total Reserves: $10,
> Total Loans: $90,
> Total Money Supply: $100

Step 3: Next, a second bank takes the $90 in deposits, holds $9 for its reserves, and lends the other $81.

> Total Reserves: $19,
> Total Loans: $171,
> Total Money Supply: $190

Step 4: Repeat Step 3. A third bank takes the $81 as a deposit, holds $8.10 for its reserves, and lends out $72.90.

> Total Reserves: $27.10,
> Total Loans: $243.90,
> Total Money Supply: $271

Step 5: Repeat Step 3 again. A fourth bank takes the $72.90 as a deposit, holds $7.29 for its reserves, and then lends $65.61.

> Total Reserves: $34.39,
> Total Loans: $309.51,
> Total Money Supply: $343.90

Step 6: Repeat Step 3 and so on until the limit is reached,

> Total Reserves: $100,
>
> Total Loans: $900,
>
> Total Money Supply: $1000

For many, this process or concept is so difficult to understand and at times, downright repulsive. A hundred dollars is turned into a thousand, by the magic of fractional reserve banking. This is the single most popular accusation made against the system.

If you notice, the bank is also portrayed as insolvent, because it has more loans than reserves. Another popular site in the internet claimed that there is an inverted pyramid between the central bank and the commercial banks, and then there is another pyramid, excuse us, another inverted pyramid between the commercial banks and the economy. They called it two inverted pyramids on top of each other. Such fancy terms, which few people will understand, are the basis of their half-truths. From mathematics point of view, pyramid upon a pyramid will crash in just a matter of days, not decades because of severe uncontrollable pyramiding. It is like an exponential graph being exponentialed twice. We also wonder how the example above will describe the situation in the UK where there is 0% reserve requirement and the bank can lend out all of its deposited money. What kind of fancy terms they will use, perhaps it is infinity and beyond or some other terms which we can never understand.

The previous steps of the misleading example is graphically presented in the series of drawings below in past tense.

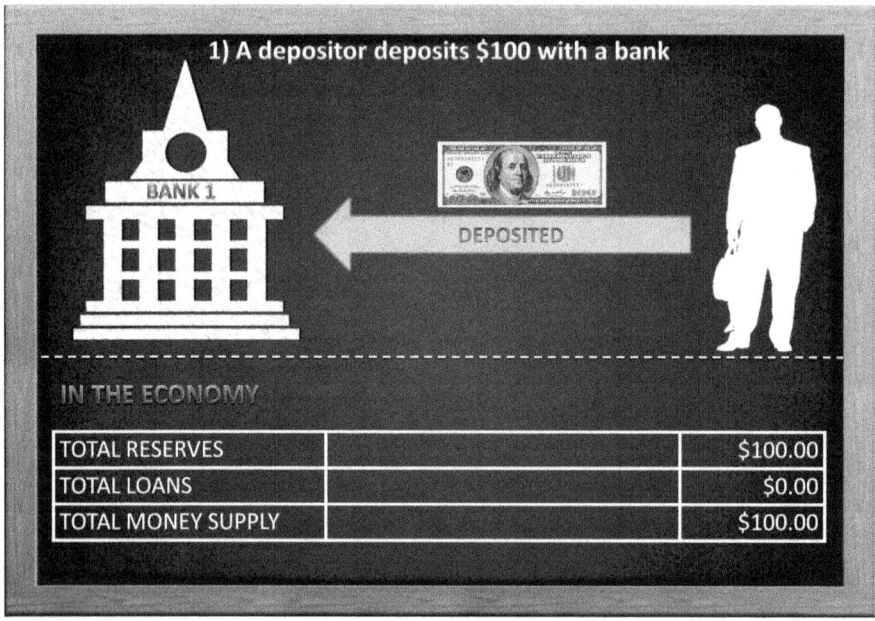

Illustration 67: Step1: A depositor deposited $100 with Bank 1. Thus, total reserves in the economy (Bank 1) became $100. There were no loans. Total money supply in the economy remained at $100.

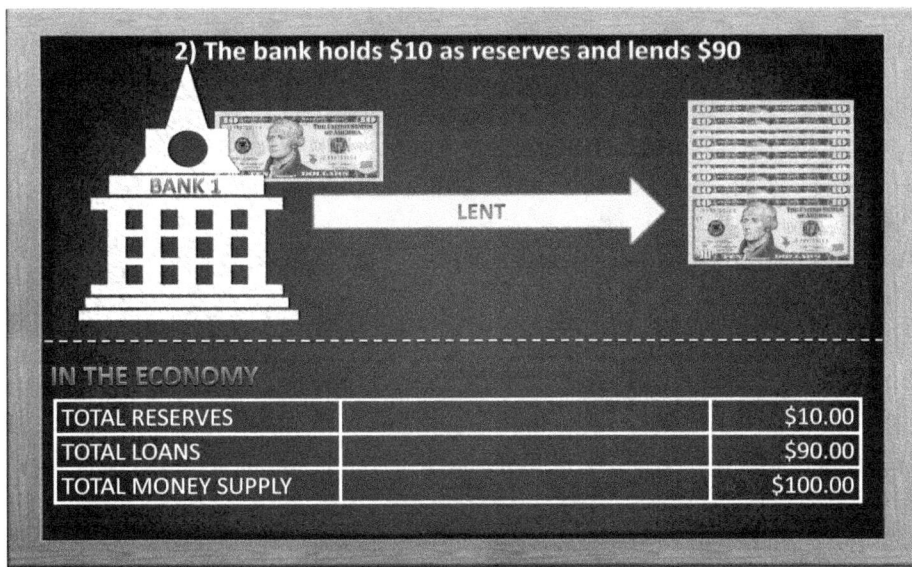

Illustration 68: Step 2: The bank held $10 for its reserves and lent the other $90 to other banks or citizens. If the borrower is a citizen, this money is temporarily holds outside of the banking system until he/she decides to deposit the money into a bank. Money supply in the economy remained at $100 (there were no other deposits). Bank 1 reserves dropped to $10 since it gave $90 as loan.

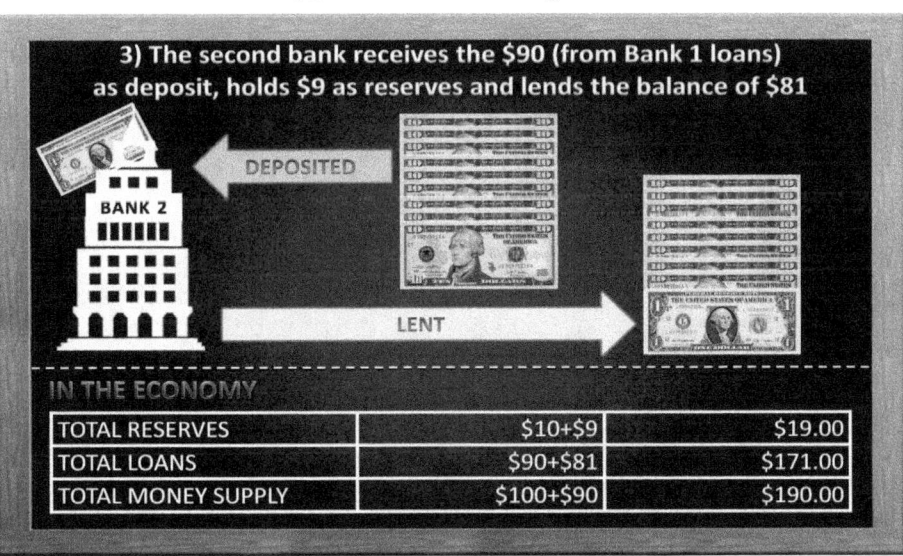

Illustration 69: Step 3 – Next, the second bank took the $90 (from Bank1's loan) in as deposits and held $9 for its reserves and then, lent the rest ($81). Total reserves in the economy (Bank 1 and Bank 2) became $19 and both banks gave loans amounted to $171. The money supply increased by $90 (due to the new deposit of $90) to $190.

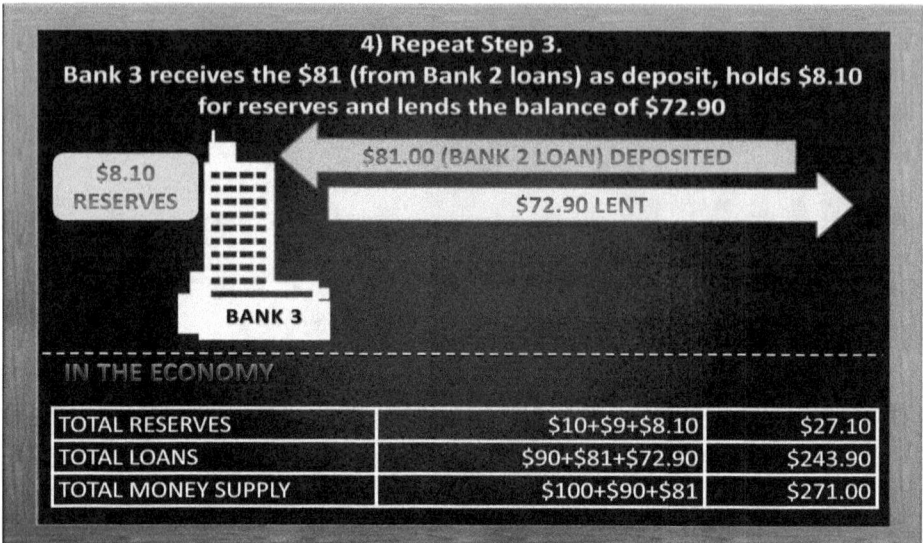

Illustration 70: Step 4: Step 3 is repeated.
A third bank (Bank 3) took in the $81 of lent money (Bank2) as its deposit. It held back the required reserves of $8.10 and lent the rest out. Total reserves held by all 3 banks became $27.10. They gave a total of $243.90 in loans. Total money supply in the economy (due to deposits) increased to $271.

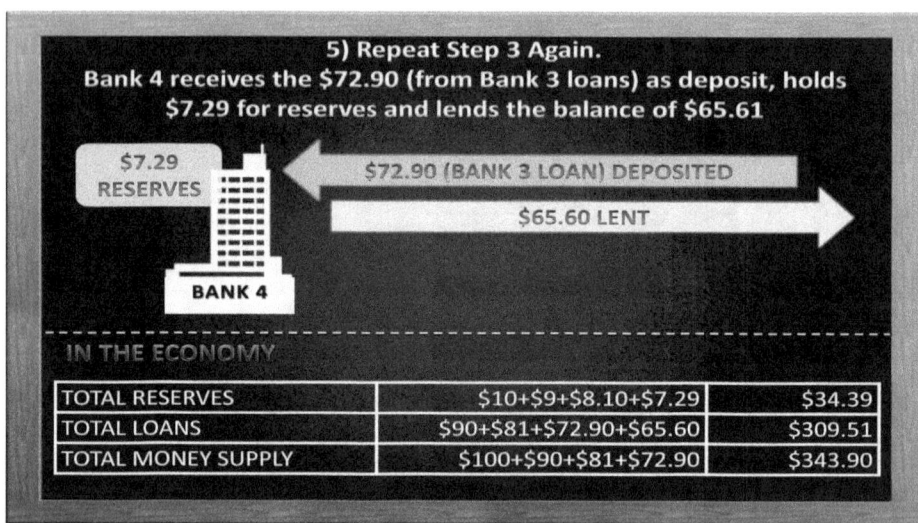

Illustration 71: Step 5: Step 3 is repeated.
A fourth bank (Bank 4) received the $72.90 of lent money (Bank2) as its deposit. It held the required reserves of $7.29 and lent the rest out. Total reserves held by all 4 banks increased to $34.39. They gave a total of $309.51 in loans. Total money supply in the economy (due to deposits) became $343.90.

IN THE ECONOMY

TOTAL RESERVES	$10+$9+$8.10+$7.29+.......	$100.00
TOTAL LOANS	$90+$81+$72.90+$65.60+.	$900.00
TOTAL MONEY SUPPLY	$100+$90+$81+$72.90+....	$1000.00

- By the magic of fractional reserve banking, a $100 is turned into $1000.
- Money created out of thin air.
- Double inverted pyramid, ready to topple

WRONG!!!!

Illustration 72:
The cycle continues until no more loans can be given out.
Maximum loan that were given out was $900 and the $100 created
$1000 in the money supply. However, as we pointed out before,
this example is misleading and the statements that describe them
are totally wrong.

Remember, these simulation of "Fractional Reserve Banking"
is wrong! Bank never gives out its reserve in one shot and
payments were never included into the simulations.

US Gov spent $1,200,000,000,000 on
recipients of SS & Medicare. That's
equivalent to $30,000 per 'head'!
Read more in Book 3
WEALTH BACKED PAPER MONEY AND
WEALTH OF THE UNITED STATES

THE RIGHT EXAMPLE OF HOW FRACTIONAL
RESERVE BANKING OPERATES

A hundred dollars is turned into a thousand, by the magic of fractional reserve banking. This is commonly parroted by many authors and designed to mislead people.

Let us assure you, that fractional reserve banking "creation of money" is perfectly acceptable, due to the reasons that we will show below. Most examples found in other books and especially the internet, will leave out the complete story and thus, make it more difficult to fully comprehend what actually is happening in the fractional reserve banking system. By leaving out some important items, the reader will not be able to understand the real reason why the banking system even works.

We will first attempt to show you a simplified way of how fractional reserve banking operates by having only one sole bank in the following economic model so that it is easy to comprehend. We will then take it step by step, with increasing complexity, yet still easy to follow. To enhance and ensure your full understanding of the examples, please visit our website at **http://sites.google.com/site/259trillionvs5trillion and download the free accompanying lessons movie presentation materials.**

Lesson 5: Fractional Reserve Banking In Action

Let us start with the bank injecting its own money worth 100 into the bank. The bank will now have a total deposit of 100 and the total money supply in the banking system is 100 as well. The actual cash in the bank is 100 and the bank has zero liabilities as no loan is made just yet. Actual cash reserve to loan ratio is 1.0 or 100%.

	Total Deposit Level	Total Loans	Total Money Supply	Actual Cash in Hand (in Banks)	Banks Liabilities (due to deposit)	Cash to Deposit Ratio (SRR)
Bank's Own Money	100	0	100	100	100	1.000

Illustration 73: Simulation of Fractional Reserve Banking (Simple) —The Bank started its business by injecting its own money of $100

Let's assume that the statutory reserve ratio (SRR) or the cash reserve limit is 0.1 (or 10%). The bank is now ready to lend money, so it started to issue loans. Borrowers started to obtain loans from the bank. The impact to the bank is as follows:

	Total Deposit Level	Total Loans	Total Money Supply	Actual Cash in Hand (in Banks)	Banks Liabilities (due to deposit)	Cash to Deposit Ratio (SRR)
Bank's Own Money	100	0	100	100	100	1.000
a borrower borrowed $10	100	10	110	90	100	0.900

Illustration 74: Simulation of Fractional Reserve Banking (Simple) A borrower borrowed $10 of the Bank's money

A borrower who borrowed 10 from the bank will cause the total loan extended by the banking system to go up from 0 to 10. Money supply due to the banking system grows by 10 to 110. The bank is holding less actual cash in its hand, it is now only 90 instead of 100. The bank still has the same liability, which is the deposit of 100 made earlier, so there is no change to the liability of the bank. The actual deposit to loan ratio (or cash reserve ratio) is now 0.9 or 90%. If more borrowers come and borrow money from the bank, the following will happen:

	Total Deposit Level	Total Loans	Total Money Supply	Actual Cash in Hand (in Banks)	Banks Liabilities (due to deposit)	Cash to Deposit Ratio (SRR)
Bank's Own Money	100	0	100	100	100	1.000
a borrower borrowed $10	100	10	110	90	100	0.900
a borrower borrowed $10	100	20	120	80	100	0.800
a borrower borrowed $10	100	30	130	70	100	0.700
a borrower borrowed $10	100	40	140	60	100	0.600
a borrower borrowed $10	100	50	150	50	100	0.500
a borrower borrowed $10	100	60	160	40	100	0.400
a borrower borrowed $10	100	70	170	30	100	0.300
a borrower borrowed $10	100	80	180	20	100	0.200
a borrower borrowed $10	100	90	190	10	100	0.100

Illustration 75: Simulation of Fractional Reserve Banking (Simple) After 9 borrowers, the Bank will reach its maximum lending limit set by the Central Bank

The bank now reaches its maximum lending limit set by the central bank. The bank only has 10 actual cash in hand. The cash to deposit ratio (SRR) is 0.1 or 10%. Essentially the bank is holding 10 for every 100 of deposit as actual cash in hand. Looking the example in a different way, the bank, which is having a liability of 100 (due to deposit of 100) had extended 90 worth of loans. The money supply, has grown from 100 to 190 due to the loans extended. Is the bank insolvent? Many people say so, but in reality, the bank is not insolvent. It has assets in excess of its obligations. Whenever a borrower asks for a loan, the bank will swap the money it extended with a collateral from the borrower. An asset such as a house will do just fine. Every loan extended will have an asset to cover for it. The bank actually has, from the beginning, a surplus in assets. The anti fractional banking group will say that the bank is suppose to have 100 cash reserve for 100 worth of deposit, i.e. 100% cash reserve. These groups **always** **confuse money with wealth** (explained thoroughly in the first book of the series, **The Conundrum Of Assets & Money**). Stop thinking money as wealth, and **start thinking of money as a medium; for exchanges and transactions.** When you deposit 100 into a bank, you are not putting the money into the bank, you are merely carrying a representation of the asset you hold (a house etc. in the economy) and deposit that into the bank.

Another way to look at money is by looking at it as un-numbered coupons representing a portion of an asset in the economy. When this coupon is deposited into the bank, the bank will log it as an entry into an account, and the coupon will no longer be needed and thus be free for use for something else, such as lending. The bank can lend all of the coupons it collected, and if someone come to the bank and requests their coupons back, the bank will collect them from those it has lend out to. The coupon by itself, has no value of its own and the asset's value it represents, can change in value, therefore the value of money can change. It is the central bank's job to maintain the value of the money in the economy.

Let us now look at the asset side of the bank.

A new category is added to the previous table as below:

	Total Deposit Level	Total Loans	Total Money Supply	Actual Cash in Hand (in Banks)	Banks Liabilities (due to deposit)	Asset of Banks (due to Own Cash and Loans payable)	Cash to Deposit Ratio (SRR)
Bank's Own Money	100	0	100	100	100	100	1.000
a borrower borrowed 10	100	10	110	90	100	100	0.900
a borrower borrowed 10	100	20	120	80	100	100	0.800
a borrower borrowed 10	100	30	130	70	100	100	0.700
a borrower borrowed 10	100	40	140	60	100	100	0.600
a borrower borrowed 10	100	50	150	50	100	100	0.500
a borrower borrowed 10	100	60	160	40	100	100	0.400

Continue on the next page.......

a borrower borrowed 10	100	70	170	30	100	100	0.300
a borrower borrowed 10	100	80	180	20	100	100	0.200
a borrower borrowed 10	100	90	190	10	100	100	0.100

Illustration 76: A new Category —Assets of Banks is added to the previous table (Illustration 75)

The assets of the bank continue to increase, in tandem with the amount of loans extended while its cash reserve will decline. The net effect is that the asset of the bank will not change, it will stay at 100 throughout, but the composition is slowly changing from cash heavy to asset heavy. **Banks are unique that customers' deposits are considered as liabilities and loans extended out are considered as assets,** which is the total opposite of typical businesses where deposits will be considered as assets and loans as liabilities. Loans extended by banks originated from the cash in hand (from deposit side) which is swapped for another form of asset (such as the house mentioned earlier).

Whenever a loan is extended, the borrower will either spend it, or deposit the money into his or her account— which is none other than at the bank itself. If the borrower spends the money, the seller who receives the money will eventually make that deposit, you guessed it, at the bank as well. Therefore, we need to include deposits made to our simulation, to better reflect the actual working of the banking system. All of our examples shown here exclude interest or profit for the bank, so that the reader can easily understand the main objective of the simulation. Although interest or profit inclusion is rather a simple entry into the example, the simulation in our computer became vastly complex and will be confusing for beginners to follow. We will explain later in this book what will happen to interest and why interest is needed by banks.

The following expanded simulation will now closely resemble the actual workings of the banking system in real time. Let's go through it slowly and we will explain one by one along the way.

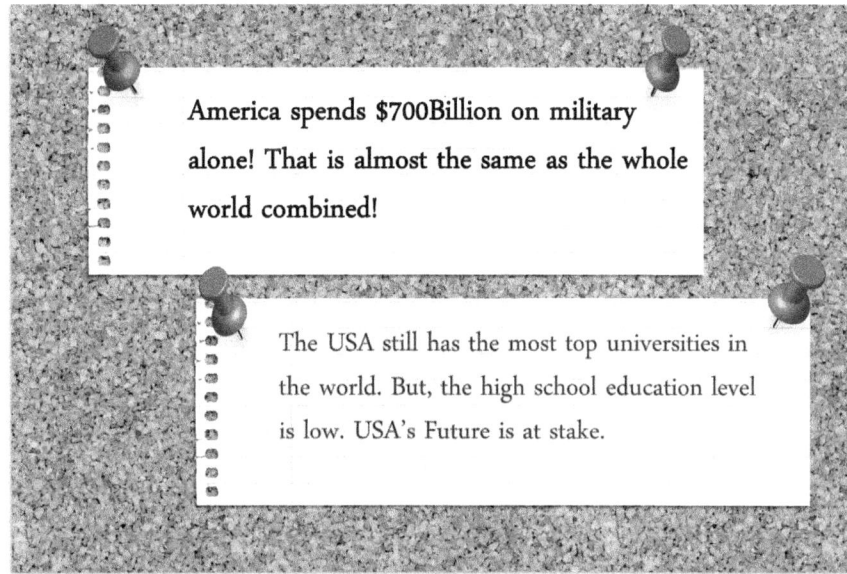

We start once again with the bank depositing its own 100 into the bank. Now several new categories are added into our simulation, to better reflect the actual situation in the banking system. When that deposit of 100 is made, there is a net inflow into the banking system (+100) which is reflected in the Net Money In/Out of Banking System Due to Loan or Deposit category. Another added category is the Actual Loan To Deposit Ratio. Since no loan is made just yet, it is zero at the moment.

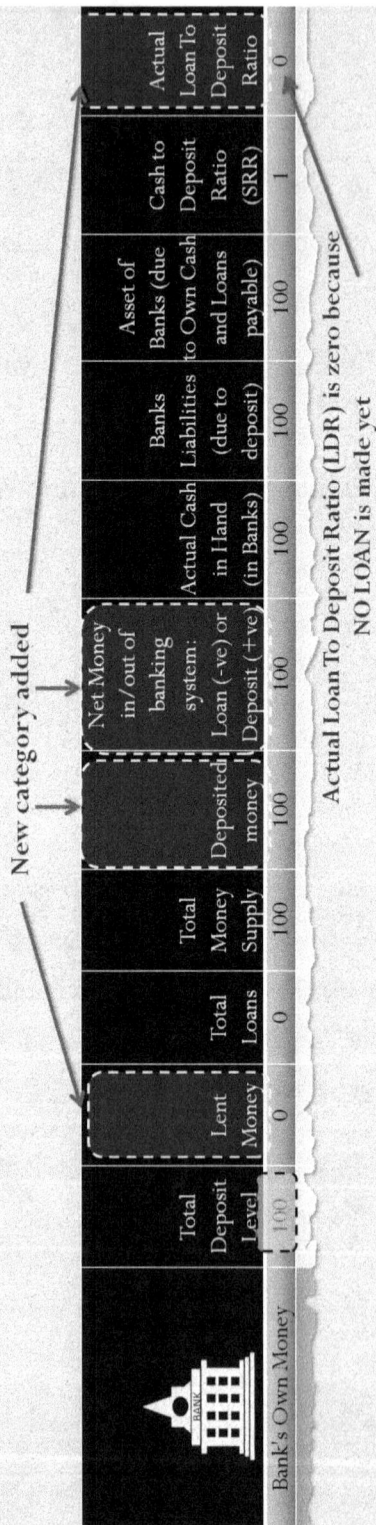

Bank's Own Money	Total Deposit Level	Lent Money	Total Loans	Total Money Supply	Deposited money	Net Money in/out of banking system: Loan (-ve) or Deposit (+ve)	Actual Cash in Hand (in Banks)	Banks Liabilities (due to deposit)	Asset of Banks (due to Own Cash and Loans payable)	Cash to Deposit Ratio (SRR)	Actual Loan To Deposit Ratio
	100	0	0	100	100	100	100	100	100	1	0

New category added

Actual Loan To Deposit Ratio (LDR) is zero because NO LOAN is made yet

Illustration 77: Simulation of Fractional Reserve Banking – Bank injected its own money of $100 to start its business

Now a borrower comes in as expected, wanting to borrow money and in exchange, provided a house as a collateral.

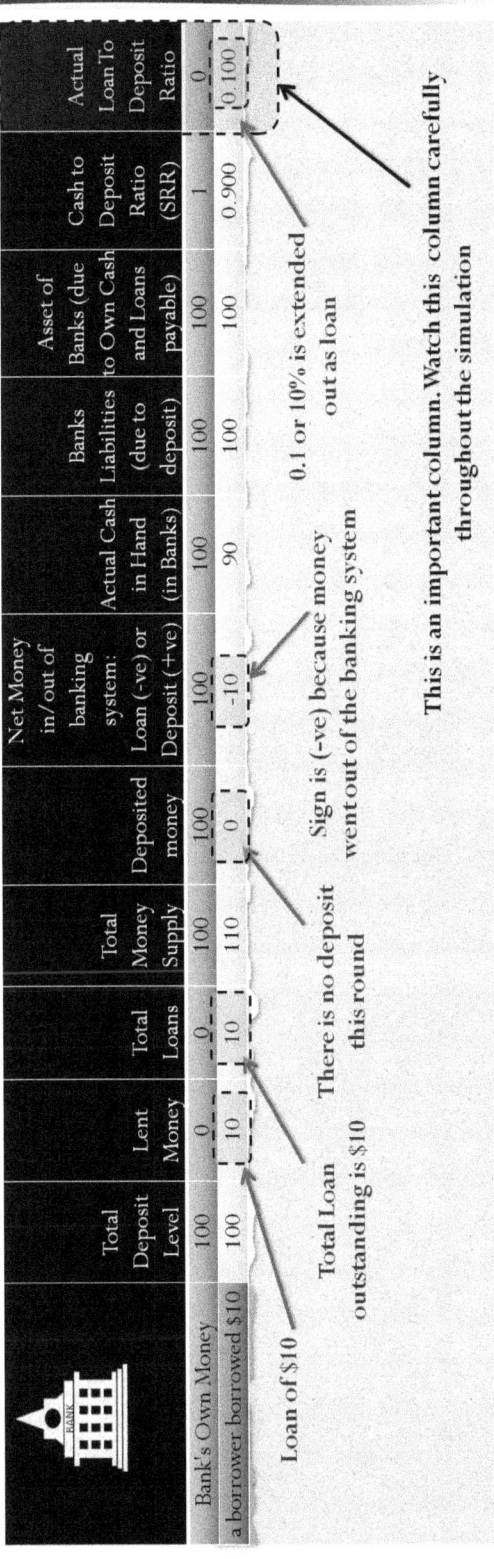

	Total Deposit Level	Lent Money	Total Loans	Total Money Supply	Deposited money	Net Money in/out of banking system: Loan (-ve) or Deposit (+ve)	Actual Cash in Hand (in Banks)	Banks Liabilities (due to deposit)	Asset of Banks (due to Own Cash and Loans payable)	Cash to Deposit Ratio (SRR)	Actual Loan To Deposit Ratio
Bank's Own Money	100	0	0	100	100	100	100	100	100	1	0
a borrower borrowed $10	100	10	10	110	0	-10	90	100	100	0.900	0.100

Loan of $10

Total Loan outstanding is $10

There is no deposit this round

Sign is (-ve) because money went out of the banking system

0.1 or 10% is extended out as loan

This is an important column. Watch this column carefully throughout the simulation

Illustration 78: Simulation of Fractional Reserve Banking – A borrower borrowed $10

There is a total of 10 of money lent out with total outstanding loan at 10 as well.

There is no deposited money in this round, so deposited money is zero.

There is a Net Money In/Out of The Banking System Due to Loan or Deposit, of –10. The sign is –ve, since money went out of the banking system due to a loan given.

Since there is a loan outstanding, the Actual Loan To Deposit Ratio is no longer zero, it is at 0.1 or 10%, **essentially meaning that 10% of the money in the bank is extended out as a loan. This is an important indicator and it is put at the last column for that reason.** Please check it out thoroughly throughout this part, and you will understand why the banking system is always solvent and never gives money it does not have.

Now, a depositor (can be the very same borrower earlier) makes a deposit into his or her account

	Total Deposit Level	Lent Money	Total Loans	Total Money Supply	Deposited money	Net Money in/out of banking system: Loan (-ve) or Deposit (+ve)	Actual Cash in Hand (in Banks)	Banks Liabilities (due to deposit)	Asset of Banks (due to Own Cash and Loans payable)	Cash to Deposit Ratio (SRR)	Actual Loan To Deposit Ratio
Bank's Own Money	100	0	0	100	100	100	100	100	100	1	0
a borrower borrowed $10	100	10	10	110	0	-10	90	100	100	0.900	0.100
A depositor deposit $10	110	0	10	110	10	10	100	110	110	0.909	0.091

No borrower this round

Deposit of $10 is made

Sign is (+ve) because money went into the banking system

Actual Cash in Hand went back to the original $100

Illustration 79: Simulation of Fractional Reserve Banking – A deposit of $10 is made

Total Deposit Level increased by 10 due to the deposit of 10 made.
There is a net inflow of money into the banking system, signified by the +10 at the Net Money Out/In column.
Actual Cash in Hand in the bank increased by 10 due to the deposit of 10 made. It went back to its original level of 100.

On the next cycle, another borrower comes in, and borrowed money.

	Total Deposit Level	Lent Money	Total Loans	Total Money Supply	Deposited money	Net Money in/out of banking system: Loan (-ve) or Deposit (+ve)	Actual Cash in Hand (in Banks)	Banks Liabilities (due to deposit)	Asset of Banks (due to Own Cash and Loans payable)	Cash to Deposit Ratio (SRR)	Actual Loan To Deposit Ratio
Bank's Own Money	100	0	0	100	100	100	100	100	100	1	0
a borrower borrowed $10	100	10	10	110	0	-10	90	100	100	0.900	0.100
A depositor deposit $10	110	0	10	110	10	10	100	110	110	0.909	0.091
a borrower borrowed $10	110	10	20	120	0	-10	90	110	110	0.818	0.182

Total Loan of $20

Illustration 80: Simulation of Fractional Reserve Banking – Another borrower borrowed $10

There is a loan of 10 made in this round, bringing the Total Loans to 20.

The borrower deposits the money into his or her account.

	Total Deposit Level	Lent Money	Total Loans	Total Money Supply	Deposited money	Net Money in/out of banking system: Loan (-ve) or Deposit (+ve)	Actual Cash in Hand (in Banks)	Banks Liabilities (due to deposit)	Asset of Banks (due to Own Cash and Loans payable)	Cash to Deposit Ratio (SRR)	Actual Loan To Deposit Ratio
Bank's Own Money	100	0	0	100	100	100	100	100	100	1	0
a borrower borrowed $10	100	10	10	110	0	-10	90	100	100	0.900	0.100
A depositor deposit $10	110	0	10	110	10	10	100	110	110	0.909	0.091
a borrower borrowed $10	110	10	20	120	0	-10	90	110	110	0.818	0.182
A depositor deposit $10	120	0	20	120	10	10	100	120	120	0.833	0.167

Illustration 81: Simulation of Fractional Reserve Banking – $10 is deposited back into the Bank

The cycle will go on until a limit is reached. Let's take a look how it progresses.

Continue from Illustration 81.....

	Total Deposit Level	Lent Money	Total Loans	Total Money Supply	Deposited money	Net Money in/out of banking system: Loan (-ve) or Deposit (+ve)	Actual Cash in Hand (in Banks)	Banks Liabilities (due to deposit)	Asset of Banks (due to Own Cash and Loans payable)	Cash to Deposit Ratio (SRR)	Actual Loan To Deposit Ratio
a borrower borrowed $10	120	10	30	130	0	-10	90	120	120	0.750	0.250
A depositor deposit $10	130	0	30	130	10	10	100	130	130	0.769	0.231
a borrower borrowed $10	130	10	40	140	0	-10	90	130	130	0.692	0.308
A depositor deposit $10	140	0	40	140	10	10	100	140	140	0.714	0.286
a borrower borrowed $10	140	10	50	150	0	-10	90	140	140	0.643	0.357
A depositor deposit $10	150	0	50	150	10	10	100	150	150	0.667	0.333
a borrower borrowed $10	150	10	60	160	0	-10	90	150	150	0.600	0.400
A depositor deposit $10	160	0	60	160	10	10	100	160	160	0.625	0.375

Continue on the next page......

Continue from last page.....

a borrower borrowed $10	160	10	70	170	0	-10	90	160	160	0.563	0.438
A depositor deposit $10	170	0	70	170	10	10	100	170	170	0.588	0.412
a borrower borrowed $10	170	10	80	180	0	-10	90	170	170	0.529	0.471
A depositor deposit $10	180	0	80	180	10	10	100	180	180	0.556	0.444
a borrower borrowed $10	180	10	90	190	0	-10	90	180	180	0.500	0.500
A depositor deposit $10	190	0	90	190	10	10	100	190	190	0.526	0.474
a borrower borrowed $10	190	10	90	200	0	-10	90	190	190	0.474	0.526
A depositor deposit $10	200	0	100	200	10	10	100	200	200	0.500	0.500
a borrower borrowed $10	200	10	100	210	0	-10	90	200	200	0.450	0.550
A depositor deposit $10	210	0	110	210	10	10	100	210	210	0.476	0.524
a borrower borrowed $10	210	10	110	220	0	-10	90	210	210	0.429	0.571
A depositor deposit $10	220	0	120	220	10	10	100	220	220	0.455	0.545
a borrower borrowed $10	220	10	130	230	0	-10	90	220	220	0.409	0.591
A depositor deposit $10	230	0	130	230	10	10	100	230	230	0.435	0.565
a borrower borrowed 10	230	10	140	240	0	-10	90	230	230	0.391	0.609
A depositor deposit $10	240	0	140	240	10	10	100	240	240	0.417	0.583
a borrower borrowed $10	240	10	150	250	0	-10	90	240	240	0.375	0.625
A depositor deposit $10	250	0	150	250	10	10	100	250	250	0.400	0.600
a borrower borrowed $10	250	10	160	260	0	-10	90	250	250	0.360	0.640
A depositor deposit $10	260	0	160	260	10	10	100	260	260	0.385	0.615
a borrower borrowed $10	260	10	170	270	0	-10	90	260	260	0.346	0.654
A depositor deposit $10	270	0	170	270	10	10	100	270	270	0.370	0.630
a borrower borrowed $10	270	10	180	280	0	-10	90	270	270	0.333	0.667
A depositor deposit $10	280	0	180	280	10	10	100	280	280	0.357	0.643

Continue on the next page.....

BANK	Total Deposit Level	Lent Money	Total Loans	Total Money Supply	Deposited money	Net Money in/out of banking system: Loan (-ve) or Deposit (+ve)	Actual Cash in Hand (in Banks)	Banks Liabilities (due to deposit)	Asset of Banks (due to Own Cash and Loans payable)	Cash to Deposit Ratio (SRR)	Actual Loan To Deposit Ratio
Continue from last page…..											
a borrower borrowed $10	280	10	190	290	0	-10	90	280	280	0.321	0.679
A depositor deposit $10	290	0	190	290	10	10	100	290	290	0.345	0.655
a borrower borrowed $10	290	10	200	300	0	-10	90	290	290	0.310	0.690
A depositor deposit $10	300	0	200	300	10	10	100	300	300	0.333	0.667
a borrower borrowed $10	300	10	210	310	0	-10	90	300	300	0.300	0.700
A depositor deposit $10	310	0	210	310	10	10	100	310	310	0.323	0.677
a borrower borrowed $10	310	10	220	320	0	-10	90	310	310	0.290	0.710
A depositor deposit $10	320	0	220	320	10	10	100	320	320	0.313	0.688

Total Loans

Liabilities due to deposits

Total Assets

As you can see by now, the amount of Actual Cash in Hand remains steady.

This simulation will continue further as long as the limit set by the Central Bank is not reached

Illustration 82: The Right Simulation Of Fractional Reserve Banking (with deposits and loans)

It must be clear by now that the amount of Actual Cash in Hand in the bank **always remains steady.** Loan to deposit ratio continue to increase, while the inverse of it, the Cash Reserve to Loan ratio continue to decrease.

Let's do a quick check for solvency.

The bank has 320 in deposits, with 220 in total outstanding loans. Very solvent and healthy indeed. Cash in hand remains at 100 with 320 worth of assets in the books (including the cash of course). The bank has extended 68% of its deposits as loans, which is the 220 of loans divided by the 320 of deposits.

Now let's simulate to the end!

	Total Deposit Level	Lent Money	Total Loans	Total Money Supply	Deposited money	Net Money in/out of banking system: Loan (-ve) or Deposit (+ve)	Actual Cash in Hand (in Banks)	Banks Liabilities (due to deposit)	Asset of Banks (due to Own Cash and Loans payable)	Cash to Deposit Ratio (SRR)	Actual Loan To Deposit Ratio
From an initial deposit of $100 of banks own money, after 73 borrowers and 73 depositors.....											
A depositor deposit 10	840	0	740	840	10	10	100	840	840	0.119	0.881
a borrower borrowed 10	840	10	750	850	0	-10	90	840	840	0.107	0.893
A depositor deposit 10	850	0	750	850	10	10	100	850	850	0.118	0.882
a borrower borrowed 10	850	10	760	860	0	-10	90	850	850	0.106	0.894
A depositor deposit 10	860	0	760	860	10	10	100	860	860	0.116	0.884
a borrower borrowed 10	860	10	770	870	0	-10	90	860	860	0.105	0.895
A depositor deposit 10	870	0	770	870	10	10	100	870	870	0.115	0.885
a borrower borrowed 10	870	10	780	880	0	-10	90	870	870	0.103	0.897
A depositor deposit 10	880	0	780	880	10	10	100	880	880	0.114	0.886
a borrower borrowed 10	880	10	790	890	0	-10	90	880	880	0.102	0.898

Continue on the next page.....

Continue from last page.....

BANK	Total Deposit Level	Lent Money	Total Loans	Total Money Supply	Deposited money	Net Money in/out of banking system: Loan (-ve) or Deposit (+ve)	Actual Cash in Hand (in Banks)	Banks Liabilities (due to deposit)	Asset of Banks (due to Own Cash and Loans payable)	Cash to Deposit Ratio (SRR)	Actual Loan To Deposit Ratio
A depositor deposit 10	890	0	790	890	10	10	100	890	890	0.112	0.888
a borrower borrowed 10	890	10	800	900	0	-10	90	890	890	0.101	0.899
A depositor deposit 10	900	0	800	900	10	10	100	900	900	0.111	0.889
a borrower borrowed 10	900	10	810	910	0	-10	90	900	900	0.100	0.900
A depositor deposit 10	910	0	810	910	10	10	100	910	910	0.110	0.890
a borrower borrowed 10	910	10	820	920	0	-10	90	910	910	0.099	0.901
A depositor deposit 10	920	0	820	920	10	10	100	920	920	0.109	0.891
a borrower borrowed 10	920	10	830	930	0	-10	90	920	920	0.098	0.902
A depositor deposit 10	930	0	830	930	10	10	100	930	930	0.108	0.892
a borrower borrowed 10	930	10	840	940	0	-10	90	930	930	0.097	0.903
A depositor deposit 10	940	0	840	940	10	10	100	940	940	0.106	0.894
a borrower borrowed 10	940	10	850	950	0	-10	90	940	940	0.096	0.904
A depositor deposit 10	950	0	850	950	10	10	100	950	950	0.105	0.895
a borrower borrowed 10	950	10	860	960	0	-10	90	950	950	0.095	0.905
A depositor deposit 10	960	0	860	960	10	10	100	960	960	0.104	0.896
a borrower borrowed 10	960	10	870	970	0	-10	90	960	960	0.094	0.906
A depositor deposit 10	970	0	870	970	10	10	100	970	970	0.103	0.897
a borrower borrowed 10	970	10	880	980	0	-10	90	970	970	0.093	0.907

Continue on the next page.....

| A depositor deposit 10 | 980 | 0 | 880 | 980 | 10 | 10 | 100 | 980 | 980 | 0.102 | 0.898 |
| a borrower borrowed 10 | 980 | 10 | 890 | 990 | 0 | -10 | 90 | 980 | 980 | 0.092 | 0.908 |

The bank approaches its limit of 0.9 (occasionally breaching it several times but quickly returns below when deposit is made)

Continue in next table (Illustration 84)

Illustration 83: The Right Simulation Of Fractional Reserve Banking – The Bank has reached its lending limit set by the Central Bank

The bank approaches its limit, occasionally breaching it once in a while (lower than 0.1 for cash reserve ratio or higher than 0.9 for loan to deposit ratio) when money briefly left the banking system and later reappear as fresh deposit.

	Total Deposit Level	Lent Money	Total Loans	Total Money Supply	Deposited money	Net Money in/out of banking system: Loan (-ve) or Deposit (+ve)	Actual Cash in Hand (in Banks)	Banks Liabilities (due to deposit)	Asset of Banks (due to Own Cash and Loans payable)	Cash to Deposit Ratio (SRR)	Actual LoanTo Deposit Ratio
Continue from last table											
A depositor deposit 10	990	0	890	990	10	10	100	990	990	0.101	0.899
a borrower borrowed 10	990	10	900	1000	0	-10	90	990	990	0.091	0.909
A depositor deposit 10	1000	0	900	1000	10	10	100	1000	1000	0.1	0.5

Total Deposit   Total loan   Actual Cash In Hand is still $100   Total Asset

The bank finally reaches its limit of 0.9.
It cannot lend anymore. 90% of its deposit is lent out.

Illustration 84: The Right Simulation Of Fractional Reserve Banking – Toward the end of the simulation/ iterations

Finally, the bank reaches its limit, set by the central bank. Let's do a quick check. The bank has 1000 in deposits, with 900 in total outstanding loans. Still solvent indeed. Cash in hand, amazingly still remains at 100. It now has 1000 worth of assets in the books. The bank has extended 90% of its deposits as loans.

From the original 100, money is used as a medium of exchange, repeatedly as can be seen from the example above, exchanging between depositors and borrowers. The bank connects the depositors and the borrowers.

This lesson is available in a downloadable video presentation form, which will increase your understanding even further.

Now, in case a non engineer or technical person happen to read this book, we've decided to remove 'numbers' from this simulation, and show how the bank accumulates assets.

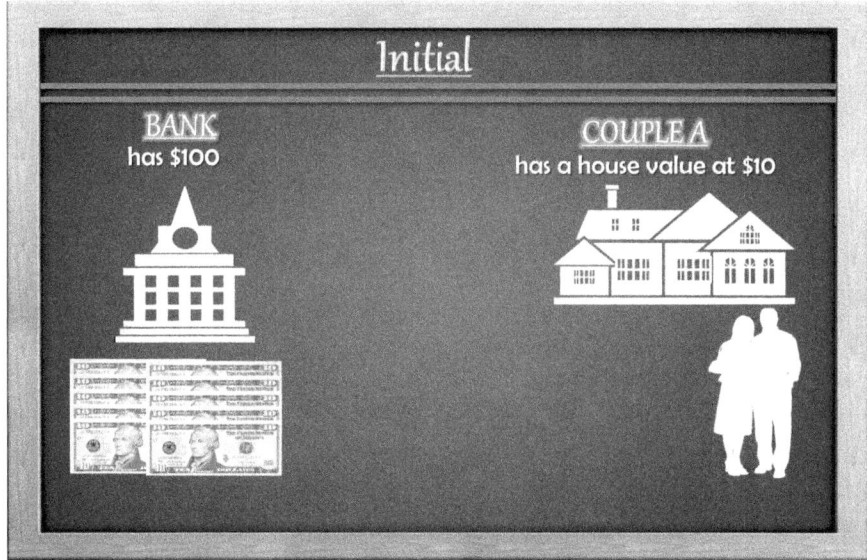

Illustration 85: Initially, bank has its own money (deposit) of $100 and a couple has a house, valued at $10 , but no cash.

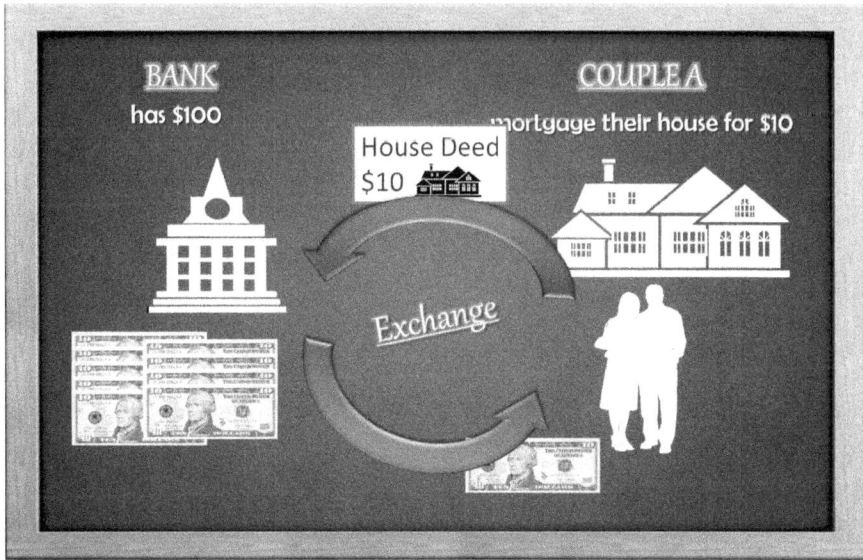

Illustration 86: Couple A mortgaged their house to the bank and received $10 and retained the use of the house. Bank received the house as collateral.

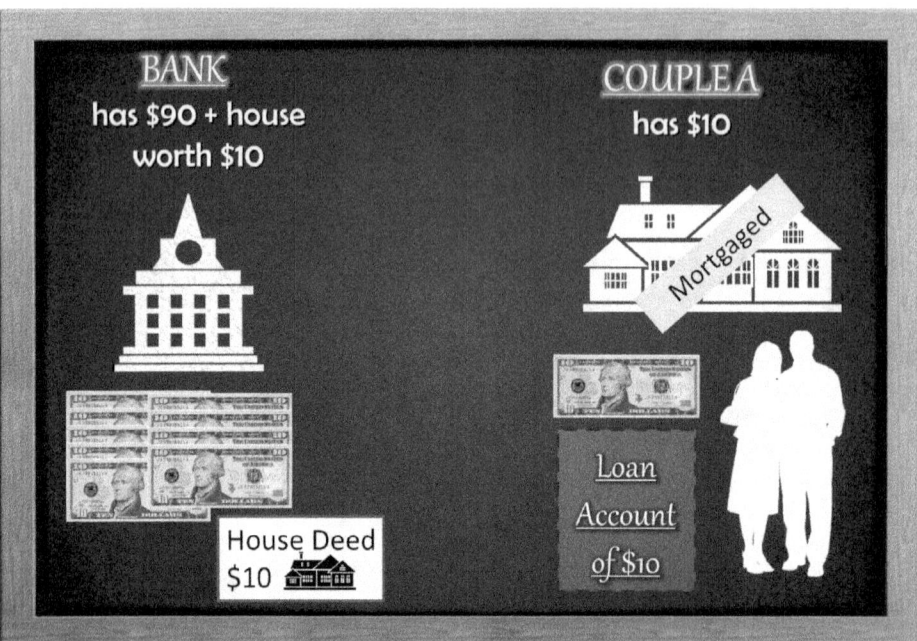

Illustration 87: Now, the bank has $90 and a house worth $10. Couple A has $10 and a loan account of $10, but they retained the use of their house.

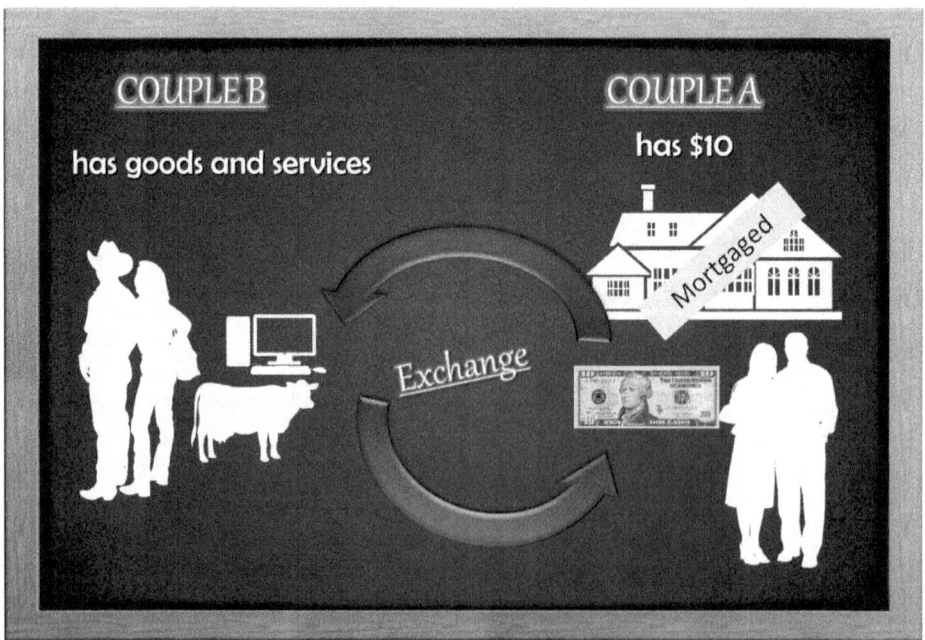

Illustration 88: Couple A bought goods and/or services from Couple B for $10. Their loan money of $10 is now with Couple B.

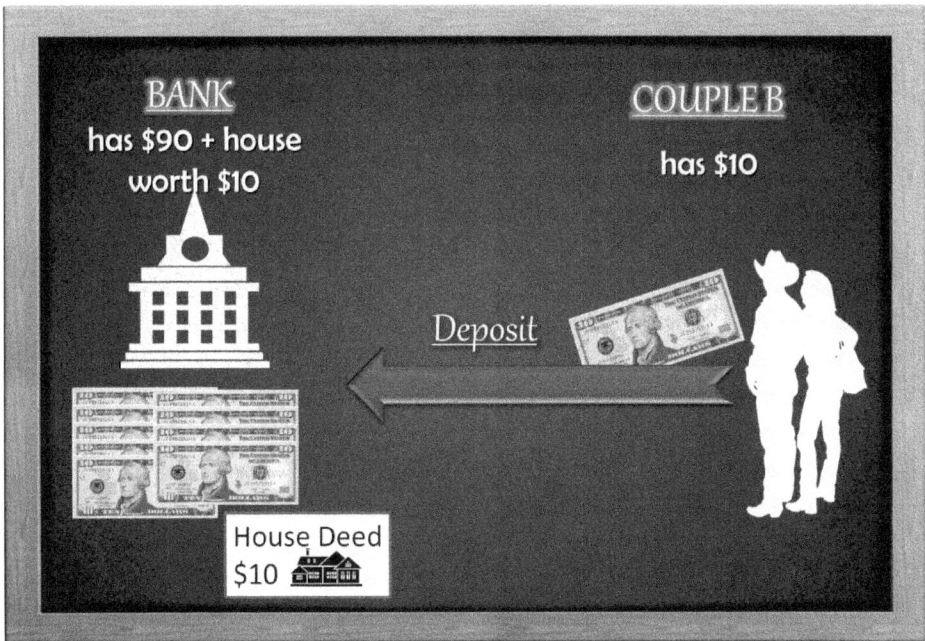

Illustration 89: Couple B then deposited the $10 they received for providing goods and services into the Bank which has $90 cash and $10 in hard asset.

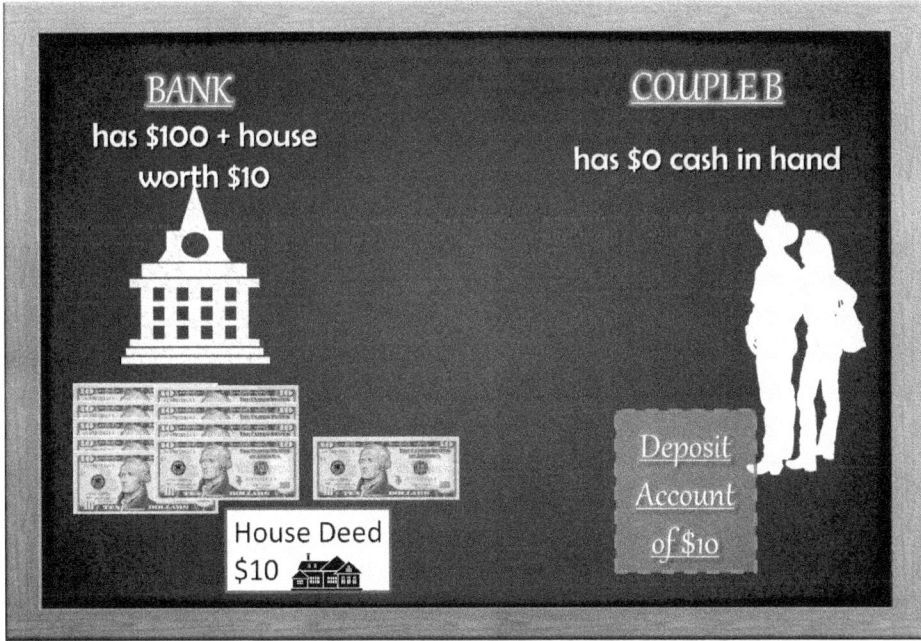

Illustration 90: Now, bank has $100 and $10 hard asset. Couple B has $0 in cash but have a Deposit Account of $10 with the Bank that they can withdraw anytime they want.

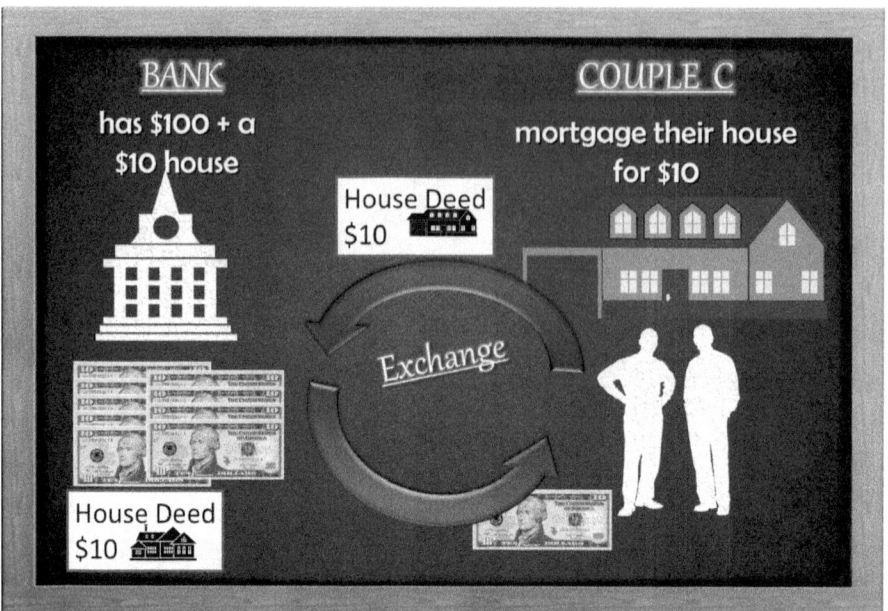

Illustration 91: Couple C mortgaged their house to the Bank and received $10 and retained the use of the house. Bank received the house as collateral.

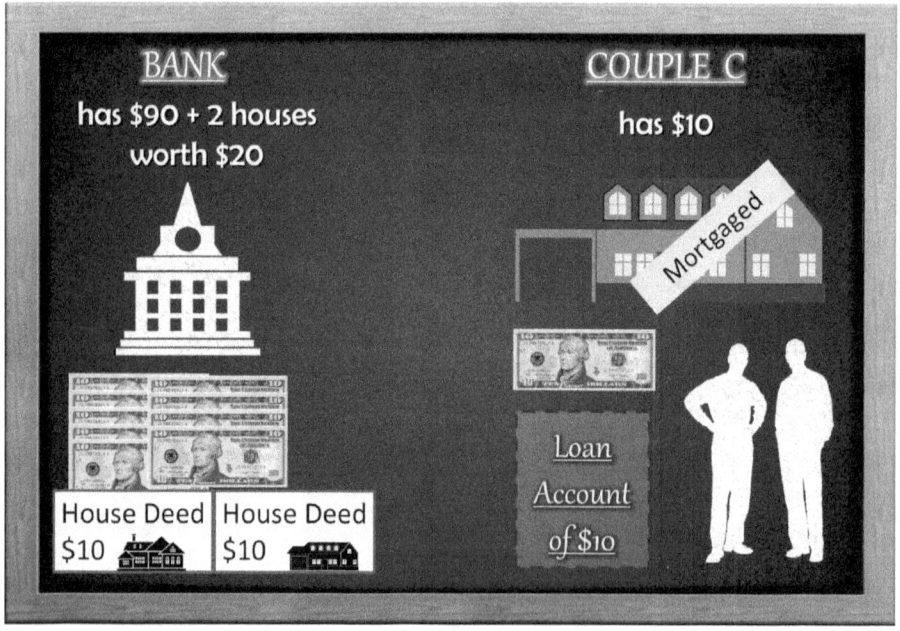

Illustration 92: Previously, Bank has $100 in cash and a house worth $10. Now, the Bank has $90 and 2 houses worth $20. Couple C now has $10, and a loan account of $10, but they retain the right to use their house (as long as loan payment is being made).

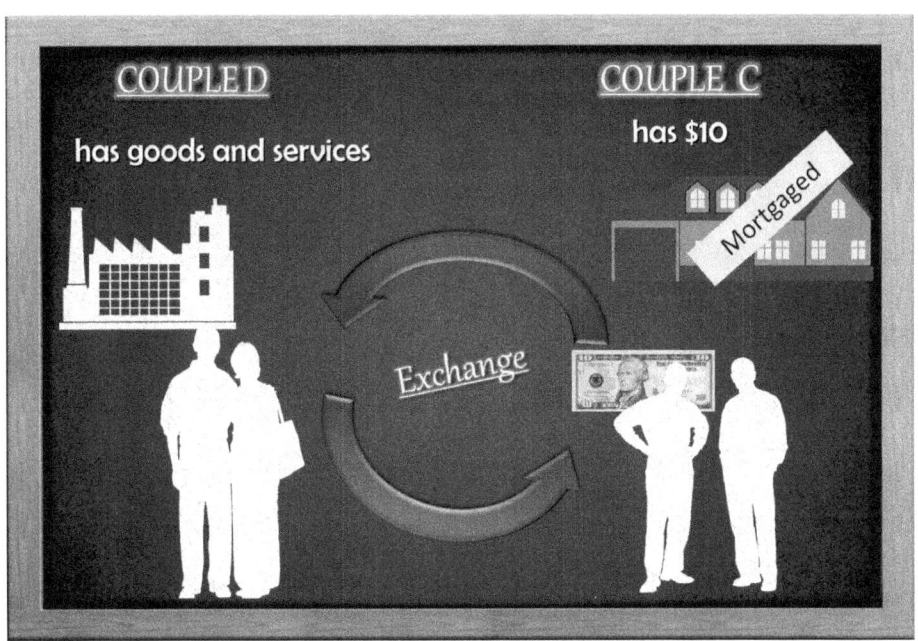

Illustration 93: Couple C paid $10 to Couple D, for the goods and services provided to them

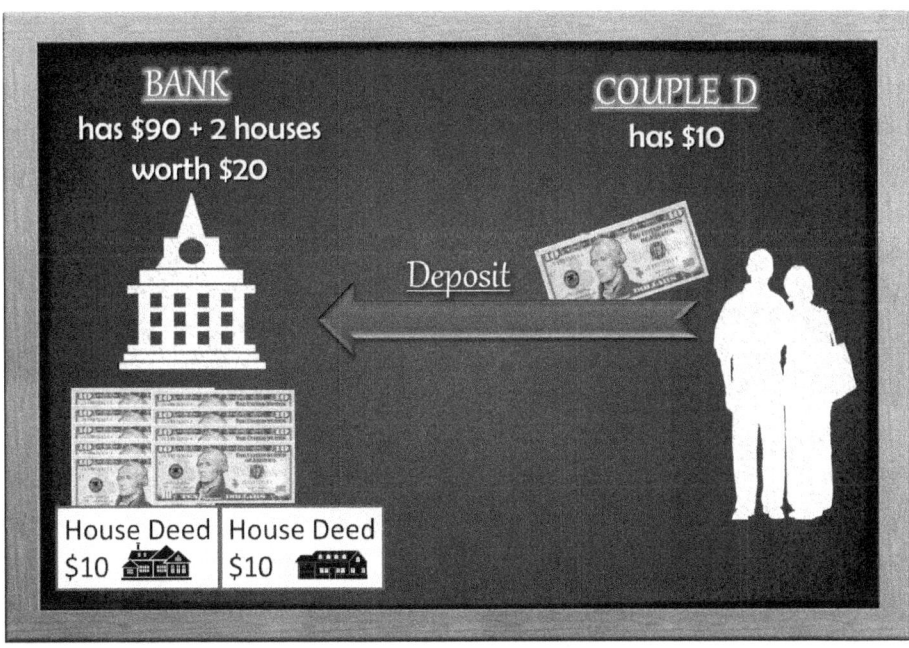

Illustration 94: Couple D then deposited their money into the Bank which has $90 in cash and 2 houses worth $20.

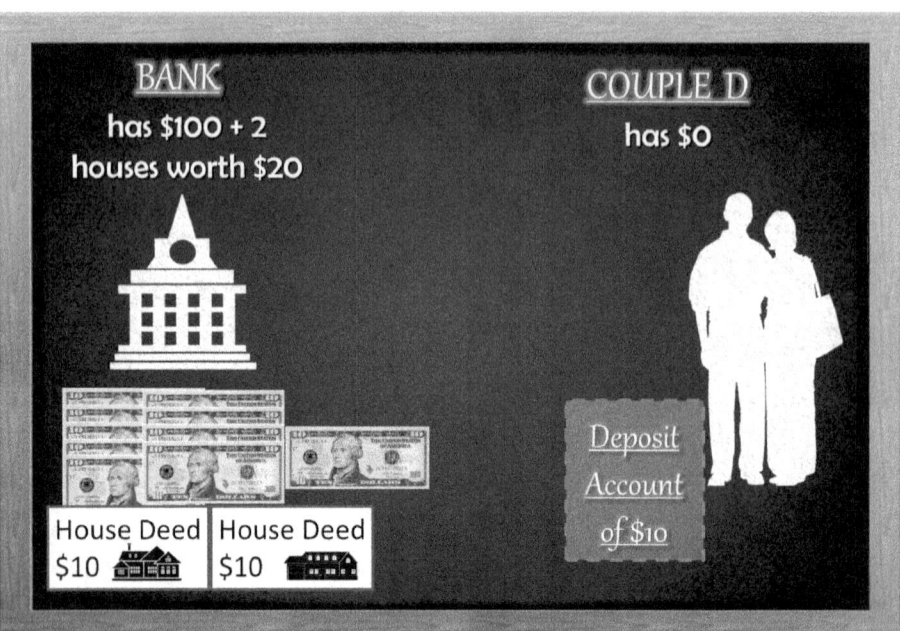

Illustration 95: Bank now has $100 in cash and houses worth $20 (or net asset of $120). Couple D has $0 in cash but has a deposit account with the bank.

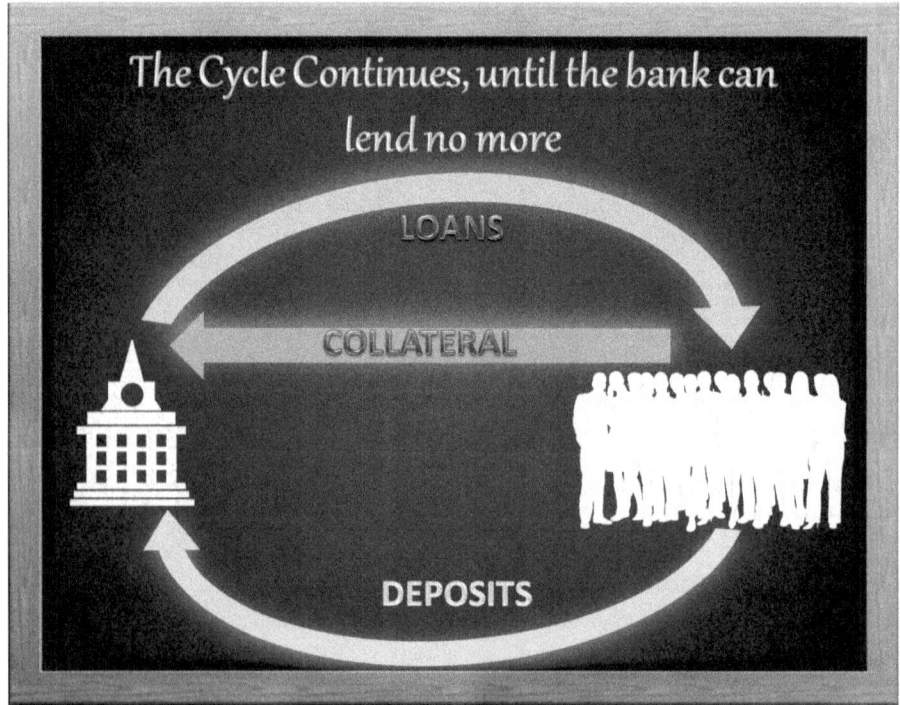

Illustration 96: The cycle will continue with many borrowers taking loans and depositors depositing money into the Bank.

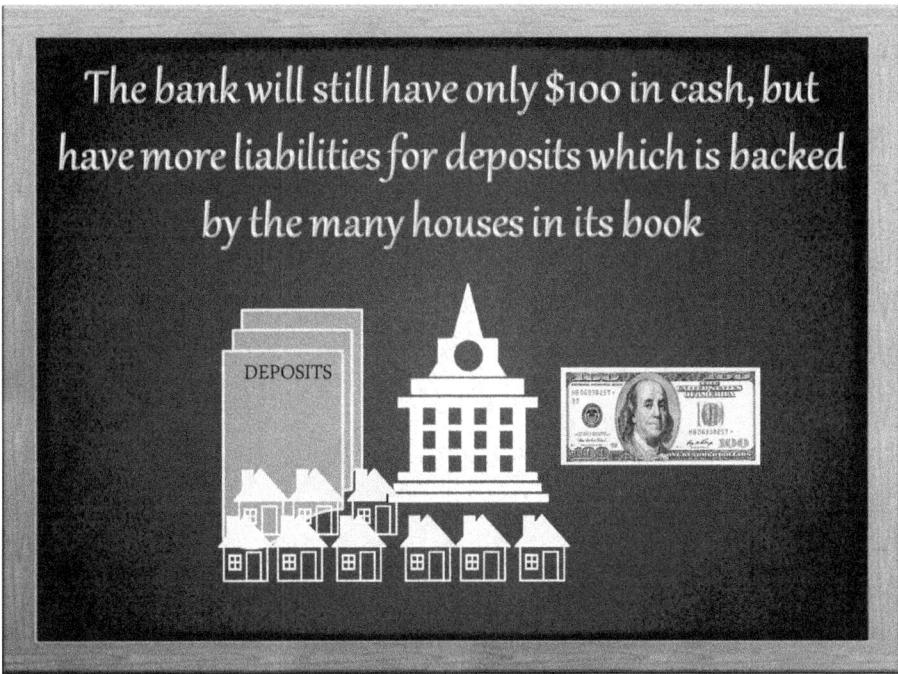

Illustration 97: At the end, the Bank will still have only $100 in cash and also more liabilities for the deposits which is backed by the many houses in its book.

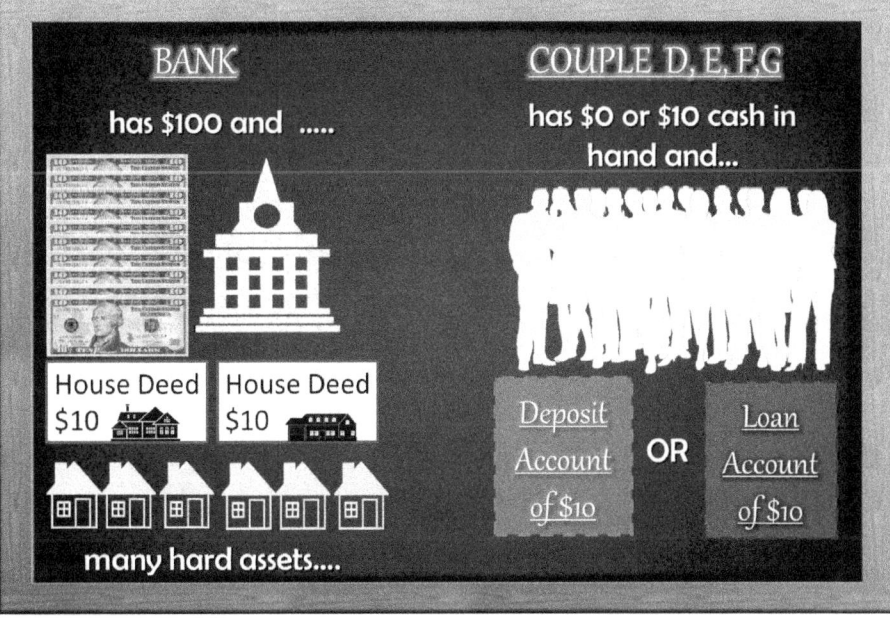

Illustration 98: Bank has $100 in cash but its deposits is backed by the assets it holds. The bank can give back the deposits when loans are repaid or the assets are liquidated.

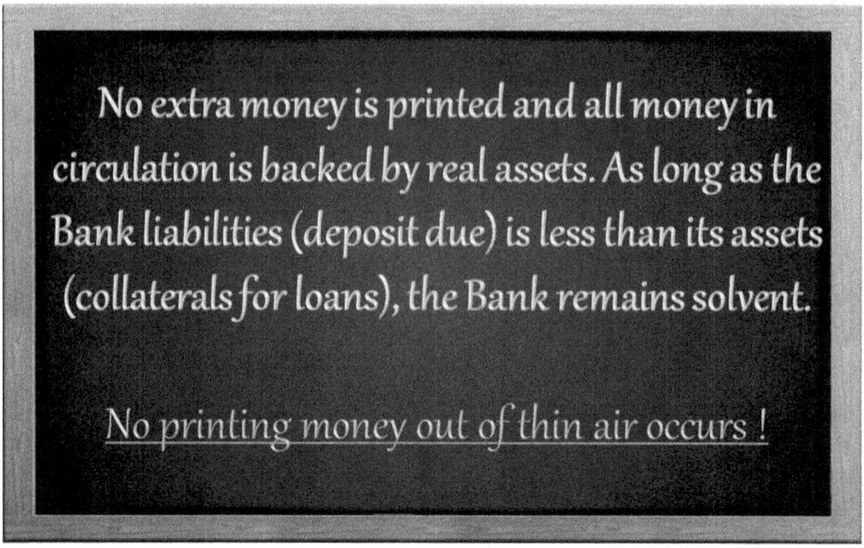

No extra money is printed and all money in circulation is backed by real assets. As long as the Bank liabilities (deposit due) is less than its assets (collaterals for loans), the Bank remains solvent.

<u>No printing money out of thin air occurs !</u>

Illustration 99: No money is printed out of thin air. If Banks can print or create money out of thin air, they would not need depositors. The depositors enable the banks to give out loans. No depositors = No loans!

The examples showed that banks are merely an agent of **connecting savers and borrowers**, making profit from the interest or 'profit' spread. This is the main function of a bank in the economy. Our example also proves that money is not asset, it is merely a medium used for conducting transactions of mortgaging the houses. The amount of money need not increase as long as there is enough money in circulation to meet all transactions demands. In the example above, there was no need to increase the money supply. As you might have thought out already, the money supply will need to be increased if there are many more people and houses involved.

Once the limit set by the central bank is reached, the monetary base could expand no more. If the central bank did not set any limit, a bank can continue to give out loans as long as it can cover any losses (due to non payments) with its own money. Since we already knew that money is neither asset nor wealth, it does not really matter how much money the bank is keeping. **What's important is how much assets it has.** Well that is one of the logic behind fractional banking. In the UK and some other countries, their banks can give out 100% of their deposit as loans, as long as the bank has enough capital. Remember money is only as a medium of exchange? It still is and also as a temporary store of value. If a bank has little cash, but rich in assets, it can sell it to the central bank anytime in exchange for cash. There won't be a liquidity problem even during a bank run. However, if the bank has more liabilities than assets, problems are sure to follow. Even a good bank, may experience such a situation whenever its assets (the loans given) are not being paid back, and may ends up having more liabilities than assets. Therefore, it actually does not matter what is the limit of the loans that can be given out by banks, what's important is that it always has more assets than liabilities.

As the economy grows further, an increase in the economic wealth results, however if currency in circulation does not follow suit, it will automatically create deflation. This is because with more assets and market participants out there, there would not be enough currency to enable all transactions; therefore the value of the currency will rise, or in short, deflation will take place. At this juncture, the monetary base needs to expand. This is the job for none other than the central bank. It can print money and swap assets. As in the US, the Fed will directly purchase treasury securities to inject money directly into the hand of the government, which the government will immediately spend. The Total Money Supply will continue to increase, mirroring the state of the economy. It can decrease as well, as has been demonstrated many times throughout the years. The injection or increase will need to be managed carefully, by the central bank, via asset purchases from commercial banks, to match the growth of the economy. The hard part of being a central banker, is managing the whole monetary system to ensure balance is maintained between money creation or destruction and the actual wealth or need of the economy.

 In our example above, the rate of increases are steady and logical. **The bank do not lend out everything it has in one go,** it will give out the loans, in a stepwise manner, to many borrowers. Concentrating one very large loan into one borrower is risky and unwise, and a prudent bank will not do it. Therefore the earlier example of **"The Wrong Example of How Fractional Reserve**

Banking Operates" where the bank who initially received 100 in deposit and immediately lent out all but 10 of it, **is not a practical example and the first wrong assumption of the anti fractional reserve banking groups.**

Another silly argument of the anti fractional reserve banking is why there is even a need to go for 'fractional reserve banking' in the first place? Why don't we go for 100% reserve, without any fraction, without any need to have less cash compared to outstanding loans? The answer is really rather simple.

Imagine a banking system with 100% reserve. A customer who deposited 100 into the bank, the money will be kept and stored in a safe place. Zero loans will be given out, since all 100% need to be saved. The bank cannot do its original function of connecting savers with excess funds to needy borrowers with new wealth generation ideas, it merely becomes a place to safe-keep money. The problem of 100% reserve system manifests itself in the monetary system by soaking in a lot of cash (a thousand percent or more than existing money supply will be required), money sitting in the banks, not doing anything will be commonplace and widespread, making those money useless and unproductive. New businesses can't get their capital, house builders cannot mortgage their houses and the economy will be stagnating and will decline. Banks basically cannot be banks; the purpose of banks is not just for safekeeping money as the anti fractional banking group thought, they also channel depositors' money for productive uses, as a capital for new projects etc. which is good for the economy.

The economy will not be able to function efficiently in a 100% reserve banking system and will forever be doomed in a backward state with difficult environment. No entrepreneurs will be funded and no new ideas can be explored. The end result is economic malaise, and slow descends into a deprived state. Everything will be expensive and the age of abundance we are so accustomed to today, will become the age of great scarcity instead.

Those short thinking but busy anti fractional reserve banking groups do not realize that **safekeeping money is not cheap,** there are many costs involved in safekeeping money in banks. Buildings, guards, security systems, storage and vaults, accountants, computer systems, auto teller machines and other elaborate systems will be required and need to be paid for. This will not come cheap and the bank will have to charge its customers, for keeping their money safely. This is not a good proposition for the banks' customers. **Imagine keeping your money in a bank, paying a 1% fee on it, year in, year out. After several years, there will be less money in your account than when you actually first put it in.** Of course people will start to hoard their cash under their pillows; the monetary demand will shoot through the roof, and managing the money supply will become impossible for the central bank and the government. Imagine that 95% of the money out there is stored under pillows and mattresses, and they can come out en masse, anytime! The other side effect of this is that robberies will be rampant in the economy.

We are basically recommending that banks keep a high percentage of their asset in super safe government securities only, while the rest can be used for higher return areas (higher risks of course) such as mortgages of non government backed variety. Banks should be prudent and understand that not all deposits should be lent out, in pursue of profits.

Lesson 5

Federal Government debt is $49,180 per American. But do you know the wealth of American, per head? Find out the answer in Book 3!

CONGRATULATIONS!
Lesson Completed

Lesson 6. Loan Repayments In Fractional Reserve Banking

Let's simulate the situation where the borrowers start to pay their loans.

	Total Deposit Level	Lent Money	Total Loans	Total Money Supply	Deposited money	Net Money in/out of banking system: Loan (-ve) or Deposit (+ve)	Actual Cash in Hand (in Banks)	Banks Liabilities (due to deposit)	Asset of Banks (due to Own Cash and Loans payable)	Cash to Deposit Ratio (SRR)	Actual Loan To Deposit Ratio
A depositor deposit $10	1000	0	900	1000	10	10	100	1000	1000	0.1	0.9
Borrower Withdraw and REPAY $10	990	0	890	990	0	0	100	990	990	0.10101	0.899

From an initial deposit of $100 of banks own money, after many depositors and borrowers, the Bank finally reaches its Reserves Limit.

Limit reached

Total Deposit decreases by $10 – withdrawal

Total Loans decreases by $10 – loan is paid off

No money goes in or out of the banking system (withdraw and repay loan at same instance)

Bank assets shrinks as collateral is returned (loan paid)

LDR improves. Drops below Limit

Illustration 100: The Right Simulation Of Fractional Reserve Banking – The first borrower withdraws his money and pays off his loan

When a borrower withdraws money from a one bank banking system, then pays off his or her loan to the bank, several things happened. The Total Deposit Level decreases by 10 as money is withdrawn, Total Loans decreases by 10 as loan is being repaid and the Total Money Supply shrinks by 10, as money is being extinguished by the loan repayment. No money goes in out or out of the banking system, so the Net Money In/Out is zero. There is no change to the bank actual cash in hand. The bank's assets shrink in tandem with the repayment and the Actual Reserve to Loan Ratio and the Actual Loan to Deposit Ratio both improves, signaling a renewed capability to lend.

If all borrowers started paying off their loans, the following will happen:

Continue from the previous table (Illustration 101)

A borrower withdraw and REPAY $10	980	0	880	980	0	0	100	980	0.102	0.898
A borrower withdraw and REPAY $10	970	0	870	970	0	0	100	970	0.103	0.897
A borrower withdraw and REPAY $10	960	0	860	960	0	0	100	960	0.104	0.896
A borrower withdraw and REPAY $10	950	0	850	950	0	0	100	950	0.105	0.895
A borrower withdraw and REPAY $10	940	0	840	940	0	0	100	940	0.106	0.894
A borrower withdraw and REPAY $10	930	0	830	930	0	0	100	930	0.108	0.892
A borrower withdraw and REPAY $10	920	0	820	920	0	0	100	920	0.109	0.891
A borrower withdraw and REPAY $10	910	0	810	910	0	0	100	910	0.110	0.890
A borrower withdraw and REPAY $10	900	0	800	900	0	0	100	900	0.111	0.889
A borrower withdraw and REPAY $10	890	0	790	890	0	0	100	890	0.112	0.888
A borrower withdraw and REPAY $10	880	0	780	880	0	0	100	880	0.114	0.886
A borrower withdraw and REPAY $10	870	0	770	870	0	0	100	870	0.115	0.885
A borrower withdraw and REPAY $10	860	0	760	860	0	0	100	860	0.116	0.884
A borrower withdraw and REPAY $10	850	0	750	850	0	0	100	850	0.118	0.882

Continue on the next page…

Continue from the page before ......

	Total Deposit Level	Lent Money	Total Loans	Total Money Supply	Deposited money	Net Money in/out of banking system: Loan (-ve) or Deposit (+ve)	Actual Cash in Hand (in Banks)	Banks Liabilities (due to deposit)	Asset of Banks (due to Own Cash and Loans payable)	Cash to Deposit Ratio (SRR)	Actual Loan To Deposit Ratio
A borrower withdraw and REPAY $10	840	0	740	840	0	0	100	840	840	0.119	0.881
A borrower withdraw and REPAY $10	830	0	730	830	0	0	100	830	830	0.120	0.880
A borrower withdraw and REPAY $10	820	0	720	820	0	0	100	820	820	0.122	0.878
A borrower withdraw and REPAY $10	810	0	710	810	0	0	100	810	810	0.123	0.877
A borrower withdraw and REPAY $10	800	0	700	800	0	0	100	800	800	0.125	0.875
A borrower withdraw and REPAY $10	790	0	690	790	0	0	100	790	790	0.127	0.873
A borrower withdraw and REPAY $10	780	0	680	780	0	0	100	780	780	0.128	0.872
A borrower withdraw and REPAY $10	770	0	670	770	0	0	100	770	770	0.130	0.870
A borrower withdraw and REPAY $10	760	0	660	760	0	0	100	760	760	0.132	0.868
A borrower withdraw and REPAY $10	750	0	650	750	0	0	100	750	750	0.133	0.867
A borrower withdraw and REPAY $10	740	0	640	740	0	0	100	740	740	0.135	0.865
A borrower withdraw and REPAY $10	730	0	630	730	0	0	100	730	730	0.137	0.863
A borrower withdraw and REPAY $10	720	0	620	720	0	0	100	720	720	0.139	0.861

As borrowers continue to repay the loan, Total Loans and Total Money Supply continue to go down

The Loan to Deposit Ratio will improve

Illustration 101: The Right Simulation Of Fractional Reserve Banking –All borrowers started to pay off their loans

The Loan to Deposit Ratio will continue to improve, shifting further from the limit set by the central bank.

Near the end of the repayments, what will happen to the banking system? The continuation of loan repayments will extinguish money as follows:

Further repayments were made, until..........

A borrower withdraw and REPAY $10	260	0	160	0	100	260	260	0.385	0.615
A borrower withdraw and REPAY $10	250	0	150	0	100	250	250	0.400	0.600
A borrower withdraw and REPAY $10	240	0	140	0	100	240	240	0.417	0.583
A borrower withdraw and REPAY $10	230	0	130	0	100	230	230	0.435	0.565
A borrower withdraw and REPAY $10	220	0	120	0	100	220	220	0.455	0.545
A borrower withdraw and REPAY $10	210	0	110	0	100	210	210	0.476	0.524
A borrower withdraw and REPAY $10	200	0	100	0	100	200	200	0.500	0.500
A borrower withdraw and REPAY $10	190	0	90	0	100	190	190	0.526	0.474
A borrower withdraw and REPAY $10	140	0	40	0	100	140	140	0.714	0.286
A borrower withdraw and REPAY $10	130	0	30	0	100	130	130	0.769	0.231
A borrower withdraw and REPAY $10	120	0	20	0	100	120	120	0.833	0.167
A borrower withdraw and REPAY $10	110	0	10	0	100	110	110	0.909	0.091
A borrower withdraw and REPAY $10	100	0	0	0	100	100	100	1	0

Total Loans goes to zero and Total Money Supply goes back to the Initial $100   The Loan to Deposit Ratio goes to zero

Illustration 102: The Right Simulation Of Fractional Reserve Banking – When the last borrower has repaid his loan, all levels return to initial level, $100 Bank's own money

The banking system goes back to its original condition! Total deposit level goes back to 100. All other categories including the Cash Reserve and the Loan to Deposit Ratio revert to their original condition (or value).

It was totally untrue that money in the modern banking system will simply grow and grow exponentially, due to the 'printing money out of thin air' and many other incorrect accusations. It is **totally bogus** to say that debt will result in more debt because in order to pay that debt, ever more money in the form of interest are needed. In fact, as we had just seen above, the banking system goes back to its original condition when all outstanding loans are paid. As we mentioned earlier, when we include the element of interest (with a more complicated simulation), we found that the system still behaves the same way. The interest is the profit made by both parties and realized when new wealth is added. If there is no new wealth added, the interest will either be extinguished (bankruptcy) or other wealth will be used to cover the interest and capital repayments.

This lesson is available in a downloadable video presentation form, which will increase your understanding even further.

CONGRATULATIONS!
Lesson Completed

We have shown in our various examples that paper currencies do have actual and real wealth supporting its existence. Modern banking allows the expansion and as well as shrinkage of the monetary base as and when required, which cannot be readily performed if gold or other commodity is used as money.

Now it is easy for us to explain what exactly wrong with the incorrect claim made by the earlier article on page 113 (Illustration 55).

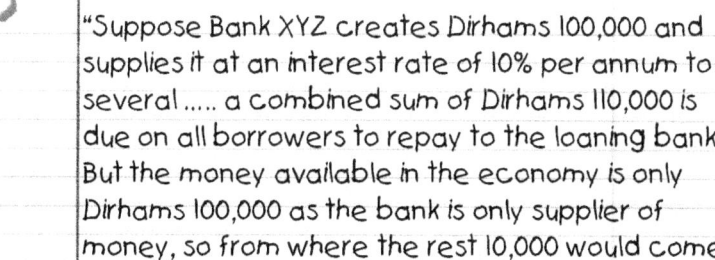

"Suppose Bank XYZ creates Dirhams 100,000 and supplies it at an interest rate of 10% per annum to several..... a combined sum of Dirhams 110,000 is due on all borrowers to repay to the loaning bank. But the money available in the economy is only Dirhams 100,000 as the bank is only supplier of money, so from where the rest 10,000 would come that is the difference in the borrowers intake and total repayment amount...... from NOWHERE. Yes,

The claim by the author was totally wrong and we presumed this is because of lack of understanding of the banking system and the economic system. When they describe the example as above, **they did not mention one important step** in our modern banking system.

The following tables describe **what they** typically mention about how the banking system functions The table must be read line by line, step by step starting from the top.

(Typical Anti Fractional Reserve Bank's Balance Sheet)	Cash		Bank's Core Ratio	
	Deposit	Loans	Cash Reserve	Loan to Deposit Ratio
Latest Bank Balances	1,000,000	900,000	0.10	0.90
Deposit Withdrawal	-100,000			
Immediate Loan Repayment		-100,000		
New Bank Balance	900,000	800,000		
Interest on Deposit	18,000			
Interest on Loans		48,000		
Latest Bank Balances	918,000	848,000	0.08	0.92
Deposit Withdrawal	-100,000			
Immediate Loan Repayment		-100,000		
New Bank Balance	818,000	748,000		
Interest on Deposit	16,360			
Interest on Loans		44,880		
Latest Bank Balances	834,360	792,880	0.05	0.95
Deposit Withdrawal	-100,000			
Immediate Loan Repayment		-100,000		
New Bank Balance	734,360	692,880		
Interest on Deposit	14,687			
Interest on Loans		41,573		
Latest Bank Balances	749,047	734,453	0.02	0.98
Deposit Withdrawal	-100,000			
Immediate Loan Repayment		-100,000		
New Bank Balance	649,047	634,453		
Interest on Deposit	12,981			
Interest on Loans		38,067		
Latest Bank Balances	662,028	672,520	-0.02	1.02

Illustration 103: Describes what typically explained by anti fractional reserve banking group on why there is 'not enough money' existed to pay back all loans and interests in the economy

They are saying that there is not enough money in the banking system. This is an interesting claim, and they also normally add conspiratorial theories such as the banks are out to get all of the assets of others. We had showed the claim that banks did not make money by bankrupting their customers earlier in this book, and thus answered one of their claims. Now let's answer where the money to pay off loans and the interest will come from. The example above showed how the money supply is decreasing and there won't be enough money to pay off debts. The core ratios all turn for the worse, cash reserve went negative.

Is this claim really true?

Of course it is not. The following series of tables will describe **very accurately** what actually happen in the banking system, and which part was omitted by them. In this example, when the bank receives payments, it will make— surprise, a profit! Who receives the profit? None other than other individuals in the economy, they of course, redeposit their profit into the bank. Another group of people is the suppliers and contractors of the bank, which are categorized as business expenses for the bank. Well, this group of suppliers and contractors also has accounts in the bank, and they of course will deposit their profits into the bank.

	Cash		Bank's Core Ratio	
	Deposit	Loans	Cash Reserve	Loan to Deposit Ratio
Latest Bank Balances	1,000,000	900,000	0.10	0.90
Deposit Withdrawal	-100,000			
Immediate Loan Repayment		-100,000		
New Bank Balance	900,000	800,000		
Interest on Deposit	18,000			
Interest on Loans		48,000		
Bank's Operating Costs (paid to others)	19,318			
Profit (paid to Bank's Shareholders)	10,682			
Latest Bank Balances	948,000	848,000	0.11	0.89

Redeposit into bank Conveniently not included

$ 48,000	Interests On Loans
-$ 18,000	Paid to Interests On Deposits

$30,000	Balance is paid to others (salary etc) AND Shareholders, (which deposited them back into the Bank)

Deposit Withdrawal	-100,000			
Immediate Loan Repayment		-100,000		
New Bank Balance	848,000	748,000		
Interest on Deposit	16,960			
Interest on Loans		44,880		
Bank's Operating Costs (paid to others)	18,136			
Profit (paid to Bank's Shareholders)	9,784			
Latest Bank Balances	892,880	792,880	0.11	0.89

Continue on the next page....

Deposit Withdrawal	-100,000			
Immediate Loan Repayment		-100,000		
New Bank Balance	792,880	692,880		
Interest on Deposit	15,858			
Interest on Loans		41,573		
Bank's Operating Costs (paid to others)	16,884			
Profit (paid to Bank's Shareholders)	8,832			
Latest Bank Balances	834,454	734,453	0.12	0.88
Deposit Withdrawal	-100,000			
Immediate Loan Repayment		-100,000		
New Bank Balance	734,453	634,453		
Interest on Deposit	14,689			
Interest on Loans		38,067		
Bank's Operating Costs (paid to others)	15,556			
Profit (paid to Bank's Shareholders)	7,822			
Latest Bank Balances	772,520	672,520	0.13	0.87

Bank's Core Ratios never deteriorates.

Illustration 104: What actually happens to the interest money and why there will always be money to pay back interests on loans

As can be seen, there was no instance where the bank core ratios deteriorate, in fact steadily improves as loans are being paid. Money is clearly being extinguished which is typical when loans are being paid (refer to our previous examples). **A category typically omitted by other writers is the redeposit into the banking system**. It is true money was withdrawn, but then it is redeposited into the bank. The bank's shareholders took profit and put the money in their account, none other than in the bank itself. Service providers and other operating costs are paid by the bank to many companies and these monies, eventually make their way back into the bank, as deposits. The earlier claim by the internet writer that additional money (dirham) needed for the borrowers are not correct, as money is readily available as deposit in the banking system in excess of the loans outstanding.

The claim from Hazariba.com (in Illustration 55) does merit some additional explanation from us. Their claim that there is not enough money in the economy to pay back the loans issued as well as banks are cheating their clients by extending loans that are un-payable so they will default on their obligations and thus surrendering their assets, is so misleading that this argument must be struck out by us not once, but several times so that the argument will be buried deeply and remain so forever.

When borrowers obtained loans from the bank, they will use it for generating new wealth. The new wealth will be used to pay off the loan and the interest; there will be plenty of left over from the new wealth. A borrower that uses the money to plant crops in his farm, will generate wealth several times over than the amount borrowed. There is no problem to pay out the loans.

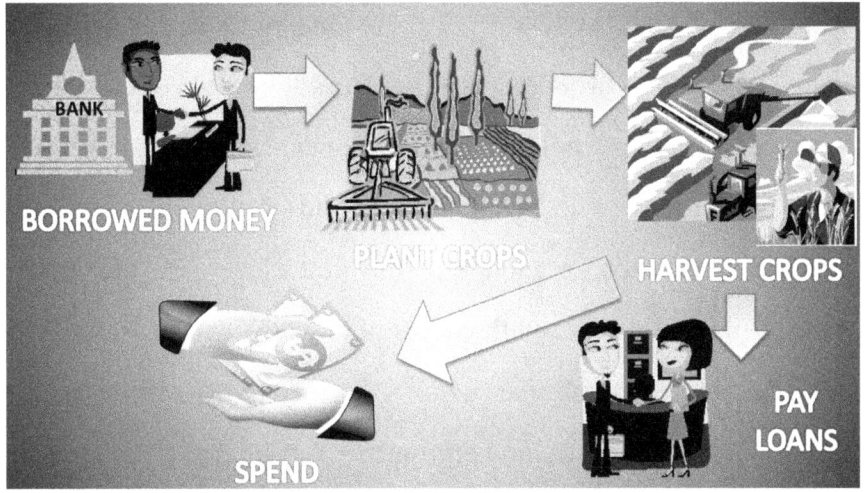

Illustration 105: A farmer borrowed money from a bank for crop planting. When harvesting time comes, he will add wealth into the economy solely by his action. Money supply can increase due to this added wealth, the farmer will pay off his original loan plus the interest with his profits, and there will be plenty of leftovers to spend.

When borrowers could not generate wealth and lost money in the process, there is no way for them to pay off their outstanding loans. As an example, the borrower who borrowed to plant crops in his farm but the crops did not survive and multiply, will be unable to pay off his loan. Wealth is destroyed in the process because resources were already taken in. This is the only instance where borrowers will not be able to pay off their loans, though shortage of money is not one of it. This correction in wealth (when wealth is destroyed either through calamities, wars, wrong decisions, poor resources allocations) is a fact of life (we can never predict what lies in the future) and is part and parcel of dealing with money. That is why the risks associated with giving loans are high. A lifetime worth of savings could be wiped out in an instance. In the example where the farmer was unable to pay off his loan, did he lose all his money? He did not lose all his money because it was not his money in the first place. He uses other peoples' money (people with excess of cash —the depositors) and thus, he need to reimburse them. One way to do it is by giving back the land, machines and equipment that he had bought using borrowed money (OPM). It is fair, and the failure of his crop is not the fault of the lenders.

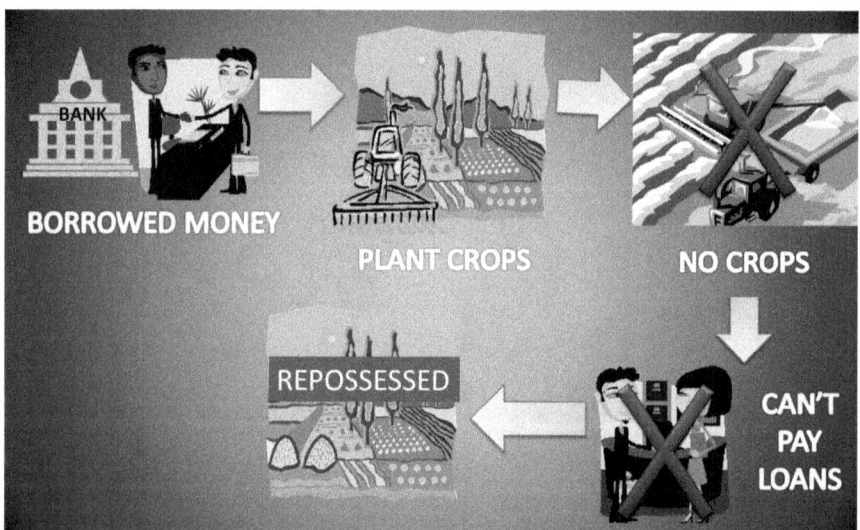

Illustration 106: If the farmer's crop fails to grow, wealth will be destroyed (loss of spent resources). The farmer will not be able to pay his original loan and his land may be repossessed by the bank to pay back the depositors (original owner of money for which the farmer used to buy the land). The land does not belong to the farmer at all, as the farmer did not lose anything in the process contrary to what people might say.

What if there are no lenders? Then the farmer can never be a farmer and buy lands to plant crops. He will never be able to amass enough money NOW to use as capital. Wealth can take a long time to be realized. That is why buying something really big (e.g. house, land) will take almost nearly the whole of the working life! However, by getting LOTS OF CASH NOW, using his profit he can always pay back the loan and interest A LITTLE BIT, OVER A LONG TIME (25 – 30 years). We don't see why this is bad. Enticement must always be given, else there will be no lenders.

In the following series of illustrations, we show that there will be no instance of 'no money in the economy' and in fact, the amount of money in the economy will stay within a constant band, during the borrowing and lending activities. In order to simulate the silly claim from such websites, we will use the 100,000 dirham loan as example.

In the example, the people in that economy created wealth totaling 110,000 dirham. Also claimed by the website, Bank XYZ is the sole creator of money so it printed that money (backed by the asset in the economy) and then put it in its vault (though in reality banks cannot print their own money without permission). In order for the people to trade between them and ensure all assets are utilized to the fullest and by the best people, they went to Bank XYZ and borrowed the necessary money for enabling trades. They extracted 100,000 dirham from their assets that worth more than that (banks always give slightly less money than the assets value). Let see what happen:

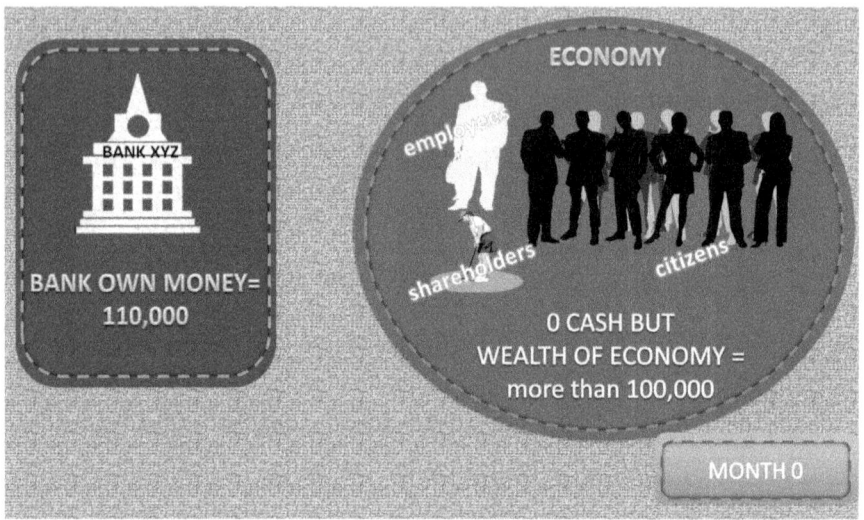

Illustration 107: Initially, Bank XYZ has 110,000 dirham. The people in the economy have no money but they have created 100,000 worth of wealth (asset).

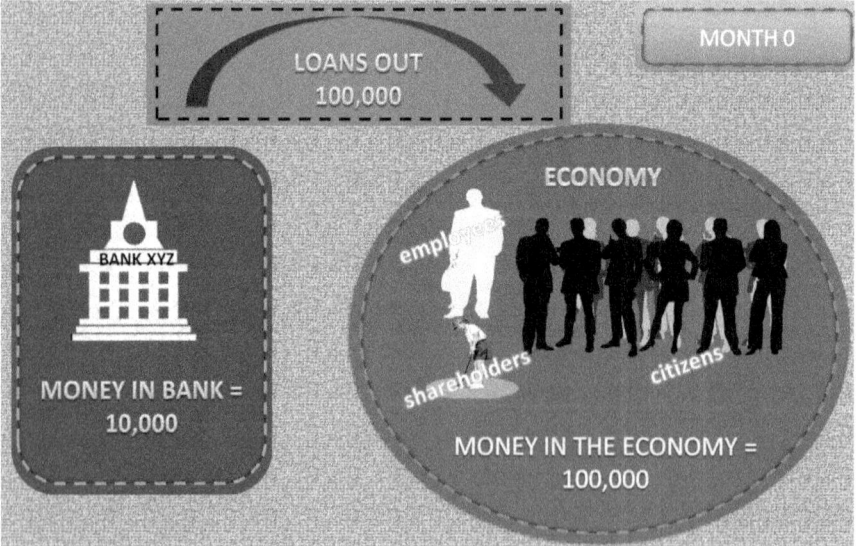

Illustration 108: The people in the economy mortgaged their assets worth 100,000 and received 100,000 dirham in loans at fixed 10% per annum interest.

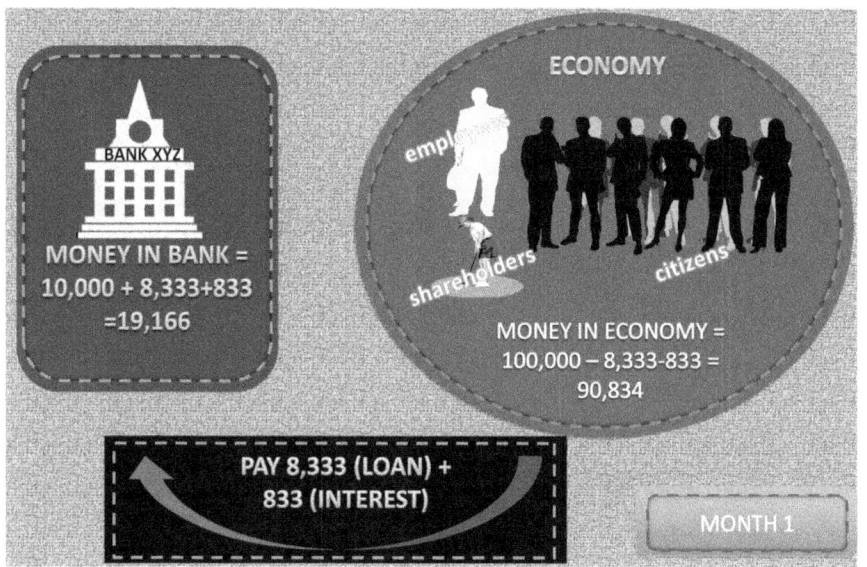

Illustration 109: Early of the month, borrowers pay 8,333 dirham of loans and 833 dirham of interest. Bank would have 19,166 dirham and money in the economy would decrease to 90,834 dirham.

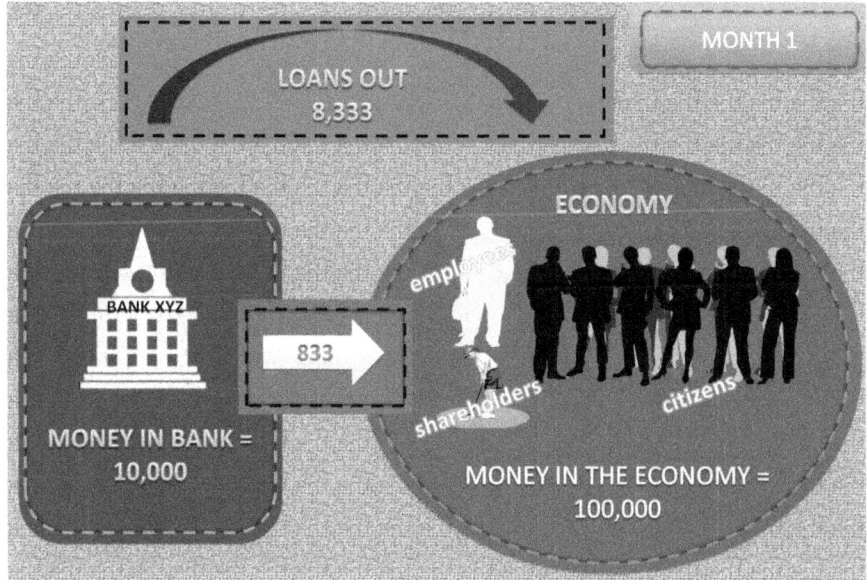

Illustration 110: At the end of the month, Bank XYZ would return 833 of the profit to its worker and shareholder (they are part of the economy). A new loan of 8,333 would also be issued as wealth of economy grows each month.

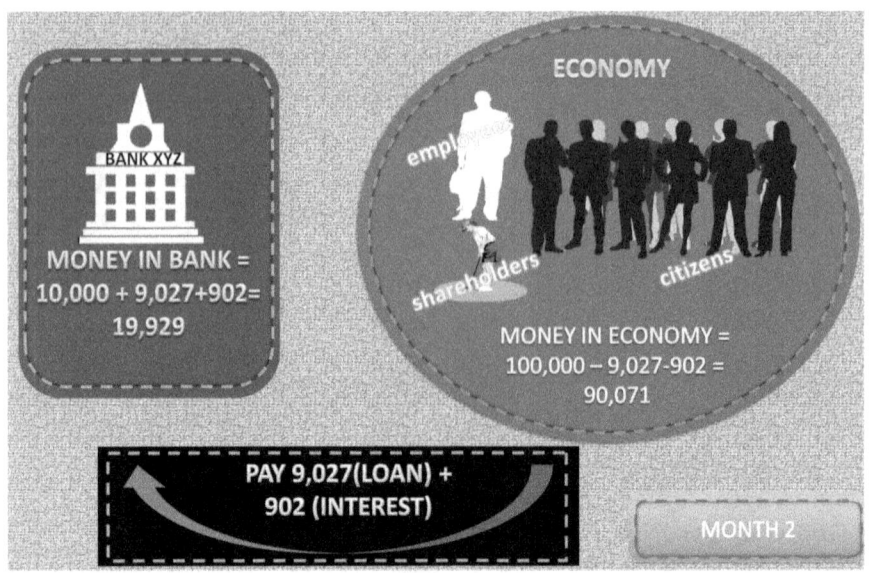

Illustration 111: Early of Month 2, borrowers would pay 8,333 (initial loan) + 694 (new loan) of loans and 833 + 69 in interest. Banks cash increases to 19,929 dirham and money in the economy goes down to 90,071 dirham.

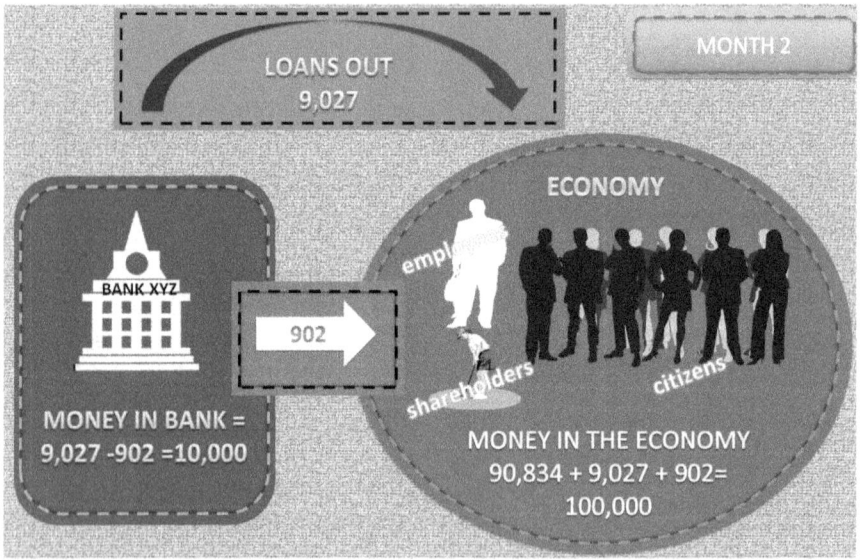

Illustration 112: At the end of month 2, Bank XYZ would return 902 of the profit to its worker and shareholder (they are part of the economy). A new loan of 9,027 would also be issued as wealth of economy grows each month.

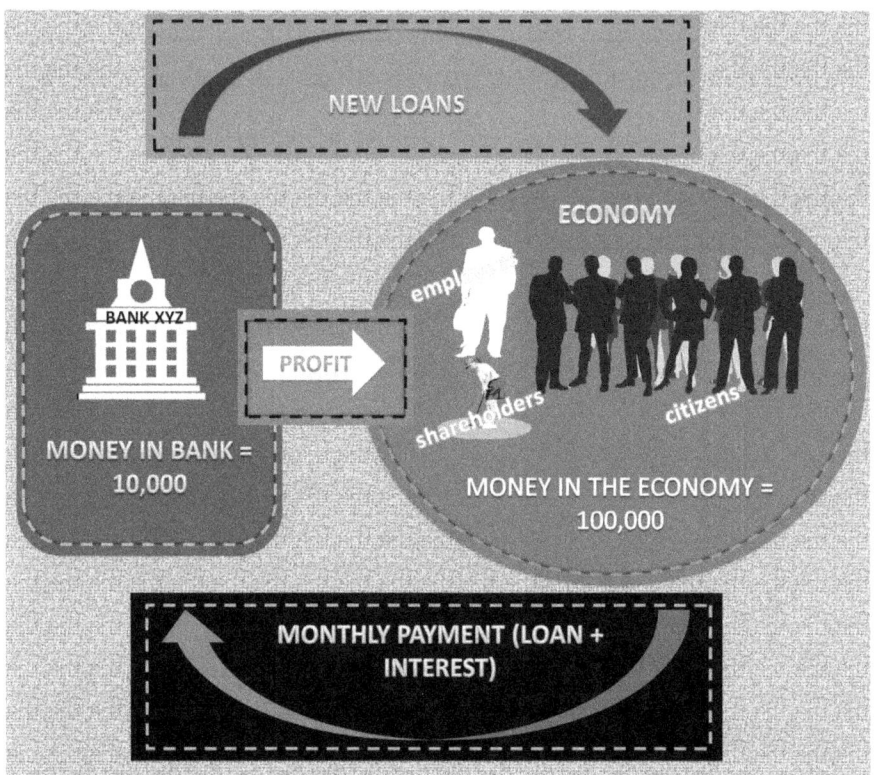

Illustration 113: This cycle can continue forever. There is no instance where there is no money in the economy to pay off the interest. No new money would be printed.
However, when wealth grows more than money available for transactions in the economy, money must be printed or deflation would occur.

What's important in the drawings above is that the amount of money in the economy stays constant despite loan repayments together with the interest.

The previous series of illustrations are full of numbers so we make a simpler drawing to summarize the movement of money in the economy and its banking system. There are no leakages and no money lost, and certainly there won't be any instance where there is not enough money to pay for all of the debts outstanding. In the drawing below, everything is in a steady state, $10 of old loans are being repaid, then $10 new loans are issued, repeatedly over and over.

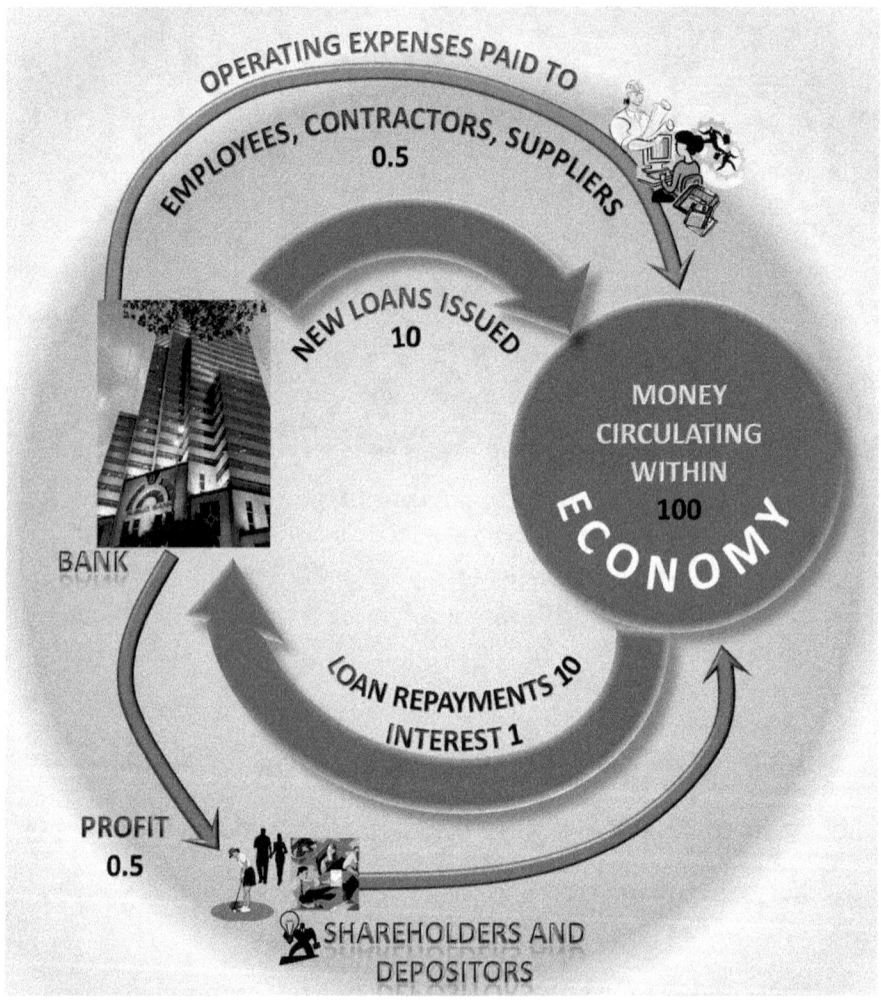

Illustration 114: Money Circulating in the economy remains constant (as long as there is enough for transaction) and repayments are returned through new loans, profit distribution and operating costs paid.

The interest portion (which is the profit) of $1 will be used to pay the bank's operating expenses of $0.5 and the remainder of $0.5 will be paid as net profit to the shareholders. The contractors and suppliers are entities that are sitting in the economy itself, so the money will flow right back into the economy. So are the shareholders, they are the economic participants themselves, so their profit money will go right back into the economy as well. The cycle will continue indefinitely.

Everything will tally and no additional money will be added or lost by the bank, despite the economy continuing to add wealth. As we explained in previous part of this **Book 2**, the wealth added typically grows exponentially, therefore the money in the economy will grow accordingly as well. For those who want a more exciting experience regarding this simulation, the reader is welcomed to visit our website at http://sites.google.com/site/259trillionvs5trillion and find the following movie presentation, **"Do Bank Loan Interest Payments Drain Money Out Of The Economy"**. The movie presentation is also useful for our next part of the book as to why interest or profit need to be paid.

We had explained earlier that banks have no reason to cheat on their clients, because they stand to lose a lot more than the clients themselves. If many of its clients went bankrupt, the bank risk holding surplus assets that not generating wealth and the remaining healthy borrowers will pay the bank with depreciated currency. It just does not make sense for the bank to risk their money this way.

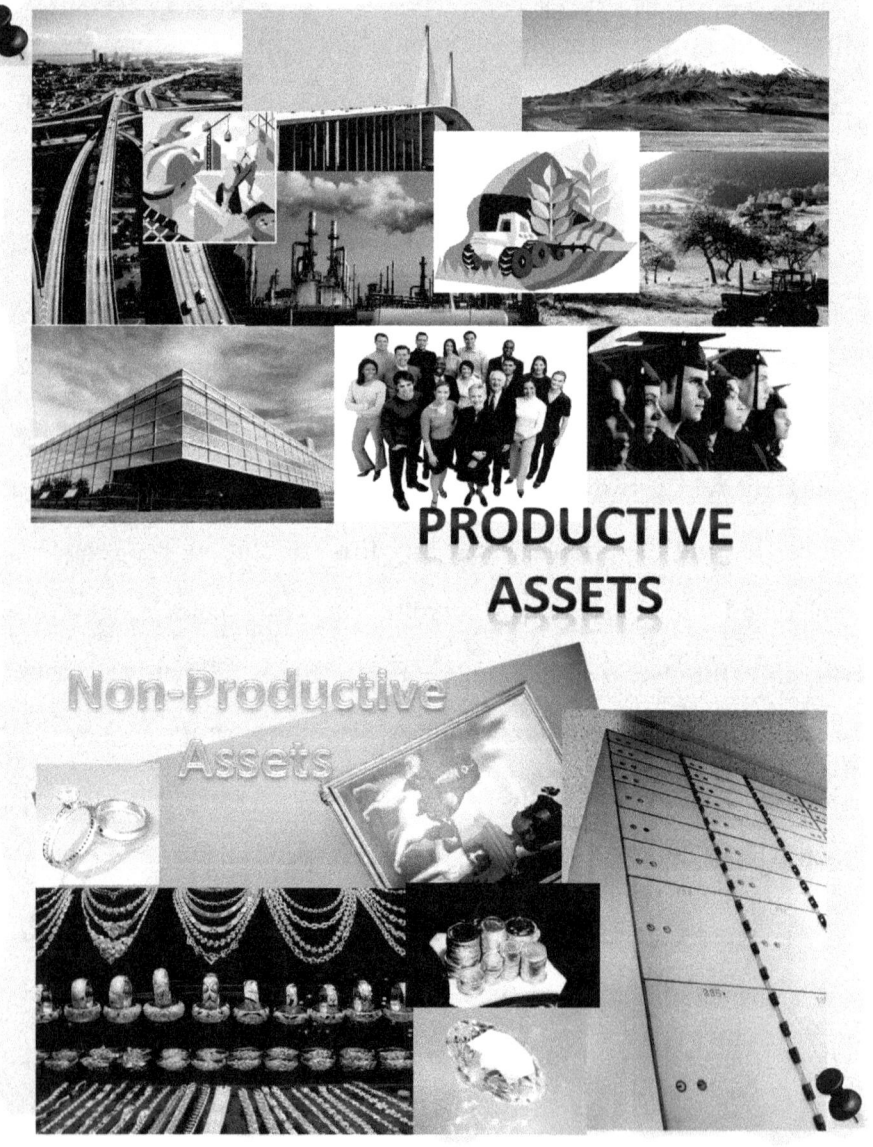

WHY INTEREST OR PROFIT NEED TO BE PAID

$\mathcal{T}$he money which workers stored in banks, will be used by the banks to lend to borrowers. Borrowers are people who have ideas, needs, which can add value to the economy, yet they have no means of achieving it due to lack of resources (i.e. capital). Such productive ideas can be financed by savers through the bank as the matchmaker, the intermediary. Anyone who has lent money knows that this business is not easy. It is actually very tough. Money lent out may be lost, may not be able to be recouped, if anything should happen to the borrower. The risk is immense. It is much more risky than a company selling a car, or selling houses. The appearance that banks will make good money during good times is because there is a need, that when times turns bad, losses will quickly mount. The money made earlier, will now need to be re-injected into the banks by the shareholders. A good bank, which performs its duties of match making nicely, will be handsomely rewarded. This reward will filter upward, to the ultimate owners of the bank (the shareholders) and downward, to the depositors who originally agreed that their money be used by those borrowers. The borrowers who successfully made new wealth, adding value to the economy, pays some of it to the bank, who also shares the profit with the owners and the depositors. These payments are in the form of interest, or profit as the term used in Islamic banking. If borrowers are unable to pay off the loans taken, the bank will step in and protect the depositors, even with its own blood (its own money that is!). The bank always sits in the middle and this ensures the safety of the depositors' money.

It is untrue that banks are taking advantage of others. Banks are providing important services to the economy. Banks are lending valuable assets of depositors, providing guarantee to it with its own blood, chase and collect payments from borrowers. Banks, do it much better than anyone can, they really specialize in this business— the banks are the best there is for this purpose. Banks do it better, especially compares to the government. If a bank rejected someone for a loan, normally it is for good reasons. If you dare, give your own money instead, to these unqualified people and see your money evaporates! When interest rate is high, banks appear to make a lot of money, however this money is used to compensate the depositors, who are suffering due to high inflation— it is not for making more profits for the bank. When interest rate is low, everyone benefited, although borrowers, or rather the bank, may start to give money away to unscrupulous people. This easy money will not be paid back, and the banks, for becoming too greedy with depositors money, was betting someone else to bail them out. That someone else, is none other than the government. Banks should be very prudent with depositors' money, and protect it to the best of their ability.

If the banks are conspiring today to steal your wealth, by giving out loans knowingly that many people will not be able to pay, **why would they lower their interest rates? Lowering their own profits?** If central banks such as the Fed are in the same conspiracy, why would the Fed reduced interest rates to very low levels? This will aid those who have no money—the masses, the borrowers. Theoretically if all is well in the economy and there is plentiful of money in surplus for investments, interest rates are bound to be low. The lower it is, the better it will be. It frees the market to decide on the level of returns it requires from such an investment. Furthermore, if there is no inflation, we see no reason to have a high interest rate environment, it does not matter whether the economy is growing nicely or in a downturn, because **economic growth is determined not by the interest rate, but by the capabilities of the people.** Interest rates should only be increased if there is inflation. Thus, it is highly illogical for banks and the Fed to be in a conspiracy together, yet they lower their own profits and do things which are good for borrowers and not themselves. Therefore such accusation does not have merit. We also showed and explained that borrowers do not actually lose money when they could not afford to continue paying off their loans because they had already received the money from the bank when the loans were first extended.

Why should borrowers pay interest to the banks? Is it possible to go for no interest loans? The explanation is really simple and it transcends religion and beliefs. If someone borrows money from you, uses it to plant crops, and made a fortune out of it, that person should pay you the original money, plus some of the profits. You had taken great risk with your money, and it is possible that the person will blow it up and pays you nothing. Thus it is only fair that if that person makes money, you are given a share of the profit, because if he doesn't, you will lose. You can of course choose not to lend that person the money, so your money will be safe but this is neither good for you, nor for that person, or the economy as a whole. It is impossible and illogical that God wishes its subjects not to help each other and share in on the profits and benefits of their own voluntary collaboration.

From the borrower point of view, if a good opportunity arises and wealth can be generated, it is only logical for the borrower to entice the lender who has the capital, to part with his money. The only way to let the lender part with his money is **to offer profit sharing potential**. If not, nobody will lend any money to potential borrowers because there are no returns offered. To make things worse for the lender, there is a large potential of losing some or all of the money in case the borrower is unable to pay back the loan for whatever reason. **This profit sharing is the interest to be paid to the lender, or in Islamic banking system, it is rephrased as 'profit'. It is one and the same, there is no difference in it.**

No matter how it is sliced, in economics, it is **impossible** to lend money at no profit to the lender. Lenders are not charities and some returns are expected. If you are the custodian of the money for your future child's education and your own retirement, it is reasonable for you to expect your borrower to pay you, plus some profit if you lend out this 'important' money. You are the guardian of someone else's future and it is prudent and proper for you to demand a return for risking the money. Otherwise, why would you lend your hard-earned money and why don't you simply plant that crop yourself? Should you decide to do it yourself, you will end up richer (or maybe poorer), but the would be borrower, **will stays poor, indefinitely.** We do not think this is what God intended for Its subjects where the rich will get richer and the poor, stays poor simply because the rich already have money with them. This is also not fair in economics and all gains and profits should be shared appropriately and not to be monopolized by the rich.

Additionally, if anyone thinks that money can be loaned at no interest and no profit, we urge this person to lend all of his or her money to others and tell them that they need not pay anything other than the principal. Tell them that they can take their time to pay it and if they lose the money, so what, nothing can be done. Better yet, inform us and we will be the first in line to borrow that money! These people continue to expound the fallacy of free interest loan and blame everyone else for not giving out such loans. **We dare them to publish their names out there and let everyone else borrow their money at zero interest. Yet, even better, they should establish their own zero interest bank and give away those loans!** These people will only talk as if they are the most righteous people on the planet, but when the time comes for them to give away the zero interest loan, they would not. Of course paying back is dependent on economic factors, luck and the acts of God are among the factors affecting people's ability to pay. If they actually create the zero interest bank, we presumed this bank will be the stingiest bank and will hardly give away its money. Nobody will then have money and economic growth will regressed.

Collection of interest or profit from a loan is therefore justified, however, if the amount imposed is more than what the borrowers generates in terms of value to the economy, it is costing the borrower its own money. This of course does not cause the wealth of the economy to increase because the borrower is using his own existing wealth and transferring it to the bank. If the borrower has no money to pay for the loan, eventually the loan is lost; the bank will have to cover the loss with its own money. This is called the 'loan loss provisions', routinely made by banks to accurately reflect and report the extent of 'losses' to their owners; the shareholders.

Logically in a modern economy, any money extended as loans, should be paid back plus a fixed amount of the generated profits with inflation adjustment agreement. This type of loan is the preferred type of loan extended by banks. If the borrower generates returns of thousands of percent, or millions of percent, the bank will still collect the same amount of interest or profit because the loan's interest is not calculated as a percentage of how much profit is made. **The borrower is free to keep most of the profits made.** The interest is paid according to an agreement, which is what the borrower originally committed. A different type of loan is also routinely extended by banks to borrowers, one that is in the form of equal risks and rewards between them. This kind of loan is typically given out in a **joint venture,** where the bank actively participates. The return can be greater for the bank, but so is the risk.

One way of looking at interest in the case of mortgages is that, interests paid are in exact proportion to the would be house's rentals payable. Let say, a borrower borrowed $300,000 to pay for a house in 25 years. Interest charge is usually 5% and that would be $1,753 a month. Of this amount, $1,250 is for the interest on the loan. You can rent a similar house in the neighborhood and the rental rates are not going to be much cheaper than the interest payment of $1,250. Assuming that rental rates are the same with interest payments, over the period of 25 years, the rental costs will be $226,000. You may rent or buy a house, but you will still need to pay (either rent or interest and both are always a cost to you). We had made detail calculations on buying versus rental, which one is better for you and it is a topic in Book 3 of this series.

Time is an important element in loan calculations. Interest payable will be more if the time is longer. However, it does not mean you will pay more interest because you will be able to earn more with the borrowed money. Our calculations showed that a loan could be dragged as long as you want it to be, if the interest is sufficiently low. Think of the possibilities of what you can do with the borrowed money (investments of course). Despite this, it is still better to pay off your loan as quick as you can if you prefer to sleep better at night.

Time value of money is real and the reason for it is because when money is lent out, the lender will lose the opportunity to use that money for something else. This lost opportunity, this loss of potential returns **must be compensated by the borrower.** Presumably, the borrower will compensate the lender by offering more returns for the use of the money. This is the typical arrangement in the marketplace. The compensation arrangement is automatically built-in in the lending agreement and it does not add costs to the borrower, especially if the borrower is borrowing under a variable rate loan. If the loan is a fixed interest loan however, the costs of this built in compensation can be massive and very significant over the long term. **Our calculations models showed that variable interest rate loan is the best type of loan for longer duration, because fairness and justice are served to both borrowers and lenders.** For the fixed, it is only good if the interest of the loan is very low (but it is only good to the borrower, not the lender, therefore fixed loans are incquitable).

When a variable rate loan's interest rate changes, it is principally due to the movement in the inflation rate of the country and secondarily due to the changes in the price of money. When the interest rate moves due to the effect of inflation, for example goes up a percent, the lender do not pocket the increase in payments in any way because the change in the interest merely compensate the lender for the loss of the money's purchasing power. If it goes down on the other hand, it compensates for the borrower's increase of purchasing power instead. In real economic sense, a variable rate loan is technically a 'fixed' loan to both the lender and the borrower because the 'margin' of the profits made by the lender will stays the same despite the changes in the inflation rate. A fixed rate loan on the other hand, does not move at all and may result in losses to the lender as well as the borrower when inflation rate changes. The comparison between a variable and a fixed rate loan of $300,000 with only interests payments made is illustrated below:

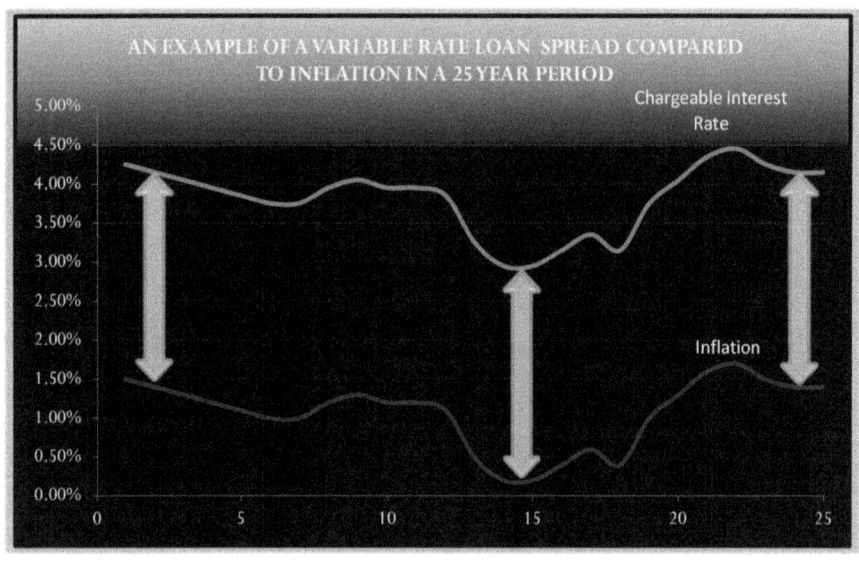

Illustration 115: Comparisons between Variable Rate Loan Spread Vs. Inflation for 25 Years

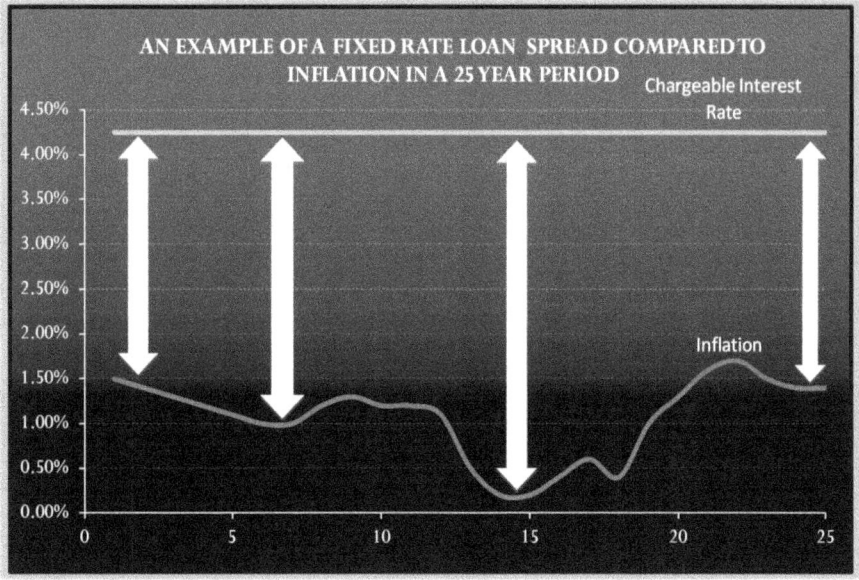

Illustration 116: Comparisons between Fixed Rate Loan Spread Vs. Inflation for 25 Years

In the illustrations above, the difference between a fixed interest rate loan and a variable rate loan is so stark it makes no sense to go for fixed interest rate at all. In the first illustration (Illustration 115) which is the variable rate loan simulated for a period of 25 years, it shows that the variable rate loan moves exactly in tandem with the economy's inflation rate, keeping the returns agreed to the lender constant (at 2.75% per annum returns). When inflation rate goes up, the rate adjusts upward, so the return to the lender is the same. Similarly when inflation rate goes down, the rate goes down as well. In both instances where the inflation rate goes up and also goes down, neither the borrower nor the lender profits from the other, i.e. at the expense of the other party. This is an equitable arrangement as it does not penalize anyone.

The fixed rate however (in Illustration 116), varies immensely as the inflation rate changes over the loan period. As the inflation rate drops towards the middle of the loan period, the profit or returns to the lender increased significantly, from 2.75% to 4.05%. But when inflation rate goes up, at one instance the borrower was paying less than planned, so the loss is to the lender. The changes in the inflation rate is posing a great risk to the lender, because there is no recourse for the lender to recover money if inflation rate goes up very high. The lender will lose. To avoid this kind of risk, the lender typically add additional layer of premium on the chargeable interest rate, normally in the range of one to two percent. This thick fat, as we shall see, will be terribly expensive for the borrower.

In the example above, both the fixed loan and the variable rate loan start at 4.25% base lending rate, with 2.75% returns per annum to the lender. During the course of the loan, the return to the lender changes wildly for the fixed loan, while for the variable rate loan, the actual interest charged by the lender to the borrower remain constant throughout the loan tenure.

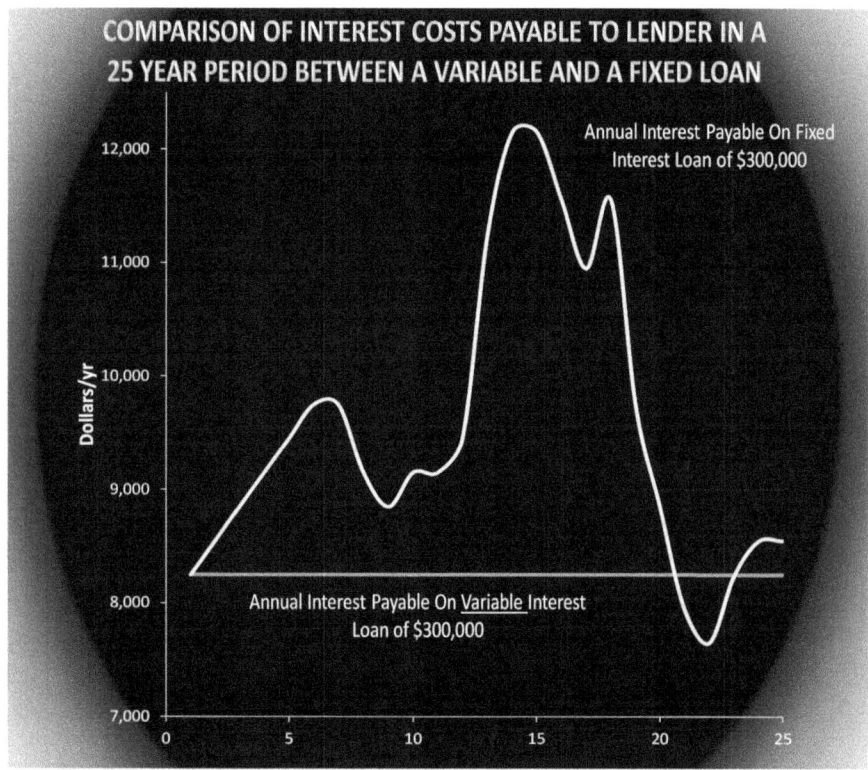

Illustration 116: Interest Costs payable to a lender over a 25 year period between two types of rate shows that variable rate borrowers actually pays the "same" while the fixed rate borrowers costs varied.

The difference between the two loans in terms of money is even more pronounced. It's $32,400 (costlier for the fixed loan) despite they both starting out at the same interest rate of 4.25% and the same interest rate margin (or profit margin) of the bank of 2.75%. The inflation rate originally starts at 1.5% and as the loan progresses, the $300,000 loan's interest payable changes for the variable rate loan. The spread on the variable rate loan is actually 'fixed' because it maintains a constant return to the lender as originally agreed. The fixed loan is different however. It is not fixed, it varies. Depending on the inflation level, one party will end up losing and the other, gaining. If interest rate is bound to be higher in the future due to higher inflation, it is prudent for the lender to demand a higher interest rate on a fixed loan. This risk specifically makes any fixed interest loan to be always comparatively higher than a variable type loan. The additional interest could be in the region of between one to two percent and in the event the 'higher' inflation never occurs, the bank will make additional and definitely a significant sums of money at the expense of the borrower. The borrower will certainly ends up paying above and beyond the originally agreed quantum of profit, or quantum of profit margin of the bank. Our example above and the dollar amount did not take into account the cost of the premium typically demanded by lenders for fixed loans, which will be between one to two percent, and at times can be even

higher. The net effect will be a tripling or quadrupling of the amount of interest payable. From a difference of 'only' $32,400, it exploded to $126,150 if a premium of only 1.25% is levied on top of the agreed return so that the overall loan rate can be fixed. You can go ahead and calculate what the difference will be if the premium is 2% or 2.5%. We are sure you will be shocked.

There are of course many factors in evaluating loan options and our focus is to illustrate a factor that is never mentioned out there. We evaluated the loan option from a neutral standpoint. We focus on fairness to both lender and borrower, where one party does not take more from the other. We understand that out there, typically reviews and recommendations are made on the borrower side alone and what will benefit the borrower, or sometimes only to the lender and what will benefit the lender more than the borrower. Hardly anyone will present a view of what is the most equitable for both parties in ALL situations.

From religious standpoint, we concluded that the variable loan is the most equitable type of loan and is the fairest of all. It does not enrich anyone and is neutral over the long term. A fixed type of loan is however is not doing justice to either party, because it can be higher than the market resulting in losses to the borrower or it can be lower than the market's price of money, that the lender will lose. **A variable rate loan will therefore eliminate the risk of time value of money to all parties, rendering the loan more 'religious' than other type of loans**. There won't be an element of usury in this type of loan arising from the time value of money at all.

You only live once and if you have to part with your hard-earned wealth for a considerable length of time, you will have less time to enjoy the wealth later on when the wealth is returned to you because you are already closer to your dying days. If you gives out a loan for 20 years, you already given up 20 years of your life from enjoying or utilizing this wealth for your own benefit. In fact, you decided to give your wealth to the borrower so he can enjoy it to the fullest instantly, right away that without it, he will have to save for the next 20 years, without that wealth to enjoy. Therefore, it is only fair that you are duly compensated with an agreed level of returns for the loan extended. It will be even worse if you die early and did not even manage to enjoy your money— but the borrower did.

Even governments do not give away free money. This is true even if they took the money from other people and hand it over to other deserving people. When politicians hand out 'free money' taken from other people (taxes and others), they still expect you to vote them and therefore it is always with a catch. It is so difficult to find a real free lunch out there, isn't it?

The public always complain that banks always took advantage of them and making lots of money, lots of profits from other people's sweats. They claim banks always made money and it is so easy for them. Our answer to this group of people and their silly claim is— Go and make your own bank because you all had found a business model that always makes money and so easy to do. Stop complaining and go open that bank! We shall see then that these same people will start to complain how tough it is, that many borrowers do not pay back their money and that all their earlier claims were false. We shall discuss this matter once more in another part of this three books series.

Many retirees spend majority of their money on health issues.

Invest in your health first by knowledge. It will save you a lot of money with tremendous returns...

Prevention is better than cure & you know your body best! Don't simply believe what others say about your condition

WHY A CENTRAL BANK IS NEEDED IN A
MODERN BANKING SYSTEM

In previous examples, the banking system is fine and dandy if there is only one bank in the system. However with only one bank, the system will be unstable, inefficient and expensive. Monopolies were shown to exhibit exactly such drawbacks, many times throughout history. Therefore several banks are needed in the economy, to create good competition and choices for depositors and borrowers alike.

In the following example, we will show why a central bank is needed and why the central bank needs to step in, to provide a temporary loan, to a bank. We are adding an additional bank into our banking system simulation presented earlier. The two banks will compete with each other, lowering their services costs to lend money to would be borrowers while greatly risking their capital as usual. Somehow, due to better 'luck', the other bank is consistently outperforming the other, and is being rewarded by the consumers, by saving more of their money in the better performing bank. Essentially, money is being transferred from one bank, to the other. To illustrate the impact and understand the outcome, let's commission a new simulation, with two banks in the economy.

Lesson 7: Why Central Bank Is Needed In Modern Banking System

In this lesson, we will have two banks, Bank A and Bank B which just open for business and put in their own money of 50 into the system.

BANK A	Total Deposit Level	Lent Money	Total Loans	Deposited money	Net Money In/out of Bank A system either due to loan (-ve) or dep (+ve)	Actual Cash in Hand (in Banks)	Asset of Banks (due to Deposit and Loans payable)	Cash to Deposit Ratio (SRR)	Actual Loan To Deposit Ratio
Bank Starts With Its Own Money	50	0	0	50	50	50	50	1	0

Illustration 117: Bank A opened for business with its own $50 deposit.

BANK B	Total Deposit Level	Lent Money	Total Loans	Deposited money	Net Money In/out of Bank B system either due to loan (-ve) or deposit (+ve)	Actual Cash in Hand (in Banks)	Asset of Banks (due to Deposit and Loans payable)	Cash to Deposit Ratio (SRR)	Actual Loan To Deposit Ratio
Bank Starts With Its Own Money	50	0	0	50	50	50	50	1	0

Illustration 118: Bank B opened for business with its own $50 deposit.

Now lending will start as usual, with the usual amount lent out.

BANK A	Total Deposit Level	Lent Money	Total Loans	Deposited money	Net Money In/out of Bank A system either due to loan (-ve) or dep (+ve)	Actual Cash in Hand (in Banks)	Asset of Banks (due to Deposit and Loans payable)	Cash to Deposit Ratio (SRR)	Actual Loan To Deposit Ratio
Bank Starts With Its Own Money	50	0	0	50	50	50	50	1	0
A borrower borrowed 10	50	10	10	0	-10	40	50	0.800	0.200

Illustration 119: A borrower borrowed $10 from Bank A.

BANK B	Total Deposit Level	Lent Money	Total Loans	Deposited money	Net Money In/out of Bank B system either due to loan (-ve) or deposit (+ve)	Actual Cash in Hand (in Banks)	Asset of Banks (due to Deposit and Loans payable)	Cash to Deposit Ratio (SRR)	Actual Loan To Deposit Ratio
Bank Starts With Its Own Money	50	0	0	50	50	50	50	1	0
a borrower borrowed 10	50	10	10	0	-10	40	50	0.800	0.200

Illustration 120: Borrowers borrowed $10 from Bank B.

As usual, someone will go back into the banks to deposit their money.

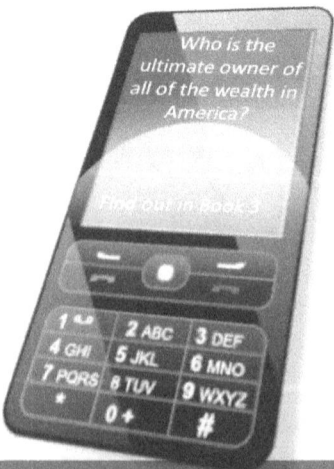

BANK A	Total Deposit Level	Lent Money	Total Loans	Deposited money	Net Money In/out of Bank A system either due to loan (-ve) or dep (+ve)	Actual Cash in Hand (in Banks)	Asset of Banks (due to Deposit and Loans payable)	Cash to Deposit Ratio (SRR)	Actual Loan To Deposit Ratio
Bank Starts With Its Own Money	50	0	0	50	50	50	50	1	0
A borrower borrowed 10	50	10	10	0	-10	40	50	0.800	0.200
A depositor deposit 6	56	0	10	6	6	46	56	0.821	0.179

Bank A only gets a deposit of $6

Illustration 121: A depositor deposited $6 into Bank A

BANK B	Total Deposit Level	Lent Money	Total Loans	Deposited money	Net Money In/out of Bank B system either due to loan (-ve) or deposit (+ve)	Actual Cash in Hand (in Banks)	Asset of Banks (due to Deposit and Loans payable)	Actual Cash Reserve to Loan Ratio	Actual Loan To Deposit Ratio
Bank Starts With Its Own Money	50	0	0	50	50	50	50	1	0
a borrower borrowed 10	50	10	10	0	-10	40	50	0.800	0.200
A depositor deposit 14	64	0	10	14	14	54	64	0.844	0.156

Bank B gets a deposit of $14, more than Bank A

Illustration 122: A depositor deposited $14 into Bank B ($8 more than Bank A).

Interestingly, the choice of these depositors are not random, the 'better' bank gets more deposit. In this case, Bank B receives more deposit than Bank A.

Bank B receives $8 more than Bank A. Let's simulate for several iterations and see what happens.

BANK A	Total Deposit Level	Lent Money	Total Loans	Deposited money	Net Money In/out of Bank A system either due to loan (-ve) or dep (+ve)	Actual Cash in Hand (in Banks)	Asset of Banks (due to Deposit and Loans payable)	Cash to Deposit Ratio (SRR)	Actual Loan To Deposit Ratio
Bank Starts With Its Own Money	50	0	0	50	50	50	50	1	0
a borrower borrowed 10	50	10	10	0	-10	40	50	0.800	0.200
A depositor deposit 6	56	0	10	6	6	46	56	0.821	0.179
a borrower borrowed 10	56	10	20	0	-10	36	56	0.643	0.357
A depositor deposit 6	62	0	20	6	6	42	62	0.677	0.323
a borrower borrowed 10	62	10	30	0	-10	32	62	0.516	0.484
A depositor deposit 6	68	0	30	6	6	38	68	0.559	0.441
a borrower borrowed 10	68	10	40	0	-10	28	68	0.412	0.588
A depositor deposit 6	74	0	40	6	6	34	74	0.459	0.541
a borrower borrowed 10	74	10	50	0	-10	24	74	0.324	0.676
A depositor deposit 6	80	0	50	6	6	30	80	0.375	0.625
a borrower borrowed 10	80	10	60	0	-10	20	80	0.250	0.750
A depositor deposit 6	86	0	60	6	6	26	86	0.302	0.698
a borrower borrowed 10	86	10	70	0	-10	16	86	0.186	0.814
A depositor deposit 6	92	0	70	6	6	22	92	0.239	0.761
a borrower borrowed 10	92	10	80	0	-10	12	92	0.130	0.870
A depositor deposit 6	98	0	80	6	6	18	98	0.184	0.816
a borrower borrowed 10	98	10	90	0	-10	8	98	0.082	0.918
A depositor deposit 6	104	0	90	6	6	14	104	0.135	0.865
a borrower borrowed 10	104	10	100	0	-10	4	104	0.038	0.962
A depositor deposit 6	110	0	100	6	6	10	110	0.091	0.909
a borrower borrowed 10	110	10	110	0	-10	0	110	0.000	1.000

Bank A reaches its loan limit.

Loan to Deposit Ratio =1 (Bank A lent all its money!)

Illustration 123: After several iteration, Bank A quickly reaches its loan limit. It has no more cash. As you can see, if there is no deposit (or less deposit), bank cannot give out loans (or only gives out small amount of loans).

After several iterations, bank A quickly reaches its loan limit due to the Actual Reserve to Loan ratio falling below 0.1. Its Loan to Deposit Ratio was sky high at 1.0, essentially lending everything it has! Of course the cash in hand dropped to zero. Let's see what happen to Bank B.

BANK B	Total Deposit Level	Lent Money	Total Loans	Deposited money	Net Money In/out of Bank B system either due to loan (-ve) or dep (+ve)	Actual Cash in Hand (in Banks)	Asset of Banks (due to Deposit and Loans payable)	Cash to Deposit Ratio (SRR)	Actual Loan To Deposit Ratio
Bank Starts With Its Own Money	50	0	0	50	50	50	50	1	0
a borrower borrowed 10	50	10	10	0	-10	40	50	0.800	0.200
A depositor deposit 14	64	0	10	14	14	54	64	0.844	0.156
a borrower borrowed 10	64	10	20	0	-10	44	64	0.688	0.313
A depositor deposit 14	78	0	20	14	14	58	78	0.744	0.256
a borrower borrowed 10	78	10	30	0	-10	48	78	0.615	0.385
A depositor deposit 14	92	0	30	14	14	62	92	0.674	0.326
a borrower borrowed 10	92	10	40	0	-10	52	92	0.565	0.435
A depositor deposit 14	106	0	40	14	14	66	106	0.623	0.377
a borrower borrowed 10	106	10	50	0	-10	56	106	0.528	0.472
A depositor deposit 14	120	0	50	14	14	70	120	0.583	0.417
a borrower borrowed 10	120	10	60	0	-10	60	120	0.500	0.500
A depositor deposit 14	134	0	60	14	14	74	134	0.552	0.448
a borrower borrowed 10	134	10	70	0	-10	64	134	0.478	0.522
A depositor deposit 14	148	0	70	14	14	78	148	0.527	0.473
a borrower borrowed 10	148	10	80	0	-10	68	148	0.459	0.541
A depositor deposit 14	162	0	80	14	14	82	162	0.506	0.494

Continue in the next page....

BANK B	Total Deposit Level	Lent Money	Total Loans	Deposited money	Net Money In/out of Bank B system either due to loan (-ve) or dep (+ve)	Actual Cash in Hand (in Banks)	Asset of Banks (due to Deposit and Loans payable)	Cash to Deposit Ratio (SRR)	Actual Loan To Deposit Ratio
Continue from the page before.......									
a borrower borrowed 10	162	10	90	0	-10	72	162	0.444	0.556
A depositor deposit 14	176	0	90	14	14	86	176	0.489	0.511
a borrower borrowed 10	176	10	100	0	-10	76	176	0.432	0.568
A depositor deposit 14	190	0	100	14	14	90	190	0.474	0.526
a borrower borrowed 10	190	10	110	0	-10	80	190	0.421	0.579

Illustration 124: After the same iteration as Bank A, Bank B's balance sheets is still healthy. It can still give more loans out.

Well, nothing much happen except that Bank B can give out more loans and has increasing level of cash in hand. The Cash Reserve Ratio is very healthy and so is the Loan To Deposit Ratio. Although the same amount of iterations happened for both banks, the difference is staggering. Bank A quickly runs out of cash, and fail to reverse the falls in deposit level while Bank B only utilizes half of its lending capacity, although their Total Loans are the same. **Let's check the amount of cash in hand at both banks, it is 90 + 10 - 100 (use the last depositor deposit row). This still showed that even with two banks, no additional money is printed and certainly, no money out of thin air is printed.** Most of the cash is moved by borrowers and depositors to Bank B.

Each individual bank in this two banks economic simulation shown in the example above ends up with different core ratios, one is rather terrible and the other is excellent. The central bank however has a higher level view of the whole banking system and has a consolidated numbers for all banks. The consolidated figures are shown below (it is similar to the one bank example shown much earlier).

ECONOMY MONEY SUPPLY	Total Deposit Level	Lent Money	Total Loans	Deposited money	Net Money In/out of Bank A system either due to loan (-ve) or dep (+ve)	Actual Cash in Hand (in Banks)	Asset of Banks (due to Deposit and Loans payable)	Cash to Deposit Ratio (SRR)	Actual Loan To Deposit Ratio
Bank A & Bank B	300	0	200	20	20	100	300	0.333	0.667

Illustration 125: Central Bank's eagle's eye view of the banking system

From an eagle's eye view of the banking system, the central bank will see that the whole banking system is in good condition, although one bank is having trouble. Even if that bank collapses, it is not that big of a problem for the system because the overall key ratios of the system are still very healthy. Usually, what will happen in the economy is that the central bank will ask the healthier bank to acquire the ailing bank. The merging of the two banks will be all right for the banking system and no depositors will lose their money. In fact, the very reason Bank A was doing poorly in the first place is due to competition, not due to an unhealthy economy or its banking system. Although banks are being protected by the central bank in many ways, they will still succumb to the forces of capitalism.

In our example above, despite the difference of deposit level between the banks, the quality of their loans extended are the same (assuming they apply the same standard for loan approvals). Remember that loans extended are the assets of the banks and deposits are the liabilities. Therefore, the assets of the banks are similar. Yet, as we can see, Bank A experienced a sort of 'mini' bank run and lost a lot of deposit, which ended up at the other bank. If the withdrawals of deposits continue, it will be necessary for the bank to ask for capital injection from its shareholders, or simply swap its assets with the central bank for money.

Should Bank A experience some non payment of its loans, it will require additional money to restore its balance sheet (to increase its loan to deposit ratio to above the minimum level). To get additional money quickly the bank can obtain a loan from the other bank, or directly from the central bank. When a bank goes to another bank to borrow money, this is normally called 'overnight lending'. In Malaysia, this rate is called the 'Overnight Policy Rate'. In the USA, it is called the 'Fed Funds Rate'. This is the floor of the interbank rates for borrowing money from each other. (Take note that borrowing from other countries is a totally different ball game and the basics and reasoning are not the same. The 'Libor' or 'London Interbank Rate' is what bank lends to each other, globally and will depend on many other factors and typically, there are no central banks involved).

The central bank monitor each bank in the economy closely—in fact very closely. During the day, hourly or even minute by minute monitoring of banks' balances and reserves is conducted by the central bank. During the close of the business day, each bank assess whether they have sufficient cash reserve as required by the central bank. Banks that do not have enough cash reserve just like Bank A in our example above, will have to borrow from other banks that have surpluses. If those banks refuse to lend their surpluses, the deficit bank can always go to the central bank and request for a temporary 'loan'.

The central bank will accept, knowing that overall, in the whole economy, the loans are still serviceable and profitable, so long as the economy continues to generate wealth (or still growing). In the event the economy is not growing and wealth is being destroyed, there is little guarantee that the loan extended can be paid back, especially if it involves a very large scale of loan. When a loan cannot be paid back, the generated wealth basically evaporates. The created money will then be extinguished.

Stopping this process will create further imbalance, and possible inflation due to excess liquidity in the system.

Bank B continues to have excess money and will be able to lend it out to anyone, including to the other bank. The Fed knows this of course, therefore, has little fear in extending loan to Bank A. Bank A could be a very well run bank and have no higher risk than Bank B, however due to depositor preferences, deposits were moving into Bank B in greater numbers. This imbalance will eventually result in Bank A having problem with diminishing cash reserve and may give the impression that it is going under. However in reality, there is always a reason why such migration exists, whether it is temporary or systemic and long term. The money migration into other banks will worsen the bank critical ratios and will eventually cause it to seek 'assistance' as described earlier. This 'assistance' is of course in the form of borrowed money. When a bank seeks assistance by borrowing money from another bank, they will negotiate on the interest rate or profit. As mentioned, the central bank has a heavy hand here, whereby it routinely advertises its 'Overnight Rate' or 'Fed Funds Rate'. This 'official' rate will influence the negotiation between the two banks because the borrowing bank can always go to the central bank if the lending bank wanted to give a loan of higher interest (or profit), higher than the rate offered by the central bank. This powerful yet simple rate setting method has significant repercussions in the banking system and the general economy. The central bank uses interest rates to ensure proper functioning of the economy according to economic data and needs of the economy. The topic of interest rate and its impact to the economy is very widely discussed, however to a beginner or someone who routinely being confused by incomprehensible terms and jargon spurned out by economists, academicians and analyst, then this book will be a valuable reference.

Interest rate (or profit rate) is basically the cost of borrowing short term money. The higher the interest rate, the higher the cost of borrowing money. When the central bank increases the interest rate, banks have the option of increasing their own interbank lending, or just keeping the rate as is. However, why would the bank do so if the central bank is offering a higher rate? The end result; all banks will follow closely the central bank offered interest rate. Banks with surplus money, will enjoy greater returns on their surpluses, while banks with little reserve, will need to pay even more. The situation will be utterly different at the front lines with customers, borrowers and depositors. Banks with surpluses of reserves, do not have to follow the central bank interest rate and are rather free to lend at any interest rate they want. Banks that do not have enough reserve, will only lend at a higher level than the official central bank interest rate, otherwise it will begin to lose money. Check out your favorite bank's critical ratios and figure out whether they are routinely borrowing money from other banks. Then check out their base lending rate to borrowers. Normally it is higher than other banks. Based on this fact, banks with surplus of funds, are not obligated to set their lending rates to borrowers at the rate sets by the central bank. This is the reason why you will see banks do give lower interest than the standard base lending rate, e.g. "interest rate of minus 1.5% of BLR". Contrary to what many people believed, interest charged on borrowers are not dictated by the central bank.

Naturally, everyone wanted low interest rate, the lower, the better. This is very true and good for borrowers. Low interest rate in the economy shows that there is ample capital for use. If however, capital is scarce, borrowers will have to compete for that limited amount of money available. Borrowers who think they can make more money with the borrowed money, will tend to offer higher returns to the lenders. They will then get that scarce money. This very fact is one of the fundamental of capitalism; the best endeavor with the greatest returns potential are naturally selected by the economic participants. It is good for the economy as a whole. For the banks, higher central bank interest rate is a reason to increase their lending interest rate, which hurt borrowers. Again, the bank with surpluses at hand, will enjoy significant return on their money and they actually do not really need to follow the central bank official rate. These banks will appear to earn more due to their cheap costs of money, but as mentioned earlier, they will have to use this money to pay out to their depositors who are suffering from high inflation. When interest rate is high, fewer borrowers will be able to take out loans, due to the high cost of money. When it is low, many will be qualified. Most banks will lend money to the hilt, which is the maximum allowed by the central bank all the time. Some good and prudent banks, always have difficulty in finding good quality borrowers to lend to. These banks will end up lending their surpluses at the interbank areas. Do you notice the talk of the town on where it is easier, sometimes much easier, to get a loan at certain bank, but not at others?

What will happen if Bank B refuses to lend money to Bank A in our example earlier? Bank A will have to go to the lender of last resort, which is the central bank. The central bank has a unique perspective on the economy, and it look at both banks. If the economy is healthy, and the rate of wealth creation is matched by the money issued, then technically all banks are healthy in the economy. So if one bank is suffering from money migration, the central bank has no qualm not to lend it money. If the economy is not doing well, wealth is not being created, loans may not really be backed by assets anymore, then at that point the central bank should refuse to lend money out unless the asset provided by the borrowing bank is of high quality.

So far, our banking simulation does not include the element of interest as one of the category. A more elaborate simulation will include interest/profit element as part of the factor to be considered. We have however completed this simulation as well. In order to make this book as easy as possible to be understood, this more complex simulation is omitted from the book. We can include them in a future book, or may simply publish them in our website.

Let us summarize the relations between commercial banks and the central bank as a whole in the most minimum of words.

When a commercial bank exceeded its lending limit, it will use its accumulated assets at the interbank lending market to acquire money. Banks with surpluses will lend to the bank, at a profit. This is the interbank rate, and it is a tad lower than the Fed Funds rate. The central bank controls this rate by issuing or withdrawing money (reserve). If there is no commercial bank willing to lend to the bank with a money shortfall, that bank can always go to the central bank and exchange its asset for money

(reserve) at the exact Fed Funds rate or OPR. The central bank rarely refuses to lend to such a bank, for fear of financial panic. Banks always borrow by giving up assets, and the central banks always demanded good quality assets such as government bonds and papers.

Banks must return to its mandated minimum cash reserve ratio (sometimes called as statutory reserve requirement or SRR) at the end of the day. Banks that fail to meet the minimum requirement, must borrow from other banks or from the central bank, thus the term overnight loan.

In our simulation above, as Bank A maxed out its lending limit, a potential borrower approaches it and request for a loan. The bank however have a problem, it technically cannot issue any more loans. As usual, the potential borrower is willing to cover the loan with an asset, by offering a good quality collateral (a factory for example). The bank will conduct due diligence on the asset and if satisfied, will extend the loan regardless, by tapping its dwindling cash reserve. Now the bank will exceed its limit on the loan to deposit ratio or breaches its minimum SRR. The bank must scramble and hurry to inject new capital of its own from shareholders, borrow money from the interbank market, or find new depositor to deposit new funds. If the bank fails to do any of the above, it must prepare to face the wrath of the central bank via coercion, investigation, penalties and eventually, its removal of operating license. Normally the interbank market is the quicker and easier route, so the bank will go there and ask for a loan from other banks. The other banks will require collateral for such a loan, in this case, the asset (mortgaged houses, factories, land etc.) in exchange for the money. Banks will demand a profit, and this agreed profit or interest rate will be close to the existing central bank rate; however it would be slightly lower if many banks have surplus of funds. Once the exchange takes place, the asset will no longer be booked in the bank's balance sheet, but in replacement, the just swapped cash will now sits. Its critical ratios will improve, enough to go through for the day. Now it is meeting its minimum requirement to continue operating as a sound bank.

Is government subsidy good for us and the economy? It is not because it disrupts the market's resource allocation. Find out more in Book 3

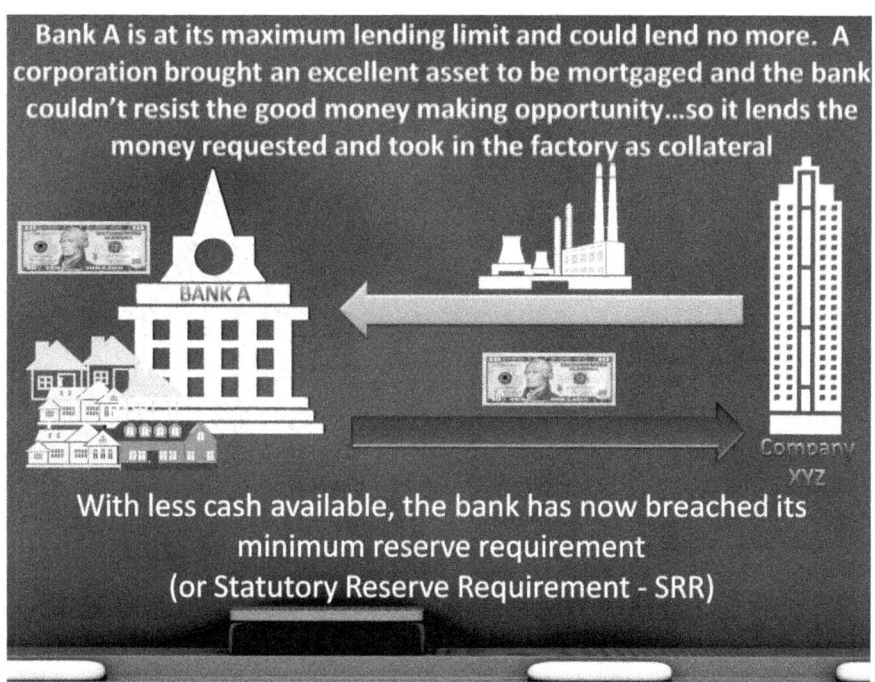

Illustration 126: Bank A breaches its SRR

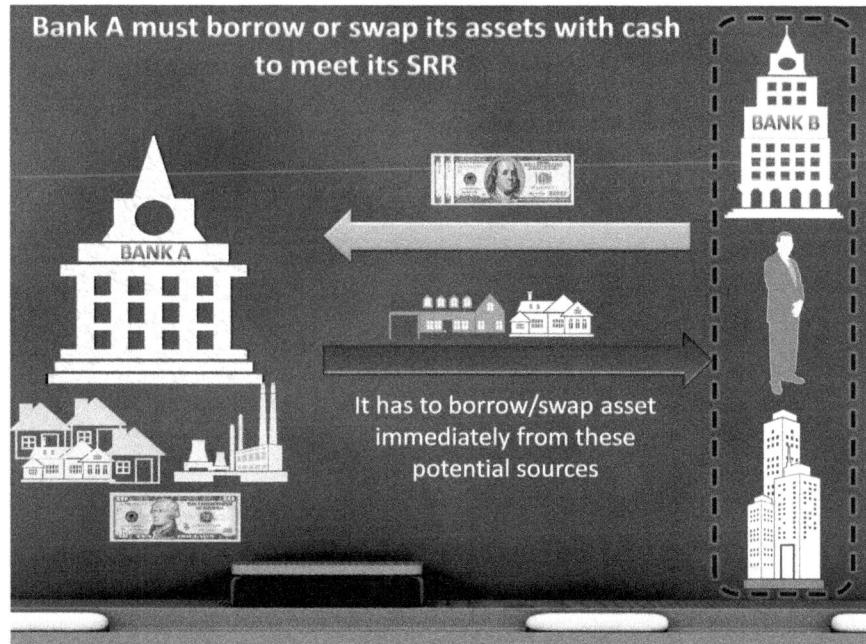

Illustration 127: It approaches other banks for interbank loans or various other investors to get the cash it needed for that day

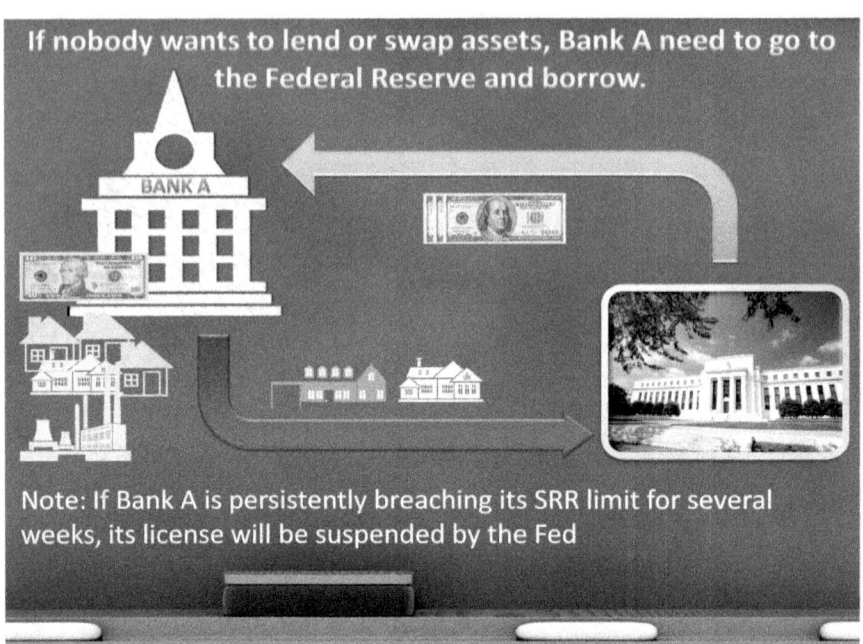

Illustration 128: Bank A approaches the Federal Reserve as lender of the last resort

As the economy grows, there are more wealth or assets created. However in the banking system, the amount of money is still as it was before. Eventually, the minimum cash reserve is also utilized for lending, signaling the economic needs for more cash.

The Federal Reserve monitors the banking system just for such a sign and will stand ready to inject new cash, with a swap with an equivalent value of asset with the needy bank

Illustration 129: When banks start coming in for loans, it signals that cash is low in the economy. The Federal Reserve needs to add more cash.

There are many countries now no longer imposing any kind of statutory reserve requirement, or set it at zero or near zero. The banks are monitored by their central banks by calculating their RWCAR (Risk Weighted Capital Adequacy Ratio). In order to explain this long abbreviation, first start with CAR (Capital Adequacy Ratio). It is the ratio of the bank's own capital to asset of the bank. Banks' assets are the loans extended to many borrowers as we mentioned earlier in this book. If there are some borrowers who could not repay their loans, this capital of the bank will be used to cover that losses, to ensure all depositors will still have their deposits. The more capital the bank has, the better the adequacy ratio would be. Borrowers are rated according to their risk profile; the risk profile is consolidated into a weighted average number, hence the term 'risk weighted'. The risks the bank is exposed to, all of it, must be taken into account to estimate the overall risk of the bank. Bank's capital consists of Tier 1 and Tier 2. Tier 1 is basically cash and Tier 2, the less liquid forms of money.

If deposits from depositors are parked in super safe government bonds, it is not included basically in the RWCAR because it is considered as no risk. With this way, it is possible for banks to lend out 100% of any deposits received. The anti fractional banking groups will have a grand 'field day', since such a bank, can appear to lend out unlimited money— without 'limits' because the statutory reserve is zero. Well actually, the bank can't lend out unlimited amount of money, otherwise its CAR will drop. This very fact will expose the lies expounded by the anti fractional banking group because using their 'misleading example' will show unlimited lending capacity, yet the banking system does not behave in that way at all. When a bank parks all of its deposits derived from depositors, into government securities, then the bank's risk is essentially the same as the government risk, or the country's. Therefore the risk of default is presumed to be very low.

		Risk Level
A bank has total deposit of	100 billion	0%
The bank parked 30% of it in government securities	30 billion	0%
The bank lent out 70% of the deposit in		
Corporate Bonds (25%)	17.5 billion	100%
Mortgage (50%)	35 billion	50%
Personal Loan / Unsecured Loans (25%)	17.5 billion	100%
The bank has a capital of	8 billion	

RWCAR = 15.2%
(minimum is 8% or maybe 10%)
This bank is having less risk compared to available capital

Illustration 130: Bank's risk factor varies depending on deposit levels, loans and investment options the bank chooses.

The risk factor can be varied according to the instruction by the central bank, or by a level based on past experience or historical data. The bank shown above is considered a safe and prudent bank as it basically keep its money in a safe environment. Using the Risk Weighted Capital Adequacy Ratio calculation as shown above, may enable the central bank to fine tune each bank risks and may decide to set a different capital requirement for each bank depending on the risks involved. Take notice that the statutory reserve requirement is no longer playing the usual role it is playing in previous models when RWCAR is applied. The calculation above assumes that all money is parked within the same country where the currency is issued and the bank is operating. When the bank RWCAR is below the minimum level dictated by the central bank, the bank will have to raise more capital, to improve its RWCAR to the minimum required. This is the money sets aside which will be used to cover any possible losses.

The difference between the two regimes (the fractional banking system using statutory reserve requirement or RWCAR) is that the bank with the SRR in fractional banking system is assumed to have minimal or no capital. In short, the bank can 'become' a bank without any money of its own, simply by setting aside some of its depositors' deposits. Basically the bank saves a portion of the money deposited into it, for contingency, in a very safe place (such as cash, government securities or with the central bank itself). The bank that operates under the RWCAR (Basel II) regime of the fractional reserve banking system however, will be able to lend out 100% of depositors money, and the classical fractional reserve banking example does not work in this case (an illusion of unlimited money creation might be portrayed and the critical ratios will be breaching their limits). In essence, the difference between the two regimes is that for the classical fractional reserve banking, the bank need not put its own money on the table while the newer fractional reserve banking regime of RWCAR, will require the bank to put up its own money on the table (but will be free to lend all deposits). It is clear that the newer regime is a lot better, because it ensure that banks do not risk depositors' money unnecessarily because they will be the first in line to cover the loss of the depositors' money, with their own. A long time ago, there were less control, and less supervision on banks, until the creation of the Fed. There were many episodes of 'bank runs', a situation where the public lost faith in a certain bank and quickly demanded full return of their deposits. This will cause severe shortfall of cash in the bank and can cause the bank to fail. There were many reasons for bank runs; one of it is that such banks were not carrying adequate cash reserves. This will make such banks to breach its loan to deposit ratio. When this happens, banks are vulnerable and if one big loan turn sour, can cause a panic when depositors scramble for their life savings. Nobody wants to be 'the' person in line when the money runs out and lose his or her deposit.

In summary, the central bank is responsible to monitor the rate of money creation to the rate of wealth creation. Any mismatch will lead to either inflation or deflation. The central bank will regulate all banks and ensure they follow the established rules. The central bank should act as a lender of last resort, only if a bank has good quality assets to swap with. Otherwise the central bank should not lend, or should only do it at a mark down. If the borrowing bank goes under, the deposit insurance scheme will protect all depositors, to a certain extent however. The government is free to reimburse depositors to the full extent of their deposit because it is responsible for managing the whole banking system (discussed at length in next topic).

Lesson 7

CONGRATULATIONS!
Lesson Completed

SOUND BANKING SYSTEM IS THE
RESPONSIBILITY OF THE GOVERNMENT

*I*n the book, "Secrets Of The Temple" by William Greider,

"Banks, large and small, were the most secure business enterprises in America, sheltered by the government from failure like no other sector of the economy. Year after year, no more than a handful of the nation's fourteen thousand banks failed, usually six or eight a year and sometimes none. In 1979, ten banks would be forced to close, all of them quite small and marginal. This compared to 1,165 mining and manufacturing companies that failed, 908 wholesale goods suppliers, 3,183 retail stores, 1,378 construction companies. Banking was safe and profitable, nearly fail-proof"

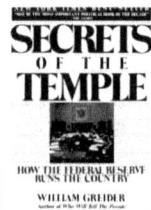

Illustration 131: A Passage From William Greider's Book, Secrets of The Temple

The statement illustrates the fact that the banking system is the responsibility of the government to manage. If the government does not manage the banking system, no party can do it for lack of authority and lack of overall view of the economy. The government is also responsible for ensuring the stability of the country; monetary stability is one such important function of the government. Promises via debts, demand deposits etc. are important promises which the government must oversee, to ensure fairness and smooth functioning of the system.

When the government of the United States decided to establish the Federal Deposit Insurance Corporation in 1933, it virtually eliminated the frequent bank panics or bank runs and this resulted in steep reduction in overall bank failures. Prior to establishment of the FDIC in 1934, the bank failure rate was 28.2% in 1933 (according to an article from http://www.cato.org/pubs/journal/cj16n1-3.html). After the establishment of the FDIC however, in 1934, the bank failure rate was only 0.37%. In fact, years after, there were minimal bank failures in the USA and every depositor in the banking system is assured that their money is safe and covered by the FDIC (up to certain limit, which covers most depositors).

This further showed that the government is responsible to manage money and ensure it is always sound in the economy. The government must regulate all banks and deposit taking institutions to ensure they are taking good care of their customers' deposits. The data shown above is obtained from the FDIC (for years after 1933) and the data prior to 1933 is from the paper *"Depression Era Bank Failures – The Great Contagion or The Great Shakeout?"* by John R. Walter.

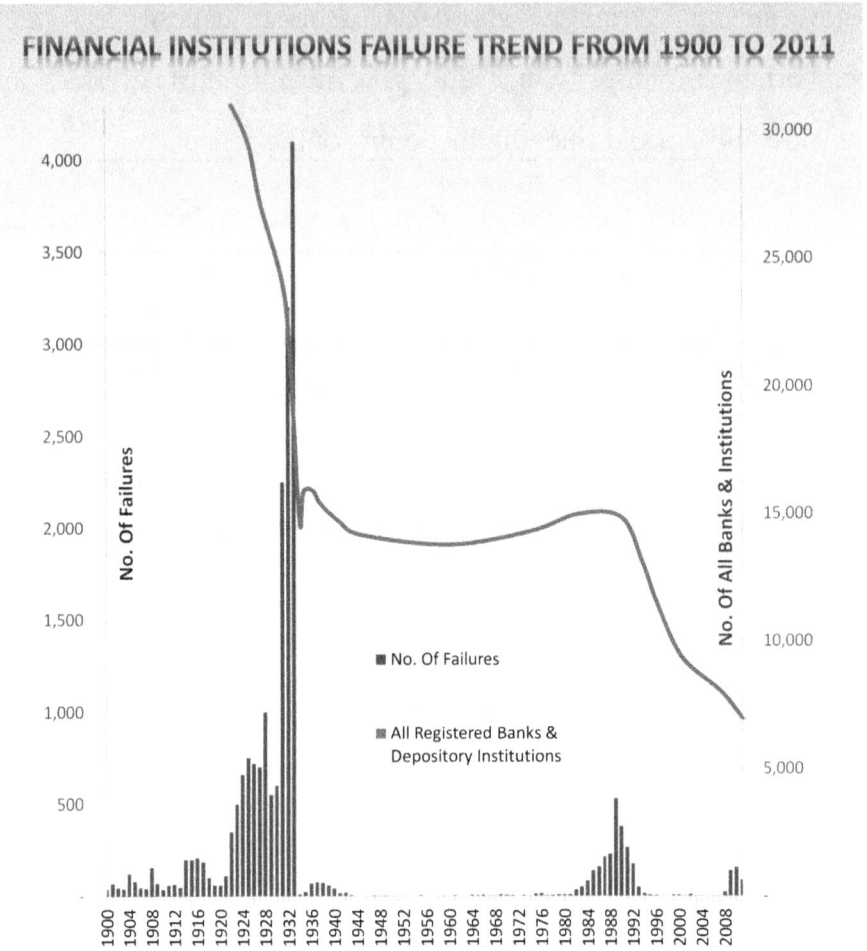

Illustration 132: Large reductions in bank's failure after the US government manages the banking system through several institutions such as the FDIC and the Federal Reserve

Before the creation of deposit insurance such as the FDIC in the US (1933 and earlier), there were many consistent bank failures and bank runs. The failures peaked during the Great Depression where a record number of more than 10,000 banks failed. Please take note that FDIC is not the sole reason why bank failures had decreased tremendously. There are other factors such as the Federal Reserve itself and several others. After the Great Depression, only a few banks will fail in a given year, which we can count using our fingers only. In 2005 and 2006, zero bank failure was recorded. In 1988, large-scale failures occurred, during the savings and loans crisis and recently in 2008, the Great Financial Crisis. During both events, only a few hundred banks failed, far lower than during the Great Depression. Without the actions taken by the Fed during both crises, a lot more banks would have failed. It will cost the government (the taxpayers) far more if the Fed is not doing its job.

At the other side of the Atlantic, in the United Kingdom, no 'bank run' has occurred in a century, owing to actions taken by the government and its central bank. However, during the 2008 financial crisis, the imminent failure of Northern Rock bank caused a bank run and forced the government to nationalize the bank and to this day remain the only bank run in the UK after the removal of the gold standard.

Government securities are considered safe because the government is effectively controlling the central bank and it has the capacity to print money at will. The printing of new money will put additional claim on the wealth of the country. If there is too much printing, the value of the currency will drop. If there is no faith on the amount of wealth backing the newly created currency plus all of the existing currency in circulation, large-scale inflation will occur. No amount of money will be enough to protect any bank within the system, unless the bank is keeping its money overseas in a different currency!

Governments of the world are ultimately to be blamed for the worst financial crisis in 2008 since the Great Depression. The party that was going on in the financial markets continued far longer than it supposed to, making the mess bigger in the end. We scouted the world for banking data and we found that they were still many countries where the banking system were hardly affected by the Great Financial Crisis of 2008, despite their economic dependents on the world at large and the eventual recession they experienced. Just like the cycle of wisdom of human beings, the Asian Financial Crisis of 1998 which turned those mighty tigers of Asia into "docile kittens", had ensured their banking systems were kept in check, due to the fear of a repeat, to this day. The current executive management of their banks surely still remembers the hardship their bank went through back then, and they're determined not to go through it again. These banks were not affected at all and their fundamentals were sound and continue to make record profits in their history.

The United States on the other hand, experienced its previous big scale banking crisis back in the early 1980s. This is a generation's worth of a gap in human memory, of human experience. The new breed of workers and managers prior to the crisis in 2008 remember only vibrant and relatively 'trouble-free' banking, and after more than a decade of uninterrupted economic growth, hardly anyone remembers what a recession was like. No preparations were made and the existing breed of economists, who supposed to scour and analyze the economic data, have only praises and vivacious forecasts. No one seen it coming (well a few did, but their voices were drowned out). We did see it coming back then, and we took all the necessary steps we think we should. We were appalled by the response of the economic community and the public in general to the financial crisis. The denial was thick and took a long time, years in fact just to disappear.

A responsible government must know how the banking system works, in order to manage it. Our analysis of the Fed's Greenspan era and a little bit of Bernanke's, found that it is not caused by the oversight of the Federal Reserve that this crisis spiraled out of control. It was due to them being human and the bureaucratic drawback imposes by the political system. Greenspan saw much earlier in 2003 and 2004 that the mortgage industry, the mortgage-backed securities and derivatives from these securities etc. were getting out of control. For example just a few years before, most housing loans were of the standard adjustable-rate mortgage (ARM) or a fixed mortgage, but during that year onward, the dominant loan type that were taken out by borrowers was of the interest only ARM with no money down, most were in the negative equity at the start, essentially betting the house price will appreciate. Paying an interest only loan on a house is just like renting, as we had shown earlier in the book. In the year 2000 and then 2001, Greenspan and the Federal Reserve's rate setting committee had slashed the fed fund's rate to very low levels. There was plenty of available capital for lending, borrowers were hesitating however. We understood that this action is not a problem and in our simulation in our book series, we concluded that the lower the interest rate, the better it is for the economy. We also concluded that in a good functioning economy where little restrictions are applied and all is well, the interest rate would tend to linger on the low side. Greenspan and the Fed were not to be blamed for the Great Financial Crisis in 2008. There is another more important factor to be blamed for the crisis. It is the human factor. We will talk a bit more about this in Book 3 of this series, so stay tuned.

The mistake of the Fed then was due to the political and bureaucracy limitation imposed by the system. There are certain areas where the Fed traditionally avoids, with good reasons. For instance, what the people of the country do with their money is really not the business of the Fed to interfere. What the government does with its money and its borrowings are not really the purview of the Federal Reserve. As much as the Fed wanted to sound the alarm bells, its hands are tied to stay within its traditional boundary. We hope that in the future, which we starting to see even now, the Fed is actually stepping out from its traditional role in its traditional boundary, and wield its immense power within the economy to prevent it from being damaged by unscrupulous people (that includes the politicians).

Greenspan back then can do only one thing to warn everybody, raising the interest rate. He did. Rates were increased repeatedly, but the problem was, it was not fast or forceful enough to shake the market. 'Measured pace' was taken by the market as 'everything is fine' and they continued to do their overly greedy practices. The US government also joined the party, turning a large budget surplus into one of the largest deficits by waging wars the country could not afford. We believed the wars can be financed much cheaply by clever use of diplomacy and democratic institutions, saving trillions of dollars and thousands of lives. The wars put a bad name on America. Americans were no longer respected the way they used to, they were seen as arrogant in their way in waging the wars and becoming a hated country for many. It is crucial this is reversed and America continues to lead the world into greater prosperity and justice for all. Just like prevention is better than cure in medicine, the same holds true in the international arena. Money and guns do not buy the things America's need or adore, but human conviction and respectful actions do.

The Fed was not supposed to interfere in the government's business of policy-making, which should be left to the politicians, and so the Fed stood and watched. Similarly in the mortgage markets, the Fed is not supposed to interfere in the non-traditional areas, such as the derivatives market. We believe that although the Fed could not interfere, it should sound the alarm bells, loud and clear. The Fed couldn't, for being too strict on the boundaries and protocols. In the future we hope the Federal Reserve Chairman and committees be allowed to speak their mind including in the non-traditional areas. In its traditional areas however, it should be more direct and forceful. When the housing loan market was turning into a badland, full of toxic products, the Federal Reserve took a view that what the banks do with their money, by giving more money to borrowers (because they have plenty of money) in excess of the houses' market value is not really an issue. We also took this same view. What or who you would like to lend your money and how much, is really not the business of the Fed. The problem will only become a problem for the Fed when it turns into a big problem such as the banks' capitals are decreasing, and their core ratios worsened. When this occurs, it is too late as the problem is already a systemic problem within the banking system. The Fed should take action much earlier, by preventing unsafe practices by banks, because ultimately the government will need to guarantee all deposits in the banking system.

Under Chairman Bernanke, we saw the Fed stepped out beyond its traditional boundary, several times. This is a great sign and the steps taken by the Fed were very carefully calculated. Bernanke and the Fed did a great job, and the feared collapse of the economy was avoided. Our forefathers back then, did design the Fed to handle many extraordinary events, without much limitation. The so called limitation are just that, traditional boundary which is traditionally followed by the Fed. Nothing specifically preventing the Fed from doing more, because it is a branch of the government and wields immense power everywhere— well everywhere that our money goes that is. We hope the Fed will worry less on deflation because our simulations showed that deflation is not the beast that we are supposed to fear at all costs. The Great Depression is not caused by deflation. The deflationary effects, were due to something else then. Preventing deflation from occurring at all costs, is not a sound strategy in our opinion. It is costly and destroys wealth by utilizing more of the un-used portion of the country's wealth.

Greed is good, was the mantra back then. We disagreed. Greed as it turns out, was never good. We need something better than that. We gave our thoughts in **Book 3** of the series. Lack of financial education, was the other problem for borrowers. They put themselves in harm's way. Banks were risking their depositors' money, into a multitude of bad lending practices, risking the whole banking system. We could not find a single banker who will calculate their lending costs in a more realistic way. They will only factor in inflation of a few percent, and that's it. They even forgot what banks are for in the first place! (find out in **Book 3**). Economists were similarly conditioned by the spectacular growth and low inflation level of the economy that they assumed it will be so, far into the future.

The problem of the Great Financial Crisis is not due to fractional reserve banking system, or due to paper money. The problem is human. The solution is therefore will also be of human origin. Greed as it is, damages the economy. It displaced and distorts wealth, where everyone is chasing for biggest returns, forgetting ethics and society. Capitalism is all for profit above everything else, which must be counter balanced with one critical factor, human desires for good of all. Money and assets, are nothing without the human element. We cannot put aside our human elements and let capitalism get a free reign. Ultimately, it will destroy what it created. When capitalism is balanced with our human nature such as 'good for all', 'best for myself and the community' we will see what the best of capitalism, and ourselves can achieve. When we wanted to go to the moon, the drive was not profit, but for survival. When we discovered the internet, it was for faster communication, not for profit. We should think more of what we can do to benefit society, and when the society benefits from our action, wealth will be created and in return, we will be rewarded.

The crisis of 2008 stemmed out of greed, for maximum profit above everything else. It went out of control. People became 'insane', blinded by potential returns, by not doing much and taking shortcuts. Some ads we saw even claim you can be rich by doing nothing. Such interesting gimmicks, but people believed them! Property experts expounded their message of easy money very hard on the gullible public. Real estate was guaranteed to make money, for anyone. We are now seeing the same lies being expounded by the gold bugs and dealers. It was of course, a big lie. Still want to believe these same people? We urge you to throw them out and forget them, educate yourself more and manage your money wisely (find out in **Book 3**!). Remember, it is not how much money you have, it is about getting able to do the things that you want to do. If the things you want to do benefits the society at large, you are bound to be rewarded.

In **Book 3** of this **259 TRILLION VS. 5 TRILLION SERIES** titled, **"WEALTH OF THE UNITED STATES – Plus Major Questions Since The Financial Crisis"**, we discussed at length on whether the government should bail out the banks or not. Although the government is responsible for the banking system, bailing them out is not one of it. The reasoning and the details are duly explained in the book. We also singled out the removal of the Glass–Steagall Act of 1930s back in the beginning of the new millennium as one of the mistakes of the government which made the economic crisis much worse than it supposed to.

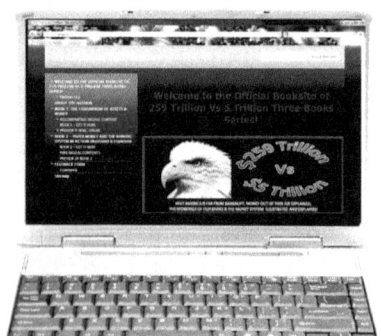

Visit
http://sites.google.com/site/259trillionvs5trillion
and get your free bonus materials.

QUICK REVIEW

*I*n order to summarize what we have presented so far, we decided to list several key points that you need to know from **Book 1 & Book 2**.

Asset is NOT money. Money is NOT asset.

 Money is only **A MEDIUM OF EXCHANGE** and **TEMPORARY STORE OF VALUE**

 Gold is a commodity, which is a form of wealth. It is not money. Gold as money will double the asset in the economy.

 Paper money has no intrinsic value. It supposed to have no value. It only represents the wealth or asset it was backed on.

 Asset can be tangible (houses, factories, lands) or non tangible (creativity, brain, productive resources).

 There are more assets than money in circulation. Money cannot be issued dollar to dollar for all wealth in the nation.

You cannot have the same asset in asset form and money form at the same time.

 OR

NOT

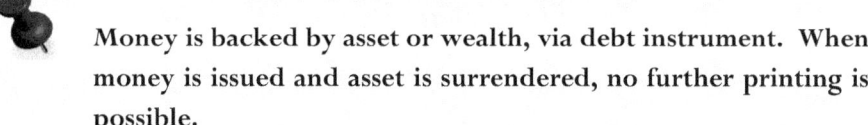 Money is backed by asset or wealth, via debt instrument. When money is issued and asset is surrendered, no further printing is possible.

Money first originated from the government. Created from assets that the government owns or created. Government distributes that money to people who participated in creating the asset.

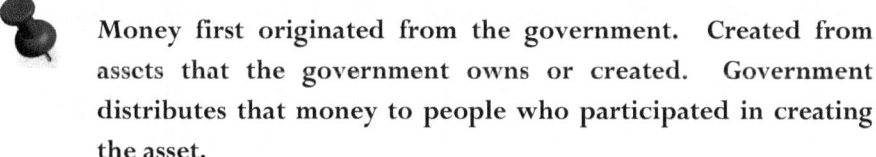 Money cannot be free. Each single currency printed must be backed by real wealth.

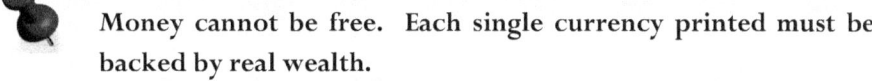 Bartering is not an efficient way of trade. Money makes trades easier and efficient.

Gold is asset. House is asset. If gold is used as money, why can't house be use as money? Or other commodities? It is unfair to limit wealth to gold. Paper money is backed by real wealth of the nation and only use for trading/exchanging of goods and services.

$259 Trillion

Vs

....."Currently, the United States total wealth is estimated to be around 60 to 700 trillion dollars, compared to net debt of less than 20 trillion dollars. Our own calculation which is more conservative, estimates the wealth at 259 trillion dollars. This wealth numbers include all financial and nonfinancial wealth. We shall go very deep into these wealth numbers in later part of this book, where we will dissect and lay bare the calculations for net wealth of Americans.".........

THE CONUNDRUM OF ASSETS & MONEY

Sharif Rahman & Amy Norwood

... "You can't have double the amount of asset, simply because the money is to be printed and be given to you, interest free. It gets even more interesting if the economy is using the gold standard. Imagine that if you have gold jewelry worth 300,000 dollars, to represent this gold jewelry in money terms, you will need 300,000 dollars worth of gold coins or bars. You will have the jewelry, plus the gold money. Something isn't right, because your asset has doubled.

When the argument of allowing the government to print money, such as during the Lincoln's era, interest free is made, what was it that is backing this money? Presumably, none, and this printing method, although patriotic in the eyes of many, are actually not sustainable. The end result was the quick demise of the then Lincoln's 'greenbacks'." ....

THE CONUNDRUM OF ASSETS & MONEY
Sharif Rahman & Amy Norwood

Sharif Rahman & Amy Norwood

GOLD CANNOT BE USED AS MONEY BECAUSE:

- Controlled by mining companies and only certain countries have it.

- Cannot be taken out of circulations and government cannot control the outflow of gold to other countries and vice versa.

- Too much resources used to mine gold and produce it as money. Too much pollution and too much energy are used.

- Commodities suffer from supply and demand problem.

- Gold cannot be used in small denomination. Gold coins are heavy to carry and hard (impossible) to authenticate during transaction.

- Gold production could not keep up with population growth and no chance in hell to catch up with GDP of the world.

A sheep is more valuable as asset than gold because it can generate new wealth. Gold does not multiply itself.

Gold standard actually still exists today, in the form of metallic coins that is not preferred by anyone and their value gyrate wildly.

Gold inflation does occurs…..as well as deflation. Read history books to find out more. Gold proponents do not want you to know the truth!

Gold stockpile could not even keep up with human population growth, let alone keeping up with wealth generated by the ever-expanding human populations.

WHY AMERICA IS FAR FROM BANKRUPT,
MONEY OUT OF THIN AIR EXPLAINED
THE WORKINGS OF ... AND EXPLAINED

.. "There are still more problems with using gold as money. If a house mortgaged earlier which was taken in terms of a few kg of gold, will need to be paid in the same amount of a few kilos of gold, imagine what will happen if the loan is taken out back in the year 2001 when gold price was low at USD280/oz and today, to pay the loan off, you will need to acquire gold at USD1650/oz, a full 6 times more than what you have borrowed it for! That will bankrupt you. Once interest or profit element is included, the loan value will be even higher, perhaps 12 to 15 times more, and there is no way for you to be able to pay it off. Can you afford to increase your monthly house payments by a minimum of 20 times? Why should you? The house is still the same, why does the payment goes up so high? Such are the possible injustices caused by using gold as money. Very dangerous and risky indeed. Gold proponents accused paper money as unstable which is a load of crap, yet their gold is so unstable, it can destroy you outright. Millions of borrowers will go bankrupt for a fault that is none of their own." ...

THE CONUNDRUM OF ASSETS & MONEY
Sharif Rahman & Amy Norwood

.... "Think it can't happen to gold? Think again. In 2011, the price of gold dropped by 23% within 2 weeks. How's that for price stability? Copper dropped 25%, in three days! Imagine that occurring to the value of your money in your hand. This is the main reason why the gold standard was replaced with fiat money, where the supply can be controlled. A commodity in which just about anyone can produce or find is very hard to control...."

... "The increase in metals prices, including that of gold, is not due to 'inflation' as claimed by many gold proponents. It was also not due to increase printing of paper money in 2008 to combat the severe financial crisis. The increase of all these metals started earlier, before the financial crisis took place. The price of gold had started to go up significantly in 2005 and reached USD600/oz in 2006, from around USD400/oz. This is already on top of the increase from its low of USD200+/oz in early 2000's. This is surely not due to monetary inflation as inflation rate was rather steady and on the low side all the while. Inflation alone cannot increase a metal's price several times over. ..."

THE CONUNDRUM OF ASSETS & MONEY
Sharif Rahman & Amy Norwood

... "At say USD1600/oz, all of the world's gold will be valued at USD 8 trillion! Well this is not that much, when compared with the total wealth accumulated in the whole planet. This calculation was done when gold prices already hitting USD1600/oz. If at the low of USD280/oz just a few years before, there will be only USD1.4 trillion of gold available in the whole world, hardly enough for commercial transactions.

Almost half of all of that gold are in the form of jewelries and about 18% are held by central banks and another 16% held by private firms or individuals for storage of 'value' purposes. So if we subtract half of the available gold that were made into jewelries from the stockpile, there will be only USD700 billion worth of gold available to go around as money during that low gold price period. It was not even enough for the use of America, let alone the whole world. In order to use this gold to replace currencies, all currencies in the world in fact, the deflation that need to occur will be truly massive." ....

THE CONUNDRUM OF ASSETS & MONEY

Sharif Rahman & Amy Norwood

THE
CONUNDRUM OF
ASSETS & MONEY

Paper money and future money fulfill all characteristics of ideal money

1) Cheap to produce
2) Can be removed or added when needed
3) Cannot be copied (anti counterfeit)

Characteristic	Paper Money	Gold
Cheap to produce	$0.09 to print a bill (Face value can be $1, $2.. $100,000 or $1billion), green	$81,250 to produce $100,000 coins! (plus tons of waste and pollutions)
Can be removed or added when needed	Federal Reserve uses interests and SRR to manage money in the economy. Monitor signs for shortages and excess every 30sec.	To add - Must be found and mined. To remove - Once in the system cannot be taken out unless made illegal and forcibly removed
Anti- Counterfeit	Only government can print and very hard to copy. Easily checked for authenticity (simply by looking and touching)	Any goldsmith can mint. Hard to check the coins for authenticity and contents purity (need fancy equipments)

 Gold does not fulfill any of the three characteristics of ideal money.

 There are A LOT MORE ASSET compared to MONEY IN CIRCULATION

Second Book Of
A Three Book Series

$259 Trillion

.... "The ascent of fractional reserve banking, overseen by a master bank (the central bank) eventually made it possible for ease of issuance and removal of money. This ability guarantees the stability of the value of the money, despite great changes in demand, during wars, large calamities and other events. This enabled paper money to obtain two of the required characteristic of ideal money. The final characteristic was soon obtained, when new anti-counterfeit technology was invented, preventing paper money from being copied and produced by anyone. With a very low production costs and the ability to be issued or removed at will, paper money has finally fulfill the ideal form of money sought after for thousands of years." .....

**PAPER MONEY AND
THE BANKING SYSTEM IN ACTION**
Sharif Rahman & Amy Norwood

Paper money is backed by assets & wealth of the nation. It is distributed into the economy via debt.

 Debt Is Only The Instrument Used To Distribute Money Into The Economy. MONEY IS NOT BACKED BY DEBT.

Asset Backed Money issued Via Debt Instrument

 Some assets or wealth that EXIST NOW is liquidated (pull out from economy and money is printed to represent them) and redistributed into the economy so that new participants can use their FUTURE wealth generating ability for trades NOW.

 Getting a loan to buy a house will never cause a loss to the borrower if the borrower fails to pay, any losses will solely be due to the declined in market price of the house and it has nothing to do with the bank, or the loan.

 Variable interest loan is the most equitable arrangement between lenders and borrowers, therefore it is also the cheapest. Only take a fixed loan if the interest rate is very low.

BOOK
2

.... "Debt is the instrument used to fairly distribute the money into the economy and this instrument, the front face of the money creation is what people typically see and they were conditioned to assume that money is backed by debt. If they will only think one more step further, just a little bit, they will be able to see that this debt was issued when an asset is produced, making our fiat paper money, to be truly backed by real asset. So just call it, "ASSET BACKED MONEY ISSUED VIA DEBT INSTRUMENT". ....

.... "The consequence of this modern function of the economy is that everything seems to be backed by 'debt'. No 'debt', no money. In reality, there are no debts, there are only assets. Money is only issued, when it is backed by real assets. In order to issue it, the asset will need to be surrendered into the system in exchange for an equivalent amount of money. There is no slavery, no conspiracy to own or steal the world...."

**PAPER MONEY AND
THE BANKING SYSTEM IN ACTION**
Sharif Rahman & Amy Norwood

Primary Function Of Money: Medium Used For Exchanging Wealth (For Trades To Occur)

 Secondary Function Of Money: TEMPORARY Store Of Value. (Not For Long Term)

 Excess money:
Should be connected to the "system"
via deposits in banks, CDs, Government
Bonds. Inflation will be auto
compensated.

AND

By investing - being owners of
Companies that generates
New wealth via shares purchase
Or direct capital injection.

 LONG TERM store of value must be in the form of WEALTH GENERATING ASSETS. E.g. Companies, Farm Land, Factories, Education.

 Gold is not a wealth generating asset.

1880	Invested In	2010
$100	Shares In S&P Companies	$4,026,000
$100	Store Under Pillow	$100 - $195,000
$100	Long Term (CD's & Bonds)	$90,100
$100	Savings Accounts	$5,070
$100	Physical Gold	$4,720

www.measuringworth.com

 Remember This? This is what happen to money when it is stored in different type of investment

 Paper money's purchasing power is compensated and will end up generate more wealth than the original value.

 US Dollar is issued at no cost and no interest to the government. It is free to distribute and spend.

 There are enough money to pay for all loans and interests because interests come from newly created wealth. They will collectively re-enter the economy promptly.

 There are no other way to distribute asset as efficiently as using debt managed by private banks. Allocating free money, free resources etc. is just the same as COMMUNISM, where everybody is given equal amount of resources and cannot have more than others.

 FRACTIONAL RESERVE BANKING is NOT MAGIC. The mathematics behind it is correct. Understand it and you won't be blinded by the doom and gloom club. The bank is always solvent at all times.

 Prices of many goods went down significantly compared to years before. This is a proof that our money's value do not decline universally, and the law of supply and demand is predominant

Second Book Of
A Three Book Series

$259 Trillion
Vs
$5 Trillion

BOOK
2

... "The issuance of this money via the debt instrument is free and at no cost to the government because all of the interest payable to the Fed on the so called 'debt' is returned to the government and relabeled as 'profits'. In 2010, the Federal Reserve returned USD 89,000,000,000.00 (89 billion dollars) of profits to its only shareholder, the United States Government. This totally negate the interest payable on the so called 'mountains of debt' that is due to the money supply issuance." ...

**PAPER MONEY AND
THE BANKING SYSTEM IN ACTION**
Sharif Rahman & Amy Norwood

Banks are in the business of matchmaking. Lending excess money (wealth in liquid form from excess wealth available NOW) for redistribution to borrowers (people, companies, farmers, etc) that will generate wealth in the FUTURE. They are far from being Satan's honchos (but could be greedy just like other human)

 CENTRAL BANK (FEDERAL RESERVE) is GOVERNMENT ENTITY. It Is NOT a private bank. It Is also NOT a reincarnation of the DEVIL.

GOVERNMENT

 BANKS cannot print its own money and certainly cannot print money out of thin air. Excess deposits are returned into the economy in exchange of assets, making efficient use of TODAY'S WEALTH.

...... "The mathematical functions had proven that fractional reserve banking works and it is the fairest system of all. However it must be noted that all systems are controlled and manipulated by human beings and as such the performance of the system is wholly dependent on the driver.".......

.... "If banks can print money out of thin air, why would they need depositors in the first place? When banks were having trouble during the recent financial crisis, why did they simply not print money on their own and use it to bail themselves out? Therefore it is illogical that money can simply be printed out of thin air. Wouldn't America be the super 'duper' richest country if it can print money out of thin air and need not work anymore?" ....

PAPER MONEY AND THE BANKING SYSTEM IN ACTION
Sharif Rahman & Amy Norwood

Sharif Rahman & Amy Norwood

All Graph/Functions That Are Based On Population Growth And Productivity ARE EXPONENTIAL In Nature.

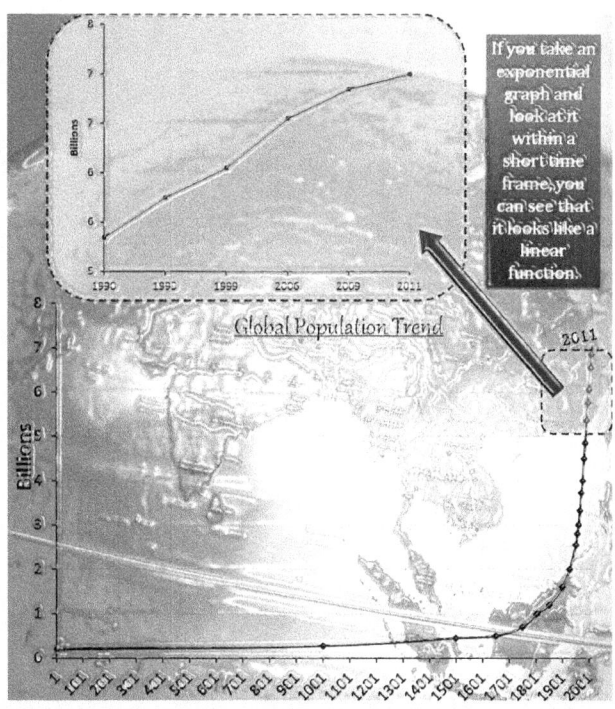

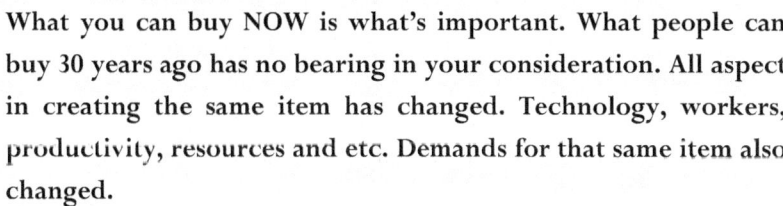

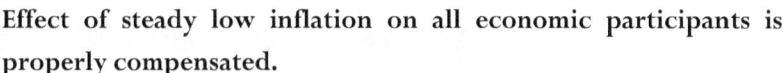

What you can buy NOW is what's important. What people can buy 30 years ago has no bearing in your consideration. All aspect in creating the same item has changed. Technology, workers, productivity, resources and etc. Demands for that same item also changed.

Effect of steady low inflation on all economic participants is properly compensated.

What value do you place on Internet Banking, online purchase, massive information exchange (internet, digital libraries)? Everything can be done, found and accessed in seconds. All the money in the world of 30 years ago would not get them this priceless innovation.

Sit and do your math. Find where the bulk of your money goes. Take it as % of income and compare with your Grandpa days. You will be surprise. Most Americans income goes toward this expense.......

..... "In bad times, people tend to blame something that they can't put a face on but as usual, it is never themselves. For example, as house prices continued to go up above and beyond the affordability level of most people and with loans that they couldn't possibly afford, many Americans continue buying homes, even houses that they knew they could not afford. Is it greed of profiting from the house appreciation or is it because of fear that house prices will continue to go up or is it because they follow those "Property GURUs" that said "Real Estate will always go up and up!" which is a very misleading statement! So who is exactly to be blamed? Ultimately, the blame fell upon each and everyone who participated in that crazy bubble blowing period. All bubbles will eventually burst, that is why, knowledge is the most important weapon in navigating the economic system and your own personal finance. Not money, not gold and certainly not greed. As we have said in Book 1, Greed Is Not Good! ....."

PAPER MONEY AND
THE BANKING SYSTEM IN ACTION
Sharif Rahman & Amy Norwood

Sharif Rahm

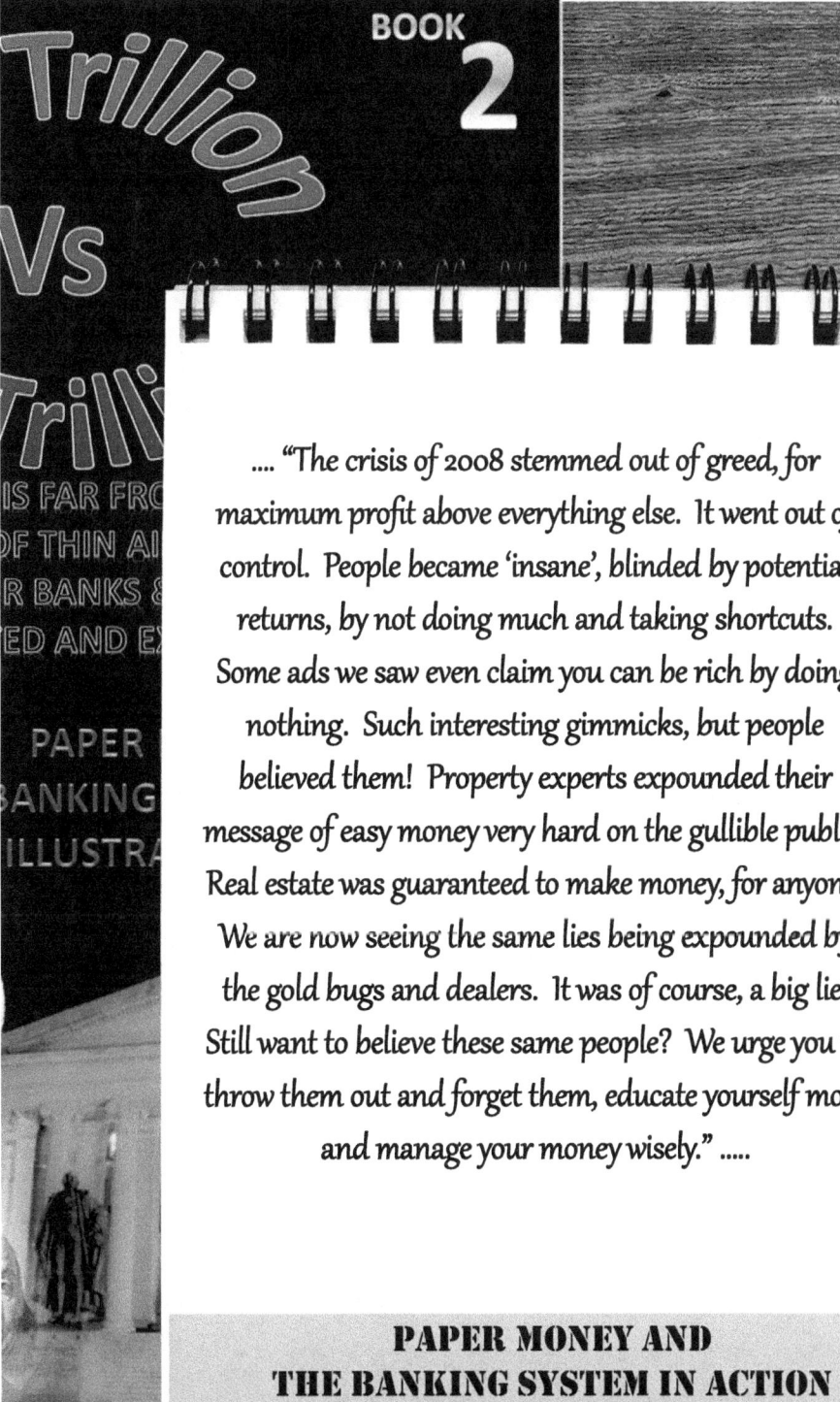

BOOK
2

.... "The crisis of 2008 stemmed out of greed, for maximum profit above everything else. It went out of control. People became 'insane', blinded by potential returns, by not doing much and taking shortcuts. Some ads we saw even claim you can be rich by doing nothing. Such interesting gimmicks, but people believed them! Property experts expounded their message of easy money very hard on the gullible public. Real estate was guaranteed to make money, for anyone. We are now seeing the same lies being expounded by the gold bugs and dealers. It was of course, a big lie. Still want to believe these same people? We urge you to throw them out and forget them, educate yourself more and manage your money wisely." .....

**PAPER MONEY AND
THE BANKING SYSTEM IN ACTION**
Sharif Rahman & Amy Norwood

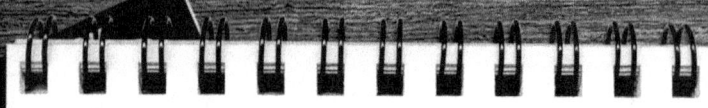

.... "If the banks are conspiring today to steal your wealth, by giving out loans knowingly that many people will not be able to pay, why would they lower their interest rates? Lowering their own profits? If central banks such as the Fed are in the same conspiracy, why would the Fed reduced interest rates to very low levels? This will aid those who have no money—the masses, the borrowers." ....

... "Therefore it is clear that there are no losses involved for people who are in foreclosures when they fail to pay their monthly payments as long as the house price is above the purchase price. If the price is lower, there bound to be losses, which can be contra out." ...

PAPER MONEY AND THE BANKING SYSTEM IN ACTION

Sharif Rahman & Amy Norwood

END THOUGHTS

$\mathcal{W}$e hope you have now understood how our fractional reserve banking system function, why 100% reserve banking is antiquated in meeting our modern economic demands, why banks are not allowed to print money on their own and many other important answers to some of the classical questions. In order to increase your understanding on the concept presented, we urge you to reread the relevant part of this book again, take your time to do it and if you still having problem understanding it, don't hesitate to go to our website and download the video presentations. With explanations in the book and the presentations, you are guaranteed to have a good learning experience.

Armed with such down to earth and simple answers, you can

now argue and debate with other people on why your views are the best and you will have the resources to back your argument up. Don't be afraid to show your support for the good things this economy is giving you, including the banking system. A lot of things will be impossible if not for our modern banking system. Young couples will not be able to buy their affordable houses while still in their twenties if not for the courageous act of the banks, making these young people spend their money on rentals instead. Without credit cards, there won't be any buffer and assistance from the economy to struggling people who are confident of their future ability to earn money but met a soft patch in their life.

Our discussions will continue into the third book in this series and in the third and final book, we shall discussed at length, yet in a simplified way the overall wealth of all Americans, combined. Here you will understand why America was called the greatest country on the planet, yet due to many doom and gloom books and reports, by the doom and gloom economists and reporters, Americans started to look down on themselves. This is unhealthy for the future of the country. America is far from bankrupt, and has a lot of potential. Doom and gloom books, usually instill fear and sells relatively well. This is not what we wanted to do. We want to show you what the real situation out there is and what we all should be doing about it. These same economists were the very ones who themselves did not see the Great Recession of 2008 and they do not understand how the economic system really functions. They were so bogged down with details, calculations and technicality with tons of jargons, they missed the big picture as well as the human side of the economy. Just stop listening to them and trust yourself more. Use our books as your best source of reference and you will understand what are the best course of actions for you to do for a better future for yourself and the world at large.

The third book is **specially** made to dispel some of the half-truths out there, starting with Keynesians economics of heavy spending. We will also discuss the issue of the 'disappearance' of the middle class because there was no real disappearance happening. We shall discuss the national debt and how to pay off the large debt of the United States and many other interesting topics, including debunking the statement that paper money value will go to zero given long enough time, the income gap between the poor and the rich and the division of the economic pie. We have dissected these issues thoroughly and we were shocked ourselves!

We will work hard to fine tune and touch up the almost

completed third book and publish it within weeks of publishing this book.

Finally, the answer of what the series title of 259 Trillion Vs 5 Trillion will be revealed!

Don't Give Up!

Sharif Rahman and Amy Norwood Maine

AUTHORS' BIOGRAPHIES

Sharif Rahman is an experienced chemical engineer graduated from Vanderbilt University with a good set of problem solving skills. He likes to jump into complicated problems and will get to the bottom of it and lay it bare for others to see in a different angle. Using his engineering knacks and other hidden 'talents', he then presented the solution in a simple way. His motto is simple, which is "Make things 'as simple as possible'". He is currently busy working full time in a power and water company as a senior manager and uses his weekends to write.

He is married to his VU sweetheart and has four kids. Together they analyzed the world in ways that few people can imagine!

FROM THE DESK OF THE AUTHOR

*A*my **Norwood Maine** graduated magna cum laude from Vanderbilt University, where she spent part of her teenage years obtaining her engineering degree. Her mathematical skills usually exceed everyone else's and her reading abilities will amazes anyone around her. Don't simply believe those old economists with thick moustaches, is her mantra. Many of them are too busy to really think through what they wrote, and they only wanted publicity and most important of all, they like to scare their readers.

Amy Norwood lent her valuable expertise to ensure this book will amazes the reader and offer a different and more down to earth understanding of our forefathers economic designs.

ALSO IN THE SERIES

BOOK 1
THE CONUNDRUM OF ASSETS & MONEY
(Kindle Edition Release in Oct 2011)
(Printed Edition Released in Nov 2011)

BOOK 3
WEALTH OF THE UNITED STATES
Plus Major Questions Since The Financial Crisis
(Slated for release in Feb 2012)

The use of paper
money and other type
of money is discussed
at length in this three
books series and
finally the answer of
whether money is
printed out of thin air
will be revealed.

The final book in the
series will discuss the
immense wealth
amassed by America
through its 230+ years
of history making it
the richest country on
the planet, plus many
major topics arisen
since the Great
Recession of 2008 such
as the myth of the
disappearance of the
middle class, the
deficit and the
national debt,
inflation or deflation,
and the distribution of
the economic pie with
very surprising
conclusion, which is
the real reason why
America is so
successful with its
free capitalism.

The truth will be
revealed

www.ingramcontent.com/pod-product-compliance
Lightning Source LLC
Chambersburg PA
CBHW051444170526
45166CB00001B/111